D1261108

WITHDRAWN
07/07/2023
SAINT LOUIS UNIVERSITY

Beyond *Woke*

Also by Michael Rectenwald from
New English Review Press:

Springtime for Snowflakes:
'Social Justice' and Its Postmodern Parentage (2018)

Google Archipelago:
The Digital Gulag and the Simulation of Freedom
(2019)

Beyond

Woke

Michael Rectenwald

LC
173
.R42
2020

Copyright © Michael Rectenwald, 2020

All rights reserved. No part of this book may be reproduced in any form or by any means, electronic or mechanical, without permission in writing from the publisher except by reviewers who may quote brief passages in their reviews.

Published by New English Review Press
a subsidiary of World Encounter Institute
PO Box 158397
Nashville, Tennessee 37215
&
27 Old Gloucester Street
London, England, WC1N 3AX

Cover Art and Design by Ari Lankin

ISBN: 978-1-943003-36-5

First Edition

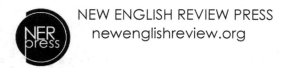

NEW ENGLISH REVIEW PRESS
newenglishreview.org

Contents

Introduction

THE FOLLOWING ESSAYS were written over the course of almost four years—from September 2016 to February 2020. They represent the development of my thinking on cultural politics in academia and more broadly. Each is a stand-alone piece and as such the book can be read in any order. The collection includes discussions of "social justice," postmodern theory, political correctness, socialism-communism, "corporate socialism," and my personal relationships with each. The essays are of varying length, ranging from two to twenty-plus pages. Only four are specifically addressed to academic audiences— "Libertarianism(s) versus Postmodernism and 'Social Justice' Ideology," "After 'Social Justice'- New Paradigms for the Humanities and Social Sciences," "Totalitarianism with Communist Characteristics, Corporate Socialism and 'Woke Capitalism,'" and "Google Marxism: Internet Ideology & the Academics Who Perpetuate It"—although many others are scholarly.

Several of the essays necessarily overlap topically in various ways, some even including verbatim repetition of short passages. While removing as much overlapping material as possible, I found it impossible to excise all repetition without doing damage to linguistic texture of the pieces. In any case, while overlap remains, the topics are addressed from varying angles.

Woke
According to the social justice creed, being "woke" is the political awakening that stems from the emergence of con-

sciousness and conscientiousness regarding social and political injustice. Wokeness is the indelible inscription of the awareness of social injustice on the conscious mind, eliciting the sting of conscience, which compels the newly woke to change their beliefs and behaviors.

Wokeness is analogous to the Christian encounter of being saved. Like being saved, being woke involves redressing transgressions through repentance and reformation. And, as the Christian is saved not by works but into works, so the newly converted social justice believers are woke not by works but into woke works.

For Christians, Christ crucified brings one's sins to mind, while also serving as a sacrifice for their absolution. Under social justice, the underprivileged do not absolve sins, but they do bring them to mind—as do other woke persons. Like the saved Christian, the social justice woke becomes penitent about previously unacknowledged sin, sin for which they must atone. Under social justice, sin is having acted carelessly from a position of privilege, without sufficient recognition or concern for those whose lack of privilege makes one's privilege possible. Under Christianity, sin is having transgressed against God, sometimes directly but often vis-à-vis others.

Setting aside metaphysical, theological, and other claims of veracity, there are empirical differences between being saved and being woke. While wokeness begins with change on the level of the individual, it is not the individual that ultimately matters according to the social justice creed. The redemption of the peculiar person, the preservation of individual selfhood—this is not at issue. Wokeness is, after all, a group phenomenon—in the sense that one is ultimately woke for the world. Wokeness does not only or most importantly alter the individual; in order to be woke, one must not only awaken, but also demonstrate a collateral commitment to make reparations for social and political injustice—to help to make a better (more just) world.

The same cannot be said of being saved. Contrary to contemporary social justice Christianity, salvation does not play out on the level of the social group. One works out one's salvation individually and not, as it were, federally. Salvation is personal, individual, singular—not collective. Under Christianity, people are not saved due to their social identity. No one is moral or good because of their membership in a social identity category.

The opposite is the case under social justice. Membership in a subordinated, oppressed social identity category confers higher moral standing under the social justice creed. Such persons are deemed to be the ethical superiors of others—just as membership confers guilt and low moral standing on members of dominant or privileged social identity categories. Under social justice, it is not what is done that matters, but who does it.

The figure of Jesus Christ, no matter what you believe about his historicity, did not address persons qua members of social groups. He addressed them as individuals whose group memberships may have impacted their values and behaviors but were not determining of their moral status. He did not admonish his followers to attend to the social identity category of others, but rather that their social identity categories ultimately should come to be of no real importance. Jesus's call was not to classes or social identity categories as such, but to the individual soul. "God is no respecter of persons" is not a call to activism for leveling the social order but rather means that worldly status and importance—or social identity—make no difference in the eyes of God. Yes, Jesus said that it is easier for a camel to pass through the eye of a needle than for a rich man to enter the kingdom of heaven. But he followed this by saying that all things are possible with God.

Beyond Woke

"Beyond Woke" implies a position better than wokeness, a perspective that may or may not be subsequent to wokeness but is certainly superior to it.

For those who have used the phrase to date, it has essentially meant "super-woke." For some, like the founders of a Facebook page "Beyond Woke," the phrase means a state of super-enlightenment, living a life devoted to going deeper. Not just being awake and aware of the wool that has been pulled over the eyes of the people, but a continual and ongoing examination of all of life and a commitment to questioning everything. It isn't just about seeing the veil, but discovering what lies beyond it and seeking both a more enlightened self and a more enlightened society. Not just aware but enlightened. Not just woke, but Beyond Woke.[1]

This passage seems to suggest an awakening into spirituality and an awareness of how the powers that be "pull the wool over the eyes of people" and dupe them into believing lies about social reality. But further inspection reveals that the founders of this page define "woke" in much the same way that it has been used by the social justice left and defined in the *Oxford English Dictionary*: "alert to racial or social discrimination and injustice."[2]

Others have mobilized the term to similar ends—to define an increased level of activism in education,[3] as well to issue admonitions about "woke-washing" or corporate virtue signaling in marketing and advertising.[4] A panel discussion on the history of woke activism has been held.[5] Duke University feminists have established a webzine devoted to going "beyond the woke headlines."[6] In short, beyond woke means hyper-woke to the woke world.

---

1 "Beyond Woke." Facebook. April 11, 2017. https://www.facebook.com/BeyondWoke/.

2 "woke, adj.2." *OED Online*, Oxford University Press, December 2018. https://www.oed.com/view/Entry/.

3 Martinez, Andrew. "When Being 'Woke' Is Not Enough." *Diverse*. March 6, 2018. https://diverseeducation.com/article/111381/.

4 "Beyond Woke: How Not to High-Jack Culture." *Amplify*. https://www.weareamplify.com/presents/beyond-woke-how-not-high-jack-culture/.

5 "Panel Discussion: 1619-2019: Beyond Woke." *Detroit Historical Society - Where the Past Is Present*. November 21, 2019. https://detroithistorical.org/detroit-historical-museum/events-calendar/events-listing/panel-discussion-1619-2019-beyond-woke.

6 "Beyond the Woke Headline." *The Muse*. https://sites.duke.edu/dukemuse/elementor-623/.

A. The Denial of Individuality and Freedom Under Social Justice

While according to at least one scholar, "the individual" as such developed historically and as a result of Christianity,[7] the figure of the individual is nevertheless non-ideological. That is, regardless of whether, and if so, over what span of time, the individual was developed or discovered, the individual is nevertheless demonstrably a non-abstract concrete particular.

Individuality is a certain basis for identity. Leaving other species aside, every person is singular, one-of-a-kind, unique. Genetic singularity is the biological correlative—some would say the basis—of uniqueness. Yet, by virtue of phenotypes and unique sets of experience, uniqueness holds even for identical twins.

Nothing about the assertion of individuality should be understood as degrading to anyone else. Contrary to social justice activists, arguing for the importance of individuality and the protection of individual expression is not a mere ruse deployed by white men to maintain their supposedly superior positions in the social order. Individuality is true for everyone, regardless of social identity.

Despite their obsession with identity itself, social justice activists erase from consciousness and consideration—supposedly for political reasons—the only certain basis for identity. Social justice politics hinges on non-familial group identity membership. Group identity is the most important for social justice ideology because social justice believers hold that group identity overwhelmingly determines what one is and may become. As such, according to social justice, group identity must determine politics as well.

But as I argued in *Springtime for Snowflakes*, identity politics solidifies the very categorization that is supposedly the source of oppression. Academic "grievance studies" devoted to this or that subordinated identity category actually solidify the supposedly subordinated categories, lending force to the containment

---

7 Siedentop, Larry. *Inventing the Individual: The Origins of Western Liberalism*. Belknap Press of Harvard University Press, 2017.

of the members therein. Identity politics lends strength to the categorical subordination of those it "serves."

But this is not the most pernicious effect of the social justice obsession with group identity. Those who conform to the dictates of social justice identity politics and group adherence tell themselves and others that their devotion to identity politics is noble. They are fighting for the oppressed, the marginalized, the subordinated. This makes social justice an alluring ideology to believers. But it hides a more fundamental reality from the consciousness of the sleepwalking woke—the terrifying aloneness and fearsome existential freedom that they must otherwise face.

By freedom, I don't mean the ability to choose, willy-nilly, from an unlimited set of possibilities—but rather the necessity that a human must choose at all. While it appears to be a contradiction to speak of freedom in terms of necessity, as Søren Kierkegaard and Jean Paul Sartre suggested, the necessity to choose is precisely what determines human freedom as such. At least since the dawning of moral conscience, each and every person has had no choice but to choose. Each person must choose at every turn. Each must exercise freedom, even when believing that the "choices" are determined. A choice may seem utterly constrained and compelled—but only because the freedom to choose meets an apparent determinism. But the belief in determinism is only possible because determinism is not absolute—although neither is freedom. Imprisonment has no meaning without relative freedom beyond the prison walls, and freedom has no meaning without the prison itself. Meanwhile, freedom holds within prison, as does partial determinism outside of prison.

Of course, many people treat freedom with little or no regard, especially those, however progressive or *avant-garde* they might imagine themselves, who depend on group membership, who place a premium on conformity with group conventions. Such as these pawn their freedom for group acceptance and safety. They engage in self-deception as they collude with the group to hide their individual and personal freedom from themselves—even or especially when not to conform would be extremely dangerous. The worthiness and nobleness of the cause provides a sufficient decoy from the truth that the will has been suborned in the process of submitting to group dictates. Yet, such individuals have acted from freedom, nonetheless.

Groups are very good at absolving individuals of responsibility for their disuse of freedom. The more authoritarian the group, the more absolution it offers the individual for surrendering his freedom. Groups that are both authoritarian and that also proffer "noble" ends are perhaps the most compelling, offering as they do two sources of compunction, including the rewards of idealism and such pretensions to correctness as to make dissent both retrograde and risky.

B. Morality from Freedom

If to be moral is to choose right acting, it follows that moral behavior is impossible without freedom. Freedom to choose, and to choose wrongly, is a prerequisite for morality. But wokeness compels choice by group pressure. It either cows one into submission prior to the act, or shames one after it.

This is why overcoming wokeness is essential and why to be truly moral is to be beyond woke. The group compulsion of wokeness precludes true moral choice, as does any herd compulsion. Thus, to be beyond woke is to leave the herd and to act from one's own freedom and without reference to the moral dictates of the group. To be beyond woke is to be an individual, to be a true moral agent, to be allowed to err honestly and without herd prevention, and to take responsibility for one's actions with reference to oneself and others. To be beyond woke is to be free.

CHAPTER ONE

I Was a Leftist NYC Prof— But When I Said the Left Was Unhinged, Colleagues Called Me a Nazi and Treated Me Like a Russian Spy[1]

W HAT'S WRONG with the American left? Suffering from Trump anxiety disorder, acting like cult members, and engaging in a new McCarthyism, the left has lost its collective mind. I saw it coming and left the left in the nick of time.

My break with the left began in the fall of 2016. I was a professor at New York University, a left-liberal, and an active social media participant. My skepticism and resentment at my political tribe's insistence that I affirm its increasingly crazy claims had been growing steadily to this point.

Much like Jordan Peterson, my tipping point involved the pronoun wars,[2] although, as you'll see, I enjoyed a more satirical approach. When the University of Michigan instituted a policy that offered students a carte blanche pronoun preference opportunity, a clever student offered "His Majesty" as his cho-

---

1 Originally published by *RT.com*. November 12, 2019. Reproduced here by permission.

2 Zivanovic, Crista. "The Pronoun Wars." *Nwitimes.com*. May 2018. https://www.nwitimes.com/the-pronoun-wars/image_2c95871b-ee1e-5f28-a70b-2435428c3c5e.html.

sen pronoun, and his blasphemous pronoun choice made the news.[3] The satirical trope hilariously underscored the absurdity of gender and pronoun proliferation, and the institutional lunacy that has attempted to keep pace with it. I posted a link to an article about the spoof on Facebook, without comment. I then proceeded to teach for the rest of the afternoon.

By the time I noticed the pandemonium, it was too late to manage it. A histrionic reaction had ensued. Hundreds upon hundreds of condemnatory threads and sub-threads multiplied beneath the link. Dozens and dozens of Facebook friends had sent private messages, demanding explanations and retractions. I was accused of betrayal, discursive violence, and transphobia.

I soon became defector from the party line and the university would come down on me like a ton of bricks...

The Left's Psychotic Break

Clearly, a collective hysteria has the left in its grip. I am not using a strict definition of the left that includes only the hardcore Antifa members, socialists, and communists, but also refer to many people formerly known as "liberals," who've since become quite illiberal. I also include former moderate centrists, who've become part of the "resistance." As an example of the latter, I point to an acquaintance I hadn't seen in years, someone I'd considered a milquetoast liberal at most, yet who now sounded like a radical leftist when remarking bitterly: "I just wish someone would put a bullet through Donald Trump's head!"

I don't blame such foot soldiers of the resistance for their viciousness. They've been led to believe that they're morally superior to Trump and his followers, despite (or perhaps because of) the fact that they harbor such violent fantasies. They are not entirely responsible for their derangement. They are unwitting dupes being whipped into frenzies by the political and media establishments. They've contracted a "contagious psychosis," wherein, as one study puts it, "certain 'unrealistic' human be-

---

3 Athey, Amber. "UMich to Profs: Don't Say 'Ladies and Gentlemen,' 'Mom and Dad.'" *Campus Reform*. November 10, 2016. https://www.campusreform.org/?ID=8372.

havior and thoughts can be transferred from one subject to another, within the intimacy of the family circle or according to an epidemic including numerous protagonists." Sounds about right.

The American Psychological Association's (APA) *Dictionary of Psychology* avoids terms like mass psychosis and contagious psychosis, likely for the same reasons that it avoids terms like "nervous breakdown." They sound too dramatic and unscientific. But the APA does use the term "collective hysteria," which its dictionary defines as "the spontaneous outbreak of atypical thoughts, feelings, or actions in a group or social aggregate. Manifestations may include psychogenic illness, collective hallucinations, and bizarre actions."[4]

With its parade of successive delusions—from the "Russian collusion" narrative,[5] to the "Russian bots" narrative,[6] and the latest, the Ukraine "quid pro quo" narrative—this seems to describe the contemporary left precisely. These narratives have in common a willful fabrication of crime stories believed to be true regardless of the lack of empirical evidence. Those who believe in these narratives merely repeat them ad nauseum in the hope that they'll become true, or at least that they'll be counted as true—which amounts to the same thing for the left, because for the left, belief equals (or is greater than) reality.

As I've suggested, the left's derangement is not limited to electoral politics. If we consider cultural politics as well, then we must include gender pluralism and transgenderism, the expanding domain of "racism," and other related phenomena.

The gender pluralist, transgender movement has resulted in a seemingly endless parade of absurdities, including but not

---

4 "Collective Hysteria." *American Psychological Association*, American Psychological Association. https://dictionary.apa.org/collective-hysteria.

5 "Trump-Russia Investigation." *CNN*, Cable News Network. May 23, 2017. https://www.cnn.com/specials/politics/trump-russia-ties.

6 Mayer, Jane. "How Russia Helped Swing the Election for Trump." *The New Yorker*, The New Yorker. July 9, 2019. https://www.newyorker.com/magazine/2018/10/01/how-russia-helped-to-swing-the-election-for-trump.

limited to the proliferation of genders[7] and gender pronouns[8] but also the claim that human sex difference is not an overwhelmingly binary system,[9] and most recently that "men can have periods too."[10] This last bit of transgender orthodoxy recently bled into mass media advertising, thanks to the feminine (not women's!) underwear company, Thinx, whose new "MENstruation" ad[11] made news when it was rejected by CBS[12] (although the network is set to consider an altered version). Ad-Age had previously reported that Bravo, E!, Oxygen, BET, MTV, VH1, HGTV, the Food Network, TLC and NBC would air the ad.[13]

Add to these symptoms of mass hysteria the contagious tendency to label anything and everything "racist," including shoes, sweaters, and stuffed animals. Commercial products deemed racist include the all-white Adidas sneakers,[14] the Adi-

---

7 "63 Genders—A New Perspective on Sex and Gender." *APath.org.* July 4, 2019. https://apath.org/63-genders/.

8 Forsey, Caroline. "Gender Neutral Pronouns: What They Are & How to Use Them." *HubSpot Blog.* September 28, 2018. https://blog.hubspot.com/marketing/gender-neutral-pronouns.

9 Fausto-sterling, Anne. "Why Sex Is Not Binary." *The New York Times,* The New York Times. October 25, 2018. https://www.nytimes.com/2018/10/25/opinion/sex-biology-binary.html.

10 Leventry, Amber. "Men Can Have Periods Too, And We Need to Normalize This." *Scary Mommy.* April 18, 2019. https://www.scarymommy.com/men-can-have-periods-too/.

11 Thinx. "MENstruation." *YouTube,* YouTube. October 3, 2019. https://www.youtube.com/watch?v=2UcwkL9zQDE.

12 Steigrad, Alexandra. "CBS Bans TV Ad That Depicts Menstruating Men." *New York Post,* New York Post. October 9, 2019. https://nypost.com/2019/10/08/cbs-bbc-america-ban-tv-ad-that-depicts-menstruating-men/.

13 Jardine, Alexandra. "The First TV Campaign for Thinx Imagines a World Where Guys Have Periods." *Ad Age.* October 3, 2019. https://adage.com/creativity/work/first-tv-campaign-thinx-imagines-world-where-guys-have-periods/2203976.

14 Jones, Charisse. "Adidas Pulls All White Sneaker Created for Black History Month in Wake of Twitter Backlash." *USA Today,* Gannett Satellite Information Network. February 13, 2019. https://www.usatoday.com/story/money/2019/02/05/adidas-pulls-white-black-history-month-sneaker-after-

das "shackle shoes,"[15] Gucci's "blackface" jumper,[16] and Prada's monkey figure[17]—all decried as racist by the Twitter Red Guards and all subsequently pulled from the market.

Meanwhile, social psychologists and political scientists have considered collective hysteria to be a characteristic of conservatives alone, with one begrudging but important exception. Four years after publishing a paper on "the relationship between personality traits and political ideologies," *The American Journal of Political Science* admitted that the article contained an ever-so-slight error.[18] When they delivered the results of their study, the authors "exactly reversed" the findings where the left and right were concerned. The periodical's editors have now issued a correction: it is liberals who exhibit the personality trait of "psychoticism" and not, as stated in the original article, conservatives. I saw this psychoticism first-hand, although I was the one called crazy.

Becoming Deplorable

Here's how the left and I parted ways. After my Facebook condemnation, I created an anonymous Twitter handle, @AntiPCNYUProf [since changed to @TheAntiPCProf] with the name "The Deplorable NYU Prof" [since changed to Michael

---

twitter-slams/2780496002/.

15 Memmott, Mark. "Adidas Cancels Its 'Shackle Shoes.'" *NPR*, NPR. June 19, 2012. https://www.npr.org/sections/thetwo-way/2012/06/19/155348916/adidas-cancels-its-shackle-shoes.

16 Hsu, Tiffany, and Elizabeth Paton. "Gucci and Adidas Apologize and Drop Products Called Racist." *The New York Times,* The New York Times. February 7, 2019. https://www.nytimes.com/2019/02/07/business/gucci-blackface-adidas-apologize.html.

17 Albanese, Chiara, and Robert Williams. "Prada Will Stop Selling $550 Monkey Figure Decried as Racist." *Bloomberg.com*, Bloomberg. December 14, 2018. https://www.bloomberg.com/news/articles/2018-12-14/prada-will-stop-selling-550-monkey-figure-decried-as-racist.

18 Verhulst, Brad, et al. "Erratum to 'Correlation Not Causation: The Relationship between Personality Traits and Political Ideologies.'" *American Journal of Political Science*, Vol 1, pp. 34–51." Wiley Online Library. John Wiley & Sons, Ltd (10.1111). August 6, 2015. https://onlinelibrary.wiley.com/doi/epdf/10.1111/ajps.12216.

Rectenwald] and began tweeting criticisms of political correctness and the adoption of "social justice" ideology in the university and beyond. I was soon discovered by a reporter from NYU's student newspaper and decided to go on the record for my views. In the interview, I criticized the adoption of the new "social justice" creed by NYU and most other North American colleges and universities, including the establishment of "bias reporting hotlines" at NYU and at over 230 other institutions, the use of safe spaces, the adoption of trigger warnings, and the now-routine no-platforming of speakers, which made it impossible for alternative perspectives to be heard on most campuses.

Although I was not fired for airing my views, my life on campus was made intolerable. Within two days of my interview's appearance, I was called into the dean's office and pressured to go on a paid leave of absence by the dean and the head of human resources. "People are concerned about you," the dean said. The implication was that I must be crazy for differing with campus orthodoxy. I was also roundly denounced by an official committee, called the Liberal Studies Diversity, Equity, and Inclusion Working Group, who ended their sentencing by declaring: "The cause of his guilt is the content and structure of his thinking." I have since dubbed them "the Conformity, Inequity and Exclusion Group." They demand conformity to their "social justice" creed, treat as less than equal anyone who doesn't conform, and attempt to exclude non-conformists from the university, and by extension, from academia at large.

When I returned from leave, I was universally shunned by over 100 fellow faculty members, some of whom wouldn't let me on an elevator with them. On the very last day of my first semester back from leave, a group of colleagues issued a series of blistering emails, attacking me for announcing on Twitter the forthcoming publication of my new book. I was called "alt-right," "Nazi," "short-pants White Devil," "fragile white male," and "Satan," among other choice slurs. I'm not exaggerating when I say that had I been a member of any other identity category, the assailants would have been summarily fired without further ado. But no. The emails continued for several days. Meanwhile, I had never once mentioned any individuals or groups by name, either in my initial interview, or in any subsequent media coverage.

My Life as A Russian Spy

Upon complaining to human resources and the equal opportunity employment officers about the abuse, nothing happened—except that my office was moved to... get this ... the Russian department! I was transferred to a completely isolated office with bare metal shelves containing none of my books, because the university refused to have them moved from my old office. I like to joke that I was treated as if I were a Russian spy, sent to my own personal gulag.

I sued the university and five of the offending colleagues for defamation. When they saw the motion to dismiss filed by NYU's army of lawyers, my attorneys refused to continue on a contingency basis and blamed my forthcoming book. The suit expired but I later negotiated a retirement settlement with the university.

Most people who hear my story do not wonder why I broke with the left when I did. They wonder why it took so long. To such people I say, consider the behavior and beliefs of the left and ask yourself how much indoctrination must have been necessary to produce such results. Then consider this: I was subjected to this very indoctrination for over twenty-five years. My escape was a minor miracle.

CHAPTER TWO

The Destruction of the Faculty[1]

I N THE FALL of 2008, I began working as a full-time faculty member in the Liberal Studies program at New York University. I was promoted to full Professor in the fall of 2016 and retired in good standing in January 2019. Thus, the tale I tell does not represent sour grapes. Rather, what follows is a jeremiad decrying the direction that academia has taken in order to underscore the threats posed to academic integrity and institutional legitimacy. Over eleven years, I watched with increasing dismay and incredulity as academic integrity, fairness, and intellectual rigor were eroded, with the implicit endorsement of administration and faculty alike. I witnessed the de-professionalization and de-legitimation of the faculty—hiring policies based on tokenized identity politics and cronyism, an increasing anti-intellectualism and ideological conformity expected from faculty and students, and the subsequent curtailment of academic freedom.

Just to be clear, most of my former faculty colleagues are well-educated, bright, and dedicated teachers. Some are also worthy scholars or creative authors. Yet, in addition to cronyism, the program's hiring practices were significantly compro-

---

1 Originally published as "The De-Professionalization of the Academy" under a pseudonym in *Quillette*, April 13, 2017. Reproduced here by permission.

21

mised, especially as a result of the premium that the university had begun to place on "diversity."

While having changed dramatically over the years, Liberal Studies at NYU represents the legacy of a remedial program that began in the 1970s. A few of its current faculty members may still be remnants of that era. Although a new, competitive bachelor's degree in Global Liberal Studies was instituted in 2009, the effects of the legacy program, along with subsequent hiring trends, added up to a professoriate of mixed credentials and accomplishments. A full listing of both full- and part-time faculty included and surely still includes at least one member whose highest degree is the B.A., with several faculty members holding M.As., along with a rather large contingent of faculty holding the M.F.A. degree. Of those whose highest degree was a B.A., or M.A., their fields of study were often unrelated to the courses that they taught. For those unfamiliar with academia, teaching with only a B.A. or M.A. degree may be possible—but only in the most exceptional cases of scholarly or creative stardom. The rule by and large has been, at least on paper, that faculty members should hold a terminal degree and the Ph.D. is the most common terminal degree.

In addition to depriving students of scholarly and pedagogic expertise, staffing the faculty with M.A.s and B.A.s must have sent a clear message to students: university accomplishments are relatively unimportant. Students might rightfully have asked why they should pursue advanced degrees or even undergraduate degrees when the university itself apparently deems such qualifications unnecessary for teaching at the university level, even in a top-twenty-five university like NYU.

This unevenness in faculty preparation would not have represented a travesty if not for the glut of highly qualified Ph.Ds. entering the job market each year, many of whom remain on the market year after year. Hundreds of newly minted and extremely impressive Ph.Ds. often go without full-time work, and some are even unable to secure positions as part-time adjuncts. Such difficulties in finding academic work are not primarily due to the "over-production of Ph.Ds.," as is commonly held. Rather, as the labor historian Trevor Griffey argues, the proximate cause is the de-professionalization of academic fields—the penchant for hiring contingent faculty without Ph.Ds., and an apparent administrative preference for under- and unqualified, inexperienced faculty.[2] In the case of NYU's Liberal Studies program, this kind of hiring proceeded apace, despite the large pool of excellent candidates with Ph.Ds., most of whom would have been more than happy to teach at NYU while enjoying its cosmopolitan environs. It is not as if these candidates did not apply for jobs in the program. They did and likely still do. But I noted that their applications were often passed over for far less qualified, even egregiously unqualified candidates.

Some of the faculty members with less than impressive credentials held and likely still hold positions of significant authority in terms of curriculum development. They served as chairs of various sub-programs within academic units and had influence over curricula, both within and beyond the program. One such faculty member—who held an M.A. degree in "Performance Studies," one of many questionable "studies" fields and one that is not even taught in the program—served on a committee responsible for making university-wide curriculum recommendations to the Provost.

My first personal and professional collision with the dismissive treatment of credentials and accomplishments in the program occurred during my second semester at NYU and involved the election of the writing faculty chair in the spring of 2009. The candidates included me and another faculty member, the same Performance Studies M.A. mentioned above. After each of us was asked to write an introduction and mission statement, the voting began. I won't attempt to reproduce our respective mission statements but suffice it to say that his was a rather flabby, loosely assembled set of supposed sentences.

---

2 Griffey, Trevor. "The Decline of Faculty Tenure: Less from an Oversupply of PhDs, and More from the Systematic De-Valuation of the PhD as a Credential for College Teaching." *LAWCHA*. January 9, 2017. www.lawcha. org/2017/01/09/decline-faculty-tenure-less-oversupply-phds-systematic-de-valuation-phd-credential-college-teaching/.

The ballot box was controlled by a faculty aide and the votes were cast manually and electronically. Upon counting the votes, the faculty aide announced that I had won by two votes. Upon hearing this, a proxy of the competitor, who had no official role in the process at all, confiscated the ballot box and absconded to her office. Subsequently, a "recount" was conducted—by whom, I never discovered. Given the confiscation of the ballots, I was obviously entitled to suspicions. I suddenly became the loser by the same margin that I had won.

In a later election for writing curricular chair, my competitor accused me in his mission statement of writing books and publishing essays. He treated these as blemishes or sins that somehow disqualified me for the position. "I haven't written any textbooks. I don't like textbooks. I don't have a Ph.D. or scores of academic, scholarly publications to my name," he wrote. These comments were made as part of a diatribe meant to diminish the importance of academic credentials and accomplishments, representing the Ph.D. and scholarly publications as pedantic, fuddy-duddy detriments rather than qualifications. As things went in the program, he won the election.

Among the writing faculty, most of whom held M.F.A. degrees, a disdain for scholarship, and in particular for Ph.Ds. in English, was palpable. This attitude was likely owing to the fact that many of the faculty with M.F.As. were required to teach first-year writing and other lower-level writing courses, while apparently believing that they were soon-to-be-discovered literary geniuses who deserved veritable sinecures within elite M.F.A. programs. They treated the writing courses in the program as if they were part of an ersatz M.F.A. program, approaching their students in introductory writing courses as if they had all been seeking, or should have been seeking, to become literary authors or columnists for *Harper's Magazine* or *The New Yorker*. This mode of instruction did a great disservice to students. I taught hundreds of students in advanced-level courses; despite having taken two writing courses and a half a dozen writing-intensive surveys before enrolling in my courses, most students came to my upper-level classes with little or no idea about how to write a scholarly essay. The hiring practices for writing instructors were often based on cronyism. One particular member of the full-time writing faculty exercised a talent for pulling strings for friends of important people with whom she sought to ingratiate herself. As such, and having some mysterious power over the deans, she managed to secure positions for new adjuncts whose qualifications were quite imperceptible. In one case, the beneficiary of the cronyism had never taught a college class, held only a B.A. in English from a mediocre middle-states institution, and had published nothing other than a few chatty, web-based editorials. Yet she was hired to teach university writing courses.

After successfully securing part-time employment for this academic labor scab, the same full-time faculty member attempted to have the equivalent of a leftist Dear Abby hired as a full-time professor in writing and journalism. This candidate's main claim to fame was having penned an advice column for the readers of *The Nation*. In her efforts to get the *Nation's* Dear Abby a faculty position, the influential faculty member was foiled by the proponents of another kind of favoritism: identity politics tokenism.

In the 2015-2016 academic year, I had been appointed by the Dean of Liberal Studies to serve as the chair for a writing hiring committee, a committee charged with hiring one full-time writing professor, someone who not only could teach first-year writing classes but also offerings in journalism.

After the first round of interviews, the committee of four met to discuss the first group of candidates before undertaking a second set of first-round Skype interviews. At that meeting, I reminded the committee of an email from one of the candidates that I had received and forwarded to them. After reading the email aloud, I argued that the missive effectively disqualified the candidate. The writing was riddled with awkward expression, malapropisms, misplaced punctuation, and other conceptual and formal problems. Rarely had a first-year student issued an email to me that evidenced more infelicitous prose. I asked my fellow committee members how we could possibly hire someone to teach writing who had written such an email, despite the fact that it represented only a piece of occasional writing. The candidate apparently could not write. I also pointed to her application letter, which was similarly awkward and error prone. One committee colleague argued that "we do not teach grammar" in our writing classes. Sure, I thought. And a surgeon doesn't take vital signs or draw blood. That doesn't mean that the surgeon wouldn't be able to do so if so required.

In the Skype interview following this discussion, a fellow committee member proceeded to attack the next job candidate, a candidate whom I greatly respected. In fact, before the interview, this colleague, obviously enraged by my criticisms of her favorite, announced that she would ruthlessly attack the next candidate—no doubt because I held the candidate in high esteem. She did exactly that, asking increasingly obtuse and irrelevant questions, while adopting a belligerent tone and aggressive posture. That candidate, incidentally, had done fascinating scholarship on the history of "the public sphere," or the very birthplace of journalism. He had earned his Ph.D. from a top-ten English department, had since accrued considerable teaching experience in relevant subjects, and presented a record of noteworthy publications, including academic scholarship and online, "digital journalism." He interviewed extremely well, except when he was harangued and badgered by the hostile interviewer. He should have been a finalist for the job. But he had a fatal flaw: he was a white, straight male.

After the interview, I chided my colleague uncompromisingly, although without a hint of bias. I believed, and still do, that her behavior during that interview was utterly unprofessional and prejudicial, and I told her so. Next, I was on the receiving end of her outrageous verbal barrage. Not only did she call me some choice expletives but also rose from her chair and was poised as if to charge me physically while flailing her limbs and yelling and swearing. I left the room and proceeded to the dean's office. I told the dean what had just occurred. He advised me to let it rest until the following week.

What happened next was telling. I was unwittingly enmeshed in an identity politics imbroglio. The woman who had verbally assaulted me was a black female and the candidate whom she championed was also a black female. I was informed by the dean that pursuing a grievance, or even remaining on the committee, was now "complicated." "Complicated?" I asked. "Complicated," he answered. I knew exactly what complicated meant. It meant that we were dealing with a member of a privileged identity category, a membership that entitled the member to all manner of outlandish and otherwise career-ending behaviors. Within a day or two, the dean recommended that I step down from the committee. I realized I was in a corner and stepped down, going from chair to non-member.

The committee went on to hire the woman in question. Since assuming her position, the new hire posted an official faculty profile linked from NYU's Liberal Studies program page. Her faculty profile page betrayed the same awkward prose, poor incorporation of quotes, and other problems of expression typical of first-year student writers, but usually not professors. The profile also included, and apparently still includes, a glaring grammatical error: "The two main objectives in teaching is…" If you point out the bad grammar, however, you will be called a racist—because "grammar is racist." Google it if you don't believe me.

To be perfectly clear, I am not arguing against the diversification of the faculty and student populations within NYU's Liberal Studies program, or anywhere else for that matter. Rather, I am suggesting that the diversity initiatives that were introduced by the university and the Liberal Studies program, and likely in most institutions of higher education, have been hastily and thoughtlessly administered and mistakenly construed, to the detriment of academic integrity and legitimate "diversity, equity, and inclusion" objectives.

Qualified academics can be found among all population groups. It is sheer cynicism to suppose that qualified candidates cannot be found among minority groups. But universities must ensure that those selected are qualified, first and foremost, not by their identities per se, but by what they know and are able to do and teach. Blatant tokenism in hiring and promotion jeopardizes the integrity of higher education and also undermines the objectives that diversity initiatives aim to promote.

Further, when markers of race, gender, gender fluidity, sexual orientation, ethnicity, religion, and other factors are deemed the only criteria for diversity, students are cheated, as are those chosen to meet diversity measures on the basis of social identity alone. Nothing is more "essentialist" or constraining than diversity understood strictly in terms of social identity categorization. Such a notion of diversity reduces "diverse" people to the status of token bearers of identity markers, relegating them to an impenetrable and largely inescapable identity chrysalis, and implicitly eliding their individuality. Meanwhile, there is no necessary connection between identity and ideas, identity and talents, identity and aspirations, or identity and beliefs.

Likewise, if academic administrators and faculty members are to foster real diversity in higher education, they must consider not only diversity of social identity but also diversity of *thought and perspective*. This is the kind of diversity that is supposed to be recognized and fostered in the first place.

CHAPTER THREE

Congratulations!

A S PART OF HIS APPLICATION to Stanford University, Ziad Ahmed, an applicant for the class of 2021, submitted the following essay in response to the prompt, "What matters to you, and why?" He later proudly posted an image of the essay on Twitter:

What matters to you, and why?
#BlackLivesMatter #BlackLivesMatter #BlackLivesMatter #BlackLivesMatter #BlackLivesMatter #BlackLivesMatter
#BlackLivesMatter #BlackLivesMatter #BlackLivesMatter #BlackLivesMatter #BlackLivesMatter #BlackLivesMatter
#BlackLivesMatter #BlackLivesMatter #BlackLivesMatter #BlackLivesMatter #BlackLivesMatter #BlackLivesMatter
#BlackLivesMatter #BlackLivesMatter #BlackLivesMatter #BlackLivesMatter #BlackLivesMatter #BlackLivesMatter
#BlackLivesMatter #BlackLivesMatter #BlackLivesMatter #BlackLivesMatter #BlackLivesMatter #BlackLivesMatter
#BlackLivesMatter #BlackLivesMatter #BlackLivesMatter #BlackLivesMatter #BlackLivesMatter #BlackLivesMatter
#BlackLivesMatter #BlackLivesMatter #BlackLivesMatter #BlackLivesMatter #BlackLivesMatter #BlackLivesMatter
#BlackLivesMatter #BlackLivesMatter #BlackLivesMatter #BlackLivesMatter #BlackLivesMatter #BlackLivesMatter
#BlackLivesMatter #BlackLivesMatter #BlackLivesMatter #BlackLivesMatter #BlackLivesMatter #BlackLivesMatter
#BlackLivesMatter #BlackLivesMatter #BlackLivesMatter #BlackLivesMatter #BlackLivesMatter #BlackLivesMatter
#BlackLivesMatter #BlackLivesMatter #BlackLivesMatter #BlackLivesMatter #BlackLivesMatter #BlackLivesMatter
#BlackLivesMatter #BlackLivesMatter #BlackLivesMatter #BlackLivesMatter #BlackLivesMatter #BlackLivesMatter
#BlackLivesMatter #BlackLivesMatter #BlackLivesMatter #BlackLivesMatter #BlackLivesMatter #BlackLivesMatter
#BlackLivesMatter #BlackLivesMatter #BlackLivesMatter #BlackLivesMatter #BlackLivesMatter #BlackLivesMatter
#BlackLivesMatter #BlackLivesMatter #BlackLivesMatter #BlackLivesMatter #BlackLivesMatter #BlackLivesMatter
#BlackLivesMatter #BlackLivesMatter #BlackLivesMatter #BlackLivesMatter

Ziad Ahmed @ziadtheactivist · Apr 1
I submitted this answer in my @Stanford application. & yesterday, I was admitted.

#BlackLivesMatter pic.twitter.com/5Et18M77bsWL

Response to the Admissions Essay, "What Matters to you, and why?"

"Stanford's" response to Ahmed's application follows:

Dear Ziad Ahmed:

We at Stanford University have given careful consideration to your application and have decided to accept you into the class of 2021. We are delighted to welcome to the university community such an innovative, articulate, academically talented and socially enlightened student as yourself. Congratulations!

Additionally, we are happy to inform you that given the content of your admissions essays, we have decided to grant you a full scholarship to Stanford University, inclusive of tuition, room, and board.

In all of the most important respects, your education at Stanford will consist of imbibing and regurgitating such social justice phrases as you have already begun to learn—although you will no doubt learn new ones, including "Hey ho! Hey ho! Charles Murray (or insert the name of other inveterate racist, fascist pig) has got to go!" and "No Trump! No KKK! No fascist USA!"

We expect that you will wish to contribute in this and other important ways to the university community during your time at Stanford. We hope you will attend events at which right-leaning speakers are able to reach the lectern, and to similarly repeat such phrases as you did in your application essay—without end, and at high volume.

Think of Stanford University as a social justice warrior incubator. Our mission is to produce students who will repeat social justice phrases without hesitation, who will refuse to listen to differing perspectives, and who will serve as carriers of this ideology to the wider society.

We are confident that you are just such a student. Again, congratulations!

Sincerely,
Officer of Admissions,
"Stanford" University

CHAPTER FOUR

On the Origins and Character of Social Justice[1]

ONE OF THE GREAT ironies of Western political history involves the term "social justice." Although a core idea within liberalism and socialism for at least 175 years, the background and origin of "social justice" was a cultural and political conservatism. The irony of the "cultural appropriation" of social justice by liberalism and socialism has recently redoubled. Suggestive of a seemingly undeniable, though intangible, good— that is, of just, fair, well-ordered, and harmonious social relations—social justice is now implicated in fierce and sometimes violent antagonisms. Social justice crystallizes in two words some of the most contentious issues roiling North American politics today. Contemporary social justice bears little resemblance to the original social justice or even more recent movements that have gone by the same name.

Social justice can be traced to nineteenth-century Catholic social theory. Coined and developed in the early 1840s by Luigi Taparelli d'Azeglio, an aristocrat turned Jesuit priest, the concept was intended to serve as s new type of justice, added to those already included in Catholic justice doctrine (commutative, distributive, and legal justice). In a five-volume magnum

---

1 Originally published by *New English Review*. August 2018.

opus entitled *A Theoretical Treatise of Natural Law Based on Fact* (1841-1843), Taparelli's "social justice" was a renovation and extension of "general justice," an ancient virtue, which St. Thomas Aquinas had adopted from Aristotle.[2]

The context for the introduction of social justice was the supposed lack of an adequate Catholic response to industrialism and urbanization,[3] with their associated social and economic symptoms—the supplanting of guild-based cottage industries by urban factories, the displacement of workers from the countryside to the metropolis, overcrowded and unsanitary conditions of urban life, and a rising population of indigent laborers. In sum, the immediate consequences of industrial development for laborers amounted to a new and expanded poverty that involved precarious and degraded ways of life. In England, this became known as "The Condition of England Question," which commentators as diverse in political outlook as Thomas Carlyle, Benjamin Disraeli, Charles Dickens, John Stuart Mill, and Friedrich Engels would directly address.[4]

Taparelli offered an alternative to the prescriptions of liberalism and socialism, the two emergent political contenders in the era, much as had Carlyle. His Catholic social justice theory

---

2 Shields, Leo William. *History and Meaning of the Term Social Justice: A Dissertation Submitted to the Committee on ... Graduate Study of the University of Notre Dame.* Forgotten Books, 2016.

3 Behr, Thomas. "Luigi Taparelli and Social Justice: Rediscovering the Origins of a 'Hollowed' Concept." *Social Justice in Context,* Vol. 1, 2010, pp. 3-16; Behr, Thomas C. "Luigi Taparelli D'Azeglio, S.J. (1793–1862) and the Development of Scholastic Natural-Law Thought as a Science of Society and Politics." *Journal of Markets & Morality,* Vol. 6, No. 1, Spring 2003, pp. 99–115, at pp. 100-101.

4 Thomas Carlyle coined the phrase "the Condition of England" in Chapter One of *Chartism* (1839). Friedrich Engels contributed in 1844 with *The Condition of the Working Class in England.* See Levin, Michael. *The Condition of England Question: Carlyle, Mill, Engels* (1998).

For primary and secondary readings on The Condition of England Question, see Rectenwald, Michael. "The Condition of England Question." *19th-Century Literary and Cultural Studies: The Condition of England Question,* Carnegie Mellon University, 2005. https://www.andrew.cmu.edu/course/76-334-734/.

aimed to protect individuals from the lottery-like conditions of laissez faire economics on the one hand, and the domination by a centralized power of the state on the other. As Taparelli saw it, laissez faire would reduce human society to atomism and anarchy, and socialism would be the inevitable response. The latter could only enforce economic equality by violating the core principles of human individuality and liberty on which his concept of social justice depended. Taparelli offered social justice as an alternative.[5]

Social justice was proffered as a fact-based theory to mitigate the evils that these twin systems failed to address. Both liberalism and socialism, Taparelli claimed, began from a philosophically materialist premise that "pleasure [is] the supreme law of nature, guiding men to their happiness."[6] From false premises, deficient analyses and prescriptions inevitably must follow; this crude materialist conception ignored the intellectual and social dimensions of human nature. Including them explained our natural propensity to identify with others, the principles of equality and reciprocity, and the charitable impulse that followed from these facts of human nature. Any comprehensive response to social crises required a grasp of these fundamental premises.

Social justice also represented a recognition that human social organization involved social groups of various sizes, beginning with the family and including churches, charitable organizations, schools, economic associations, professional and industry trade groups, workers' unions, and so forth. Social justice depended on the principle of "subsidiarity," the precept that the smallest social unit capable of undertaking a social task should indeed undertake it.[7] These groups played vital roles in social justice, yet they faced possible abolition under centralized statism, and dissolution under laissez faire. Larger, centralized social units, such as the state, should be the means of last resort. In its preference for smaller groups, subsidiarity aimed

---

5 Behr, "Luigi Taparelli and Social Justice."
6 Ibid., p. 7.
7 Ibid., pp. 6-12.

to protect the semi-autonomy and liberty of individuals, without which no justice could exist. Addressing the negative effects of unequal outcomes—including the provision of assistance to the less fortunate—was indeed part of the original social justice schema, but such measures were to be undertaken primarily at the level of individuals and charitable organizations and, only in rare cases, the state. Material, de facto equality was not the goal.

As a proposed addendum to Catholic doctrine, social justice necessarily represented human beings as equals by virtue of their shared membership in the human species, a species created by God in his image. Taparelli recognized this ultimate, abstract equality. But such equality was essentially unearthly. It represented humans as a "species being," as Marx put it, individuals who recognized their membership in a species with others.[8] For Taparelli, concrete equality was another matter altogether. Unlike contemporary social justice notions, the original social justice creed did not aim at actual, concrete equality in any dimension—either social, economic, or political. Actual human beings were concrete individuals, not living, breathing abstractions as the left figures them:

> But slow. Where is this abstract man, this replicated humanity, the notion of which has suggested to me the first lineaments of social justice? If there exist men associated with other men, they always exist in the concrete, always individuated, always endowed with forces possessing definite qualities. But when I consider men from this new perspective, where is the equality? Compare age with age, intelligence with intelligence, strength with strength, etc.; everything is disparity between men: a disparity, furthermore, that derives from nature, since it is nature that forms the individual as it does the species; or rather, let us say nature forms individuals, man perceives species. I conclude correctly, then, that all individual human beings are naturally unequal among themselves in everything that pertains to their individuality, just as they are naturally

8 Marx, Karl. "Economic and Philosophical Manuscripts of 1844." *Estranged Labour*, Marx, 1844. Marxists.org. https://www.marxists.org/archive/marx/works/1844/manuscripts/labour.htm.

equal in all that pertains to the species. And so the activity of man will be just when it is appropriate to the different rights of those with whom one is dealing. Everything in individuals is inequality, even though the likeness of their natures be total.

> This individual inequality does not contradict their equality of speciesnature, for the qualities of the individual in relation to those of the species are an addition, and if you add unequal quantities to equal ones, are not the sums unequal? For example, add to the species-property of man the individuality of son, and you will find it in regard to the father in a relationship of debtor. For to be a son means to have received one's existence, and to be a father means to have given it. Now if the giver and the receiver considered themselves only as endowed with humanity, they would be equal and they would not owe one another anything reciprocally; but if their accounts are to be in balance in light of the fact that one of the two in becoming an individual has received from the other, this other has a right to a repayment. Justice demands, then, that the son render to the father an equivalent of the existence he has received from him.[9]

Taparelli pointed to what he saw as an inevitable and historically demonstrable hierarchical tendency in human social organization. Human social hierarchy derived from differences in ability and was marked by the differential access to, and biological and legal inheritance of, material resources and social power. He compared this factual history of human social arrangements with John Locke's liberal social contract theory:

> Here in a few words is the theory of social existence based upon the facts of history, and likewise confirmed by those facts. The existence of associations of men united by nature, equal to one another in their nature, unequal in their persons, free in their power of choice and therefore in need of a principle of unity: these are the chief facts of history to which we

---

9 Quoted in Burke, Thomas Patrick. "The Origins of Social Justice: Taparelli d'Azeglio." *Modern Age*. Spring 2010, pp. 97-106, at pp. 101-102.

have applied the universal principle of duty. The results of this application are that man needs always to be governed, and so he is, in point of fact; that he who governs is stronger and at the same time possesses authority, and so he actually is; that subjects are not sovereigns, and in point of fact they are not... Compare this theory of the facts of history with the hypotheses of the social contract where man is by nature free but in fact is in chains; by right is sovereign but in fact is created by it; confers authority, but in fact has no part of that authority; has made a pact, but did no negotiating; did it to secure all his rights, and meanwhile gave them away; believes every state to be a republic, yet sees there are monarchies; believes all men are equal, yet sees everywhere a hierarchy of classes; believes it gives consent, yet sees things happen despite it; believes it gives laws, yet sees that it receives them... Compare these two doctrines, I say, and judge which of them is true![10]

The original social justice amounted to the protection and mobilization of small charitable and philanthropic organizations to address (but not eliminate) the recalcitrant social facts of individual, economic, and political inequality, which supposedly had been exacerbated under the new industrial economy.[11]

By the time it became official Catholic doctrine with Pope Leo XIII's encyclical *Rerum Novarum* (or "On the Condition of the Working Classes," 1891), the term had already changed meanings. Christian socialism, secular philosophy, and secular social theory further developed social justice in the redistributive economic direction taken by the Catholic doctrine of social justice represented in *Rerum Novarum*.

This origin story has historical value, even if only satisfying an antiquarian curiosity. On the charge of antiquarianism, I plead guilty. But I introduced it not only for its purely historical value but also to draw out a few implications that follow from the history.

First, the original version of social justice of the early 1840s differs markedly from its contemporary namesake. Although

---

10   Ibid., pp. 100-101.
11   Behr, "Luigi Taparelli D'Azeglio," pp. 104-109.

they share the concern for justice as applied to the social realm, the two are not on the same genealogical tree either philosophically or politically. They share a name but only because later movements adopted the moniker. Taparelli's social justice, which later became official Catholic doctrine, was well-articulated and intentioned, and also essentially conservative.[12] It was egalitarian only in an otherworldly sense. It included no pretense of striving for concrete equality of any kind. It relied on charity and not on state-mandated distributive measures. It had nothing to do with contemporary notions of identity. It was not socialist. In fact, Taparelli formulated social justice in large part to ward off socialism.

Second, exposure to this history shows what should be obvious even without it: the phrase "social justice" has no *necessary* meaning at all. In fact, "social justice" can and has signified many different notions, especially given that the meanings of "justice" itself have been quite varied historically and philosophically.

The third point is an extension of the first two: beware of the nominalist fallacy—beware of mistaking particular instances designated by an abstract term with the meaning of the abstract term itself. When an abstract term is used to designate a particular instance of a putatively universal concept, the instance should not be confused with the universal concept that it conjures. Charles Manson and the Family might have called their murderous campaign "social justice." That wouldn't have made it good. The American Nazi Party does invoke the term "social justice" to designate a feature of its platform.[13] The neo-Nazis' use of such a noble-sounding term should not lead to any confusion about their intent.

Another piece of political nomenclature helps to make this clear. The "progressive" movement began in the Progressive Era and included ideas we would recognize as characteristic of contemporary progressivism: progressive taxation, redistributive measures, economic safety nets, and so on. From this instance

---

12 Burke, "The Origins of Social Justice," p. 103.
13 American Nazi Party. http://www.anp14.com/platform/index.php.

a general conception of progressive politics has arisen. Yet the earliest progressive economic and immigration proposals also included eugenics proposals. Thus, the earliest progressive movement included features that were hardly "progressive" by today's standards. If we were to observe a diktat of contemporary social justice, the word "progressive" should be accompanied by a trigger warning (TW). The term should also remind us to be wary of noble ideas conjured by this and other lofty language.

Point four is another extension of the above. The contemporary social justice movement should not be accepted or supported simply because it may sound virtuous to most contemporary ears. Instead, the core ideas, epistemological assumptions, political practices, and institutional techniques should be the crux of the matter in evaluating it. In my new book, *Springtime for Snowflakes: "Social Justice" and Its Postmodern Parentage*,[14] I retrace my graduate education in literary and cultural theory and cultural studies to track the postmodern theoretical and the Stalinist/Maoist disciplinary roots of contemporary social justice.

Some will recall twentieth-century social justice movements and thereby lose the scent leading to the actual historical bases and character of contemporary social justice. The twentieth-century variant included struggles for racial justice and equality; women's rights and equality; equal economic opportunity; redistributive economic objectives; and legal and political equality, including the protection of democratic participation. Of course, both abolitionism and the Civil Rights movement were essentially social justice crusades.

But social justice has since come to be associated with new, distinct features. Whereas the campus free speech movement was a hallmark of social justice in the 1960s, violent skirmishes waged against free speech and academic freedom are now associated with the term. Events that have unfolded on college cam-

---

14 Rectenwald, Michael. *Springtime for Snowflakes: 'Social Justice' and Its Postmodern Parentage*. Nashville, TN; London, UK: New English Review Press, 2018. https://amzn.to/2toA1YE.

puses, including at Yale, New York University,[15] UC Berkeley,[16] Middlebury College,[17] Evergreen State College,[18] and many others, bear the social justice insignia.

In addition to speech codes and the demand for speech repression, social justice comes with a whole other package of beliefs and objectives. Many of these would have struck earlier social justice activists as quite alien. A dramatic shift in ideas and a new focus on social identity mark the new social justice. Social justice includes new (trans)gender theories and activism, as well as notions of "privilege," "privilege-checking," "self-criticism," "cultural appropriation," "discursive violence," "rape culture," and so forth. "Intersectionality" is the axiomatic oppression-ranking framework that establishes a new social justice hierarchy based on the multiplicities of oppression as they may intersect and affect subjects in multiple, supposedly subordinated social categories. It then inverts the supposedly existing social hierarchy on the basis of this intersectional ranking, moving those on the bottom to the top, and vice versa. This is not a temporary feature of social justice but represents a hierarchical inversion that must be maintained to engender the animus and

---

15 Chasmar, Jessica. "Conservative speaker Gavin McInnes pepper-sprayed by NYU protesters." *The Washington Times*. February 3, 2017. https://www.washingtontimes.com/news/2017/feb/3/gavin-mcinnes-conservative-speaker-pepper-sprayed-/;

Rectenwald, Michael. "Here's What Happened When I Challenged the PC Campus Culture at NYU." *The Washington Post*. November 3, 2016. https://www.washingtonpost.com/posteverything/wp/2016/11/03/campus-pc-culture-is-so-rampant-that-nyu-is-paying-to-silence-me/.

16 Bodley, Michael and Nanette Asimov. "UC Berkeley cancels right-wing provocateur's talk amid violent protest." *SFGate*. February 2, 2017. https://www.sfgate.com/news/article/Protesters-storm-Milo-Yiannopoulos-event-at-UC-10901829.php.

17 Krantz, Laura. "'Bell Curve' author attacked by protesters at Middlebury College." *Boston Globe*. March 4, 2017. https://www.bostonglobe.com/metro/2017/03/04/middlebury/hAfpA1Hquh7DIS1doiKbhJ/story.html.

18 Harris, Uri, et al. "How Activists Took Control of a University: The Case Study of Evergreen State." *Quillette*. December 26, 2017. https://quillette.com/2017/12/18/activists-took-control-university-case-study-evergreen-state/.

ressentiment necessary to continue fueling the movement. I explain the provenance of this hierarchical inversion in *Springtime for Snowflakes*.[19]

Both its epistemology and ontology—its assumptions about how one acquires knowledge, who can know, and the nature of the objects of knowledge—are enforced with authoritarianism. Claims made on behalf of correct beliefs, correct wording, and proper naming—that is, *language* itself—[TW] trump [/TW] empirical evidence and nullify scientific findings and methods in advance. Thus, social justice represents an entirely new understanding, quite distinct from previous versions. It also involves entirely different practices and methods for implementing it.

On the Internet throughout the first decade of the 2000s, although in rudimentary and often outlandish forms, many of the theoretical elements of postmodern theory appeared to have found a safe space among new and mostly non-academic believers. Surprisingly, and almost without any prior indication, by 2015-16, I noted that postmodern theory had been succeeded on campus by social justice ideology, a crude and brutish caricature of the former. Moreover, social justice believers now included university administrators.

I am not alone in describing this sudden and largely unanticipated development. Jonathan Haidt, NYU colleague, psychologist and author of *The Righteous Mind*, concurs with my assessment about the novelty of this near total takeover. The creed's terminology and mechanisms suddenly entered official university policy, mechanisms and techniques in the form of "safe spaces," "trigger warnings," "bias reporting hotlines," and the complicity of administrators in the "no-platforming" of speakers. As I show in *Springtime for Snowflakes*, behind each of these policies, mechanisms, and techniques, the markers of postmodern theory are evident.[20]

The social justice ethos had suddenly become official doctrine within university culture. On campuses across North

---

19 Rectenwald, *Springtime for Snowflakes*. pp. 73-75.
20 Ibid., pp. 46-86.

America, social justice served as a newly installed superintendent of speech, behavior, policy, and pedagogy.[21] It now goes without saying that freedom of speech, academic freedom, and freedom of inquiry have come under attack and are in full retreat in academia. And, the social justice creed has since metastasized further into the broader culture, where it has already become firmly entrenched.

By officially adopting and promoting the contemporary social justice creed, preferentially recruiting social justice novitiates and paying them to play active roles as part of an extended and extensive social justice administration,[22] the institutions of North American higher education have taken a sharp, wrong turn. They have ceded moral and political authority to some of the most virulent, self-righteous, and authoritarian activists among the contemporary left. These activists have rallied other true believers, coaxed and cowed administrators, and conduced quailing faculty to applaud or quietly assent as the intellectual, cultural, and social cargo of millennia is jettisoned so that its freight can be driven "safely" through narrowing "tunnels of oppression."[23] Having gone so far as to officially adopt a peculiarly censorious subset of contemporary leftist ideology, colleges and universities have tragically abdicated their roles as politically

---

21   A hallmark of social justice pedagogy is "progressive stacking," a method for calling on students in class based on the inverted social justice hierarchy. See Cheong, Miles. "'Progressive Stacking Is Infiltrating College Classrooms.'" *The Daily Caller*. November 2, 2017. https://dailycaller.com/2017/11/06/progressive-stacking-is-infiltrating-college-classrooms/.

22   Frommer, Rachel. "Universities Spending Big on Social Justice Initiatives," *Washington Free Beacon*, November 8, 2017. https://freebeacon.com/culture/universities-spending-big-social-justice-initiatives/.

See also: "Social Justice Education: Diversity Education's Social Justice Peer Educator Project," Washington State University. https://diversityeducation.wsu.edu/social-justice-education/; "Social Justice Advocate." Texas Tech University. http://housing.ttu.edu/docs/SJAJobDesc2016.pdf; and "Diversity Peer Educators." Harvard College, Office for Equity, Diversity, and Inclusion. https://diversity.college.harvard.edu/dpe.

23   Athey, Amber. "Tunnels of Oppression expose 'privileged' students to 'dehumanization.'" *Campus Reform*. February 3, 2017. https://www.campusreform.org/?ID=8732.

impartial and intellectually independent institutions for the advancement and transmission of knowledge and wisdom.

CHAPTER FIVE

Trigger Warnings, Safe Spaces, Bias Reporting: The New Micro-techniques of Surveillance and Control[1]

A SINGULAR ORTHODOXY has infiltrated the discursive parameters of today's universities and colleges. This orthodoxy now constitutes the ethical vocabulary of academia. Adopted from feminism, anti-racism, and LGBTQ theory and practice, the language, doctrines, and mechanisms of this orthodoxy now dominate academia's policies, procedures and handbooks. The terminology has become the vernacular among the swelling ranks of administrators, especially the relatively new cohort of chief diversity officers, directors of diversity, associate provosts of diversity, assistant provosts of diversity, diversity consultants, and so on and so on. I refer not merely to the orthodoxy of "diversity," but in particular to "diversity" initiatives as they are currently administered, using a particular set of policies, procedures, and mechanisms: trigger warnings, safe spaces, bias reporting, and the like.

While ridiculed by media outlets, and, at least where trigger warnings are concerned, disavowed by the American Associa-

---

1 Originally published by *CLG News*, https://www.legitgov.org. September 12, 2016. Reproduced here by permission.

tion of University Professors,[2] nevertheless, American colleges and universities are dominated by this ethos and its collective techne. At the University of Chicago for example, the Dean of Students, John (Jay) Ellison, Ph.D., announced[3] (to the great chagrin of some faculty and many students[4]):

> Our commitment to academic freedom means that we do not support so-called "trigger warnings," we do not cancel invited speakers because their topics might prove controversial, and we do not condone the creation of intellectual "safe spaces" where individuals can retreat from ideas and perspectives at odds with their own...

Yet, the same university has also assembled and maintains a "Bias Response Team," and "urges anyone who has experienced or witnessed a Bias Incident to report it to the Bias Response Team."[5]

As it usually happens, any perspective that deviates from this "academic" orthodoxy—or any opposition expressed by faculty members in reasoned commentary or debate about the premises of the creed and/or its techniques—is virtually proscribed in advance. Whether or not they happen to be progressives, left communists, or radicals of another stripe, potential critics rightly fear being figured as right-wing reactionaries opposed to diversity and the confrontation of oppression. Any complaints or criticisms, they fear, would be peremptorily dismissed and likely circulated among other faculty members within their own universities or in academia at large as gossip, subjecting the critic to ridicule and disrepute.

Indeed, despite the fact that a new form of policing has been surreptitiously introduced into academia at large, one would be

---

2 "On Trigger Warnings." https://www.aaup.org/report/trigger-warnings.

3 Ellison, John (Jay). "Dear Class of 2020 Student." https://drive.google.com/file/d/0BwgNV1aQVE74eGhHUXYxM2wwSTA/edit.

4 Heer, Jeet. "Minutes: News and Notes." https://newrepublic.com/minutes/136303/university-chicago-attacking-academic-freedom.

5 "Bias Education & Support Team (BEST)." https://csl.uchicago.edu/get-help/bias-education-support-team-best.

hard-pressed to find a single article, essay, or book that subjects the entire administratively controlled apparatuses of "diversity" to any kind of real scrutiny. While innumerable articles have appeared on one or another of these topics (mostly on trigger warnings and safe spaces), no one has explained the structural provenance nor analyzed the probable effects of these developments as a whole. Nor has anyone provided a theoretical or historical framework with which to understand them.

Ironically, perhaps, the most appropriate critical theoretic for grasping the structural origins, as well as the social and political implications of this new largely "academic" development, can be found within the ambit of postmodern theory itself. The new mechanisms adopted and adapted by academic administrations clearly and incredibly mirror those described in a text widely read within humanities and social science studies courses throughout American universities and beyond. Indeed, it is a wonder that no one has, until now, applied this critique to the mechanisms of this academic creed. Faculty members, graduate students, and even many undergraduates, who have had even the slightest brush with trends in the humanities and social sciences, will know to what I refer here: Michel Foucault's brilliant 1975 book, *Discipline and Punish: The Birth of the Prison*. Particularly uncanny is the resemblance of the academic mechanisms in question to the "micro-physics of power" described in the third chapter, "Panopticism."[6]

In this riveting essay, Foucault effectually describes the transmutation of power from the pre-modern to the modern period. Adducing Jeremy Bentham's architectural model of the "Panopticon," Foucault proffers what at the time was an utterly novel understanding of modern "discipline" and control. The new disciplinary mechanisms that Foucault discusses replace the earlier corporeal forms of punishment, such as quartering people in public, or branding them with the crimes they supposedly committed, and so forth. While the Panopticon was first introduced by Bentham as a model of prison, asylum, and school reform, the forms of surveillance and discipline to some

---

6   Foucault, Michel. *Discipline and Punish*, Penguin, 1979, pp 195-228.

extent prefigured by the Panopticon and in some sense preceding it, for Foucault had already metastasized beyond the prison system, becoming the general means of discipline and control in so-called "democratic" societies.

The Panopticon itself is a circular building, in which its subjects—inmates, patients, students, etc.—are arrayed in cells surrounding a central tower. The subjects can be seen at any time by a guard, who may (or may not) occupy the central tower. The captive subjects cannot see into the tower, nor can they see each other. Likewise, they are never certain whether or not they are being observed:

> Bentham's Panopticon is the architectural figure of this composition. We know the principle on which it was based: at the periphery, an annular building; at the centre, a tower; this tower is pierced with wide windows that open onto the inner side of the ring; the peripheric building is divided into cells, each of which extends the whole width of the building; they have two windows, one on the inside, corresponding to the windows of the tower; the other, on the outside, allows the light to cross the cell from one end to the other. All that is needed, then, is to place a supervisor in a central tower and to shut up in each cell a madman, a patient, a condemned man, a worker or a schoolboy. By the effect of backlighting, one can observe from the tower, standing out precisely against the light, the small captive shadows in the cells of the periphery. They are like so many cages, so many small theatres, in which each actor is alone, perfectly individualized and constantly visible. The panoptic mechanism arranges spatial unities that make it possible to see constantly and to recognize immediately. In short, it reverses the principle of the dungeon; or rather of its three functions - to enclose, to deprive of light and to hide - it preserves only the first and eliminates the other two. Full lighting and the eye of a supervisor capture better than darkness, which ultimately protected. Visibility is a trap.[7]

Although the captive individual can never verify with cer-

---

7 Ibid. p. 200.

tainty that he is being observed, the very possibility of being observed produces the intended effects of hyper-vigilance and self-circumspection on the part of the subject. As such, the subjects themselves internalize the observer, and effectively monitor and police themselves. Foucault describes the effects of this technological innovation:

> He who is subjected to a field of visibility, and who knows it, assumes responsibility for the constraints of power; he makes them play spontaneously upon himself; he inscribes in himself the power relation in which he simultaneously plays both roles [that of observer and observed]; *he becomes the principle of his own subjection.*[8]

Make no mistake, Foucault mobilizes the architectural model of the Panopticon in order to introduce his central argument—in modernity, entire societies are inscribed with, underwritten by, and even predicated upon a generalizable and generalized method of surveillance and control—Panopticism. Even the once structure-bound, institution-specific disciplinary techniques as represented so well by the Panopticon have metastasized and traveled well beyond their former institutional borders. They now permeate the entire social body. In fact, in an important section, Foucault discusses "the swarming of the disciplinary mechanisms" of Panopticism. The phrasing will invoke for contemporary readers the sentinels in "The Matrix," the legions of squid-like robots that seek out, locate, and swarm around the escapees from the matrix in sweltering masses.

For our purposes, perhaps the most salient aspect of Panopticism is the way that it makes all of its subjects into potential sentinels of surveillance: "We have seen that anyone may come and exercise in the central tower the functions of surveillance."[9] That is, anyone and everyone can be interpellated as a functionary of Panopticism. "If you see something, say something" is the mantra that effectively encapsulates this logic. Universities and

---

8 Ibid., p. 203.
9 Ibid., p. 207.

colleges employ the micro-techniques of power precisely in the fashion described by Foucault.

At this point, I should make clear a parallel between the late eighteenth/early nineteenth-century model that Foucault treats, and the contemporary devices employed in academia and beyond. A point that is often lost on many readers of Foucault's "Panopticism," especially those unfamiliar with nineteenth-century British cultural history, is that Jeremy Bentham was not some reactionary, right-wing or even conservative thinker attempting to impose a nefarious, draconian form of discipline and punishment upon the population. In fact, during his time, Bentham was regarded as a radical, what today we would call a "progressive." Bentham was known as the principle member of an early nineteenth-century group of reformers known as "the philosophical radicals." He advocated numerous liberal reforms, including "annual elections; equal electoral districts; a wide suffrage, including woman suffrage; and the secret ballot. He supported in principle the participation of women in government and argued for the reform of marriage law to allow greater freedom to divorce."[10]

My point here is that regardless of the political provenance or original intention of the repertoire of diversity mechanisms, as Foucault makes clear, such methods and techniques, whether introduced initially by reformers for progressive ends or not, can and have often been co-opted by administers of power and wielded to oppressive ends. Likewise, the origin of the new academic instruments or "micro-physics of power" in feminism, anti-racism and LGBTQ discourse and practice in no way exempts them from being employed as mechanisms of surveillance and control.

Academia has co-opted and now brandishes identity politics and its techniques of micro-power—including trigger warnings, safe spaces, and bias reporting—as means of the disciplining of the subject. Bias reporting lines are examples of the ways colleges and universities are able to enlist everyone within

---

10 "Jeremy Bentham: British Philosopher and Economist." https://www.britannica.com/biography/Jeremy-Bentham.

their ambit as sentinels of surveillance, discipline, and punishment. Bias reporting lines and reporting systems encourage everyone to act as an instrument of Panopticism, an instrument of other- and self-policing.

In terms of the academy, however, the use of such mechanisms does not represent a perversion of intent. They are coercive as such, by definition. They are part of a growing panoply of micro-techniques of power representing the appropriation and defusing of politics, rather than opposition to the systems of oppression that such politics supposedly intend to represent.

These techniques of surveillance and control recall such organizations of the nineteenth century as The Society for the Suppression of Vice, founded in 1802.[11] The only real difference involves what now count as punishable offenses. In the early to mid-nineteenth century in Britain, offenses included the production, distribution and consumption of pornography, as well as expressions of blasphemy. Today, "vices" and "blasphemies" include real or imagined "micro-aggressions," or any conceivable display of "bias," however absurdly construed. Both regimes, however, are equally religious in character, involving as they do moralistic, individualized, and personalized policing. While both are insidious, only contemporary academic Panopticism, operating under the guise of protecting and encouraging "diversity," is anathema to academic freedom and inquiry, while simultaneously undermining any potential for collective agency, or solidarity, among its subjects. Above all, Panopticism individualizes.

Meanwhile, and probably most importantly, none of this policing and self-policing will do anything to challenge or overturn "systemic oppression" in the least.[12] In fact, while serving the ideological function of obscuring supposed structural ineq-

---

11 *Society for the Suppression of Vice.* London: S. Gosnell. 1825.

12 See Wolfenden, Katherine J. "Race in Elite American Universities: Diversity as Distraction." *Inquiries: Social Sciences, Arts, & Humanities.* Vol 5, no. 2, 2013, p. 1. http://www.inquiriesjournal.com/articles/726/ race-in-elite-american-universities-diversity-as-distraction#.V9NyyemFoyl. facebook.

uities, oppression, and exploitation, they constitute their own form of oppression.

CHAPTER SIX

Libertarianism(s) versus Postmodernism and "Social Justice" Ideology

The Ludwig von Mises Memorial Lecture (2019)[1]

A PECULIAR PHRASE recently introduced into the political lexicon by media cognoscenti describes a new corporate philosophy: "woke capitalism."[2] Coined by Ross Douthat of the *New York Times*, woke capitalism refers to a burgeoning wave of companies that apparently have become advocates of social justice. Some major corporations now intervene in social and political issues and controversies, partaking in a new corporate activism. The newly "woke" corporations support activist groups and social movements, while adding their voices to political debates. Woke capitalism has endorsed Black Lives Matter, the #MeToo Movement, contemporary feminism, LGBTQ rights, and immigration activism, among other leftist causes.

How can we understand woke capitalism, is it effective, and if so, why? Meanwhile, what is now meant by "social justice"

---

1 Originally published by *New English Review*. April 2019. Also published in a slightly different form by the *Quarterly Journal of Austrian Economics*. Vol. 22, No. 2. September 24, 2019. Reproduced here by permission.

2 Douthat, Ross. "The Rise of Woke Capital." *The New York Times*. February 28, 2018. https://www.nytimes.com/2018/02/28/opinion/corporate-america-activism.html.

and is it a good thing? As it turns out, analyzing woke capitalism tells us a great deal about contemporary corporate capitalism, the contemporary political left, and the relationship between the two. It also recalls an earlier corporate leftism, as I'll discuss later. Woke capitalism also helps to make sense of the topic of my book, *Google Archipelago: The Digital Gulag and the Simulation of Freedom*—the mega-data services; media, cable, and Internet services; social media platforms; Artificial Intelligence (AI) agents; apps; and the developing Internet of Things. The Google Archipelago is not merely an amalgam of digital business interests. It operates as what Michel Foucault, perhaps the only redeemable postmodern theorist, called a "governmentality," a means of governing the conduct of populations but also the technologies of governance and the rationality that underpins the technologies.[3]

* * *

Today, I will discuss some contemporary manifestations of "social justice," but not as it plays out in the academy. Instead, my topic today is the "social justice" of U.S. for-profit corporations. Although regarded as new, I will show that "woke capitalism" is but a subset and recent type of a broader and longer-standing corporate ethos that I call "corporate leftism." As it turns out, analyzing woke capitalism tells us a great deal about contemporary corporate capitalism, the contemporary political left, and the relationship between the two. It also recalls an earlier corporate leftism. ...

Despite the initial backlash, Nike's "Believe in Something" ad campaign featuring Colin Kaepernick—whose national anthem kneel-downs brought #BlackLivesMatter protest to the NFL—dramatically boosted Nike's sales. The ad's success supported *Business Insider* columnist Josh Barro's theory that woke

---

3 Michel Foucault introduced the term "governmentality" in a series of lectures from 1977 to 1979. By the rationality underpinning technologies of governance, Foucault meant the way that power rationalizes the relations of power to itself and to the governed.

capitalism provides a form of "parapolitical" representation for corporate consumers.[4] Given their perceived political disenfranchisement in the political sphere, woke capitalism offers representation in the public sphere.[5]

With wokeness, Ross Douthat of the *New York Times* argues, corporations offer workers and customers rhetorical placebos in lieu of costlier economic concessions, such as higher wages and better benefits, or lower prices. Short of a socialist revolution, New York Congressional Representative Alexandria Ocasio-Cortez's Green New Deal seems unlikely to materialize.[6] Douthat suggests that woke capitalism works by substituting symbolic for economic value. The same gestures of wokeness may also appease the liberal political elite, promoting their agendas of identity politics, gender pluralism, transgenderism, lax immigration standards, sanctuary cities, and so on. In return, the woke corporations hope to be spared higher taxes, increased regulations, and antitrust legislation aimed at monopolies.[7]

Meanwhile, at least one woke corporation appears intent on scolding its customers. I refer to Gillette and its "We Believe" ad. Like Nike, Gillette is a subsidiary of Proctor & Gamble. First posted to its social media accounts in mid-January 2019, the ad condescendingly lectures men, presumably "cishetero" men, about "toxic masculinity." In the provocative ad, three men look into separate mirrors—not to shave but to examine themselves for traces of the dreaded condition. Voice-overs admonish men "to say the right thing, to act the right way." Dramatizations of

---

4 Barro, Josh. "There's a Simple Reason Companies Are Becoming More Publicly Left-Wing on Social Issues." *Business Insider*. March 1, 2018. https://www.businessinsider.com/why-companies-ditching-nra-delta-selling-guns-2018-2.

5 Martinez, Gina. "Despite Outrage, Nike Sales Increased 31% After Kaepernick Ad." *Time*. September 8, 2018. http://time.com/5390884/nike-sales-go-up-kaepernick-a/.

6 Levitz, Eric. "Is a Green New Deal Possible Without a Revolution?" *Daily Intelligencer*, Intelligencer. December 13, 2018. http://nymag.com/intelligencer/2018/12/what-is-the-green-new-deal-explained-revolution.html.

7 Douthat. "The Rise of Woke Capital."

bullying, mansplaining, misogyny, and sexual predation shame bad men and enjoin a woke minority of men to "hold other men accountable," or else face shame as well.

For Gillette, "shaving" now apparently means shearing away the characteristics associated with manhood now deemed pathological by the American Psychological Association.[8] To prevent the sudden onset or relapse of man-disease, self-groomers must exercise vigilance, scathing self-scrutiny, and unwavering determination. Even though their gender malignance has been "socially constructed," men are responsible for immediately discerning and excising its outgrowths. The Gillette ad thus prescribes a new gender hygienics by which such brutes can "move upward, working out the beast,"[9] becoming "The Best a Man Can Get," a newly shorn animal, or rather a new kind of man shorn of animality.

Like the Nike Kaepernick ad, the Gillette "We Believe" ad provoked significant backlash. But parent company Proctor & Gamble's executive response to the ensuing furor suggested that the corporation was willing to forgo profits for virtue points, at least for now. Jon Moeller, Proctor & Gamble's CFO, told reporters that post-ad sales were "in-line with pre-campaign levels." In advertising terms, in other words, the ad was a failure. Yet, Moeller viewed the expenditure as an investment in the future. "It's a part of our effort to connect more meaningfully with younger consumer groups,"[10] he explained, perhaps referring to those too young to sport the toxic stubble.

---

8 Pappas, Stephanie. "APA Issues First-Ever Guidelines for Practice with Men and Boys." *CE Corner*, vol. 50, no. 1, Jan. 2019, p. 34. https://www.apa. org/monitor/2019/01/ce-corner.aspx. These damaging traits include "stoicism, competitiveness, dominance and aggression."

9 Tennyson, Alfred Lord. *In Memoriam*. 2nd ed., Edward Moxon, 1850, CXV, 183. By "working out the beast," Alfred Lord Tennyson meant to eradicate the moral baseness of animal nature, rather than to establish an earthly utopia, as his predecessor William Godwin had suggested, or to remove the traits associated mostly with men due to evolutionary selection.

10 Meyersohn, Nathaniel. "Gillette Says It's Satisfied with Sales after Controversial Ad." *CNN*, Cable News Network, 23 Jan. 2019. https://www.cnn. com/2019/01/23/business/gillette-ad-procter-and-gamble-stock/index.html

Unsatisfied with the above explanations, I still wondered how and why corporations assumed the role of social justice arbiters and how and why social justice came to be the ideology of major U.S. corporations.[11] Before venturing my own theory, however, I'd like to retrace a history of corporate leftism, which will shed light on the relationship between leftism and corporatism.

Corporate leftism has a long history, dating at least to the late nineteenth and early twentieth centuries. I first recognized corporate leftism through the histories that documented the funding of the Russian and other socialist revolutions by leading U.S. capitalists and bankers. As Richard B. Spence boldly declares in *Wall Street and the Russian Revolution 1905-1925*, the term "socialist-capitalist" is not an oxymoron.[12]

Spence was not referring to so-called "mixed economies" but rather to a false dichotomy, a mating of two supposed economic antinomies, socialism and capitalism. Understanding why the term is not an oxymoron does not necessarily depend upon the historical knowledge uncovered by Spence, and before him, by Antony C. Sutton[13]—although, given that I am a historian, I found this material revealing. But the apparent contradiction in terms is based on a mischaracterization of economic opposites and a failure to detect in the original name for the field of economics, namely "political economy," the inherent possibility of such a conjunction. The real opposites are not capitalism and socialism but rather individual freedom and free markets versus centralized political control, whether statist or corporatist.

According to Sutton's *Wall Street and FDR* (1975), "corporate socialism is a system where those few who hold the legal

11   For a summary of the relationship between corporate social activism and political activists, see Lin, Tom C.W. "Incorporating Social Activism." *Boston University Law Review*, vol. 98, no. 1535, 2018, pp. 1535–1605.

12   Spence, Richard B. *Wall Street and the Russian Revolution: 1905-1925*. Trine Day. Kindle Edition. Spence, Richard B. Wall Street and the Russian Revolution, 1905-1925. Trine Day LLC, 2017.

13   Sutton, Antony C. *Wall Street and the Bolshevik Revolution*. Clairview Books, 2016.

monopolies of financial and industrial control profit at the expense of all others in society."[14] For Sutton, "The most lucid and frank description of corporate socialism and its mores and objectives is to be found in a 1906 booklet by Frederick Clemson Howe, *Confessions of a Monopolist*."[15] In attempting to validate Sutton's reference to Howe as the prototypical monopolist or even corporate socialist, I was disappointed, but ultimately found the excursion rewarding.

Beginning with Spence's Wall Street and the Russian Revolution 1905-1925, which had the same title as one of Sutton's major books except for an added date range, I searched feverishly for "Howe" and "Confessions of a Monopolist." (Actually, as is my wont, I searched electronic texts and the Kindle version of Spence, so my search produced nothing like a fever. But I *am* nostalgic for a past that I never knew, when in nineteenth century novels, the researches of fictional characters like Victor Frankenstein resulted in life-threatening frenzies.)

My problem was that I wanted to introduce corporate leftism and corporate socialism by referring to a television sitcom of the 1970s, namely, *Gilligan's Island*. Some of you will be old enough and will have hailed from backgrounds as plebeian as my own to recall this program. The situation for this "dumb TV show," as Mises Institute scholar B.K Marcus aptly put it, is a small community of seven American castaways on a deserted island. Because it aired in the early 1960s, *Gilligan's Island* is a collectivist Robinson Crusoe tale with a socialist pretext. Each character represents a different life station in an otherwise lost world of individualism, cast from a division of labor that is rendered absurd let alone inapplicable by the social and economic life on a desert isle. Since the show's creator and producer Sherwood Schwartz was at least an unconscious Marxist, the sitcom demonstrated in episode after episode that "in communist society ... nobody has one exclusive sphere of activity." Actress,

---

14 Sutton, Antony Cyril. *Wall Street and FDR*. Rudolf Steiner Press. Kindle Edition.

15 Howe, Frederic C. *The Confessions of a Monopolist*. The Public Publishing Company, 1906.

professor, millionaire's wife, and "all the rest" must "hunt in the morning, fish in the afternoon, rear cattle in the evening, criticize after dinner" (Marx, *The German Ideology*).[16] They must outgrow the limited specializations imposed on them by the capitalist order. This goes for everyone on the island, except, it seems, for the monopolist, Thurston B. Howell III.

Although their names were not identical, they were near homonyms and I'd hoped to connect Frederic Howe and Thurston B. Howell. I hadn't been so sanguine as to expect that Thurston Howell had been named directly after Frederic Howe. After all their names were spelled differently. Yet, I still hoped for some reference. And they were both monopolists. Or so I thought.

Uh oh. Spence did not mention Howe as the model monopolist or corporate socialist. In fact, he curiously omitted any reference to Howe's name and his "rule book." Coming up empty in such a cognate publication, I began to feel flush and somewhat panicky. (As you know, we humanities scholars are susceptible to hyper-emotionality.) Nor could I find any mention of Frederic Howe in connection with Thurston B. Howell at all. And, while a few early reviews of *Confessions* took the book at face value and came to the same conclusion as Sutton—that it represented the autobiography of a real monopolist giving away his secrets—even the most cursory assessment of *Doctor Frederic Howe*'s life and other works would have quickly disabused anyone but the most tendentious polemicist of the idea that Howe's *Confessions* was a rule book or how-to manual for monopolists. Howe was nothing like the corporate magnate or mega-banker that Sutton suggested he was, and so he could not possibly have helped bankroll the creation of "a captive market and a technical colony to be exploited by a few high-powered American financiers and the corporations under their control," that is, the Soviet Union. First of all, Howe had earned a Ph.D. from Johns Hopkins University. A real monopolist would wait

---

16 Karl Marx. *The German Ideology*. Progress Publishers, 1968. Marx/Engels Internet Archive. https://www.marxists.org/archive/marx/works/1845/german-ideology/ch01.htm.

for an honorary degree. Furthermore, *Confessions of a Monopolist* was not even an autobiography; it was a biting satire, a criticism of monopolies and monopolists, written by a progressive reformer and later FDR statesman. As it turned out, both Howe and Howell had been fictional monopolists.

Yet the Thurston Howell on Gilligan's island was certainly something like the stereotypical monopolist described in Frederic Howe's book. Like the character in *Confessions*, Howell's number one rule was to "make Society work for you." Thurston Howell certainly managed to command the labor and deference of his fellow islanders. As Marcus notes in "The Monetary Economics of Thurston Howell III," Howell was able to commandeer labor and goods by virtue of his off-island status, to procure goods and services by writing checks drawn on U.S. banks.[17] The fact that this fiat currency functioned in the absence of the government that backed it suggests that money operates according to a cultural, Lamarckian evolutionary process. Money's governmentally-enforced fiat characteristic is an acquired characteristic that is passed along through future generational transactions and retains these characteristics even after its basis in force disappears—at least until it is replaced, and sometimes even after that. As Mises showed, the value of a currency is historical, and the study of currencies must be historicist.

Howell's expression of monopolistic desiderata, however, is best expressed in episode 9, "The Big Gold Strike," when Gilligan, acting as Howell's golf caddie, falls into a giant hole where he notices something golden embedded in the walls of the cave. Naturally Howell recognizes gold and assumes that it is his property. After all, Gilligan was in his employ, albeit fooled by a faux fiat currency. Howell swears Gilligan to secrecy to secure his ownership against the islanders' agreement that all property on the island would be communal. But soon the mine is discovered by the rest of the community. The unreliability of the state appears to account for Howell's problem in securing exclusive

---

17   Marcus, B K. "The Monetary Economics of Thurston Howell III | Mises ..." *Mises.org.* https://mises.org/library/monetary-economics-thurston-howell-iii.

gold mining rights. Gilligan is the nominal and ineffectual President of the island and a buffoon who has no power. But Howell's failure as a monopolist is more fundamental. While he is perfectly capable to "let others work for you," he does not know the language or ways of corporate socialism and does not understand how to establish monopoly within such a state. Rather than continually yielding to expressions of blatant self-interest, a corporate socialist would couch his monopolistic ambitions in the language of equality.

Rather than Frederic Howe, King Camp Gillette would have provided a much better model for Thurston Howell—and Sutton The founder of the American Safety Razor Company in 1901, who changed its name to the Gillette Safety Razor Company in 1902, Gillette published *The Human Drift* in 1894.[18] While acknowledging that "[n]o reform movement can meet with success unless that movement takes into consideration the power of capital, and is based on present business methods, and conforms to the same laws," Gillette's *Human Drift* railed against competition, which he believed was "the prolific source of ignorance and every form of crime, and that [which] increases the wealth of the few at the expense of the many... the present system of competition between individuals results in fraud, deception, and adulteration of almost every article we eat, drink, or wear." Competition resulted in "a waste of material and labor beyond calculation." Competition was the source of "selfishness, war between nations and individuals, murder, robbery, lying, prostitution, forgery, divorce, deception, brutality, ignorance, injustice, drunkenness, insanity, suicide, and every other crime, [which] have their base in competition and ignorance." This explains the recent Gillette ad; the company has finally discovered that the root of competition, and thus, of all evil, is toxic masculinity.

But the corporate socialist King Camp Gillette may as well have patented the disposable safety razor to prevent so many desperate people from cutting their throats—at least until they

---

18 Gillette, King Camp. *The Human Drift*. The Humboldt Publishing Company, 1894.

realized the answer to all of their problems, which he had introduced in *Human Drift*: a singular monopoly, which would "naturally" control all production and distribution, specializing in everything, such that "every article sold to consumer, from the package to its contents, will be the product of the United Company." Under the United Company, the production of necessary goods, and eventually of everything, would be consolidated and centralized, eliminating the waste and hazards of the many and widely dispersed manufacturing plants and buildings of the current haphazard and chaotic system. Most cities and towns would be "destroyed," as would all competitors, as the vast majority of the population would relocate to "The Metropolis," where, powered by Niagara Falls, all production would take place and everyone's lives would center around the corporation, whose commercial and governmental power would be total.

Lest one think that *The Human Drift* represented the lark of a young idealist before he came to his senses and founded a company with almost unparalleled name recognition, Gillette went on to publish *The World Corporation* in 1910, a prospectus for developing a world-wide singular monopoly.[19] But, founding his company and patenting his razor between writing these two treatises, Gillette's biographer Russel Adams quipped, "[i]t was almost as if Karl Marx had paused between *The Communist Manifesto* and *Das Kapital* to develop a dissolving toothbrush or collapsible comb."[20]

A few passages from *World Corporation* should be sufficient to establish Gillette as the prototypical corporate socialist:

> CORPORATIONS WILL CONTINUE TO FORM, AB-
> SORB, EXPAND, AND GROW, AND NO POWER OF MAN
> CAN PREVENT IT. Promoters [of World Corporation] are
> the true socialists of this generation, the actual builders of
> a co-operative system which is eliminating competition, and
> in a practical business way reaching results which socialists

19 Gillette, King Camp. *"World Corporation"*. New England News Company, 1910.

20 Adams, Russell B. *King C. Gillette: the Man and His Wonderful Shaving Device*. Little, Brown, 1978, pp. 13-14.

have vainly tried to attain through legislation and agitation for centuries." (p. 9)

Opposition to "WORLD CORPORATION" by individuals, by states, or by governments will be of no avail. Opposition in any case can only be of temporary effect, barriers will only centralize power and cause increased momentum when they give way. (p. 62)

The corporation will dominate material but also mental production, as Gillette praises the hive mind:

"WORLD CORPORATION" represents individual intelligence and force combined, centralized and intelligently directed. Individuals are OF the corporate mind, but are not THE corporate mind. (p. 45)

And, as if anticipating Google's secret mission statement, Gillette continued:

"WORLD CORPORATION" will possess all knowledge of all men, and each individual mind will find complete expression through the great Corporate Mind.

Finally, waxing poetic in Ray Kurzweil mode, Gillette wrote:

"WORLD CORPORATION" will have life everlasting. Individual man will live his life and pass into the great beyond; but this great Corporate Mind will live on through the ages, always absorbing and perfecting, for the utilization and benefit of all the inhabitants of the earth.

It is worth noting that Gillette's business practices were not wholly at odds with the ideas in his books. True to his monopolistic impulses, he regularly filed patents, and in 1917 with the outbreak of World War I, the company provided every soldier with a shaving kit, paid for by the U.S. government. But did Gillette's expressions of corporate socialism actually help his business efforts, or merely ease his guilty conscience? We can't be sure, but speculating about the objectives of today's corporate leftists may help make sense of the rhetoric of such corporate leftists of the past.

Today's corporate social justice rebranding represents at least a rhetorical overthrow of Milton Friedman's extremely narrow view of corporate responsibility. In *Capitalism and Freedom* (1962), Friedman declared that the "one and only one 'social responsibility' of business" is to "increase profits."[21] Friedman won the Nobel Prize in Economics in 1976 and by the mid-1980s Friedman's notion of limited corporate "social responsibility" had become widely accepted.

Yet woke capitalism may still satisfy Friedman's profit-only maxim. If all the world's a stage, then the corporate mouthing of social justice bromides may be play-acting and therefore mawkish parody. To be truly woke, then, might mean that one is awake to the woke-acting corporations, the woke-believing consumers, and maybe even the demands of wokeness altogether. This explanation is consistent with the profit requirement and allows one to make short-shrift of newly found corporate virtue. It is a cynical sham and proves more than ever that the chicanery of corporations and their billionaire owners knows no bounds. This view is similar to that held by Anand Giridharadas, critic of woke billionaires and author of *Winners Take All*. [22]

---

21 In 1962, Friedman argued against the value of "corporate responsibility" that is expressed by woke capitalism. In a section entitled, "Social Responsibility of Business and Labor," Friedman wrote: "The view has been gaining widespread acceptance that corporate officials and labor leaders have a 'social responsibility' that goes beyond serving the interest of their stockholders or their members. This view shows a fundamental misconception of the character and nature of a free economy. In such an economy, there is one and only one social responsibility of business—to use its resources and engage in activities designed to increase its profits so long as it stays within the rules of the game, which is to say, engages in open and free competition, without deception or fraud." Friedman, Milton. *Capitalism and Freedom: Fortieth Anniversary Edition*. University of Chicago Press, 2002, p. 134.

22 Giridharadas, Anand. *Winners Take All: The Elite Charade of Changing the World*. Allen Lane, 2019. See Feloni, Richard. "'We're All Passengers in a Billionaire Hijacking' Says the Critic Who Has the World's Richest People

Now, as tempting as such "post-truth" cynicism may be, it doesn't explain the *promotion* of woke or leftist views by corporations and the effects that such promotions may have in making their consumer bases more leftist, a circumstance they will have to deal with at some point. Arguably, corporations would not espouse and thereby potentially spread political views merely to assuage a consumer contingent, unless said views ultimately aligned with their own interests. One is led to wonder what politics would best serve the interests of corporate leftists, especially aspiring corporate socialists.

To benefit corporate leftists, corporate socialists, or any monolithic singular producer and governmentality, a political creed would likely place a heavy emphasis on equality. Such an emphasis would likely be accompanied by shaming of the privileged along with demands that they surrender their advantages. To emphasize equality, the creed benefitting the corporate leftist would recognize refugees, the disenfranchised, and at least in theory would be internationalist rather than nationalist or nativist. While declaring equality, the political creed of the corporate leftist might nevertheless stress difference—between identity groups and even within them— and might benefit from the creation of utterly new identity types. Such a creed would consistently keep the identity groups concerned with whether or not they were losing ground to other identity groups rather than worrying about the corporate socialist. Watch words might include "equity, inclusion, and diversity." Always on the cutting edge, the corporate leftist would welcome the promotion of the new and the disruption of the old, but always with improvement in mind. A political creed that aimed at dismantling traditional gender, the family, local customs, tradition, and even historical memory would remove the last bastions against state or major corporate power. Ultimately, the corporate leftist or corporate socialist would benefit from a singular governmental monopoly, with one set of rules. As Gillette noted, ideally this global government would be the corporation itself.

Buzzing." *Business Insider*, 1 Feb. 2019. https://www.businessinsider.com/anand-giridharadas-billionaires-inequality-interview-2019-1.

Thus, woke capitalism or corporate leftism does not consist merely of rhetorical placebos, symbolic over economic concessions, or even the mere placating of liberal political elites. Woke capitalism or corporate leftism actually represents the corporate interests of the would-be monopolist, the corporate socialist, and the corporate leftist in general.

CHAPTER SEVEN

First as Tragedy, Then as Farce, Or, How I Left Marxism[1]

Af ew months ago, I was surprised and disappointed to learn that Marx's famous statement, the title of this essay and a rejoinder to Hegel's supposed remark—"that all great world-historic facts and personages appear, so to speak, twice"[2]—had been appropriated by the contemporary Slovenian Marxist and psychoanalytic theorist Slavoj Žižek, for the title of one of his books. I was disappointed because I had considered using the title myself. I was surprised because, not having read Žižek's entire oeuvre, I hadn't known of his appropriation. Further, quite apart from my own intended (and past casual) use, I was astonished to see how unselfconscious and lacking in intentional irony Žižek had been in naming a book about capitalism *First as Tragedy, Then as Farce* (2009).[3] I've used the phrase quite differently on social media: "Marx(ism): First as tragedy, then as farce"—crediting Marx for his profundity and ironically applying his observation to Marxism itself—in a boomeranging way

---

1 Originally published by the *New English Review*. January 2019.

2 Marx, Karl. *The Eighteenth Brumaire of Louis Bonaparte*. 1852. *Marxists. org*. https://www.marxists.org/archive/marx/works/1852/18th-brumaire/ch01.htm.

3 Žižek Slavoj. *First as Tragedy, Then as Farce*. Verso, 2018.

that Marx could have hardly hoped for or expected. But if this statement aptly applies to the repetition of any world-historic fact, it applies to Marxism itself.

The tragedy of Marxism has been well-documented, and despite the obstinate denial of contemporary Marxists, some of whom ludicrously hold the conspiracy theory that the documentation of historical facts amounts to "capitalist propaganda," the evidence speaks for itself, for an epochal and epic tragedy, a tragedy unmatched by any other ideologically-induced horror in human history. And the rebounding contemporary popularity of socialism-communism is certainly farcical, mostly representing LARPing[4] by theoretical and activist posers but more so the stunning historical and political illiteracy that such posturing betrays.

Yet, just over two years ago, I was a theoretical Marxist LARPer myself, I suppose. I wasn't a Stalinist or "tankie"[5] and thus didn't deny the history of Soviet, Chinese, Vietnamese, Korean, Cambodian, and Cuban atrocities. In the case of the USSR at least, I believed that the nightmare had been the result of the usurpation of a potentially social-communist revolution by the

---

4 "r/OutOfTheLoop - What Is LARPing in the Context of Online Political Discussion?" Reddit. https://www.reddit.com/r/OutOfTheLoop/comments/5xdacv/what_is_larping_in_the_context_of_online/.

5 "Tankie." Urban Dictionary, www.urbandictionary.com/define.php?term=tankie.

"A hardline Stalinist. A tankie is a member of a communist group or a "fellow traveller" (sympathiser) who believes fully in the political system of the Soviet Union and defends/defended the actions of the Soviet Union and other accredited states (China, Serbia, etc.) to the hilt, even in cases where other communists criticise their policies or actions. For instance, such a person favours overseas interventions by Soviet-style states, defends these regimes when they engage in human rights violations, and wishes to establish a similar system in other countries such as Britain and America.

"The term is used to distinguish the rare individuals with these kinds of beliefs from communists more broadly (including Communist Party members), whose adherence to Soviet doctrine and attachment to existing "socialist" states is somewhat weaker.

"It is always more-or-less abusive in the sense that those termed tankies do not use the term themselves, but it doesn't have any particular bite (unlike, say, Trot)."

Bolsheviks, whose conniving party leaders became dictatorial state leaders. In the case of China, it was a "bourgeois revolution with red flags."[6] Mao's revolutionary army hadn't consisted of the working class, which had already been decimated, but rather an amalgam of peasants and assorted "petty bourgeois" radicals with no material interest in the working-class control of society. In all cases of "actually-existing" socialism-communism, the Marxist project had been utterly foiled, or merely mimed and maimed by frauds posing as Marxists. The resultant dire consequences could and would be averted in a truly socialist-communist society of the future.

"But still, how could you have been communist," you may ask, "especially after the twentieth century?" Despite the accumulation of corpses, strangely enough, the answer is the same as it had been at the inception of Marxist communism. It is the same answer as the answer that could be given to the question, "What does it mean to be a Communist?"

I've only recently found the best answer I've seen yet—in a book referenced by Daniel Mallock in "Driven to Despair: The Return of American Socialism," an important essay published in the *New English Review* in December of 2018.[7] The book is *Witness* by Whittaker Chambers, the 1952 classic tale of a former communist who "broke"—with the party and communism itself.

A communist, Chambers held, is not merely (or necessarily) a believer in dialectical materialism, the labor theory of value, the dictatorship of the proletariat, or even the utopian promise of universal human emancipation. The basis of communism is not found in the dare and promise of the final three sentences of the *Communist Manifesto* of 1848: "Workers of the world, unite. You have nothing to lose but your chains. You have a world to

---

6 Goldner, Loren. "Notes Towards a Critique of Maoism." *Insurgent Notes*, Insurgent Notes. October 15, 2012. http://insurgentnotes.com/2012/10/ notes-towards-a-critique-of-maoism/.

7 Mallock, Daniel. "Driven to Despair: The Return of American Socialism." *New English Review*. December 2018. https://www.newenglishreview.org/ Daniel_Mallock/Driven_to_Despair%3A_The_Return_of_American_Socialism/.

gain."

Rather, a true communist is one who has examined a long-historical and still presently dysfunctional world, probably more negatively than most, and has arrived at the conviction that its rational and total remaking is both necessary and possible. Without yet giving away his eventual and ultimate objection to communism, I quote the germ of the communist creed as Chambers saw it, which I agree is its fundamental premise and claim:

> It is the vision of man's liberated mind, by the sole force of its rational intelligence, redirecting man's destiny and reorganizing man's life and the world...
>
> It challenges him to prove it [the centrality and capacity of rationality] by using the force of his rational mind to end the bloody meaninglessness of man's history—by giving it purpose and a plan. It challenges him to prove it by reducing the meaningless chaos of nature, by imposing on it his rational will to order, abundance, security, peace. It is the vision of materialism . . .
>
> Communism does not summon men to crime or to Utopia, as its easy critics like to think. On the plane of faith, it summons mankind to turn its vision into practical reality. On the plane of action, it summons men to struggle against the inertia of the past which, embodied in social, political and economic forms, Communism claims, is blocking the will of mankind to make its next great forward stride. It summons men to overcome the crisis, which, Communism claims, is in effect a crisis of rending frustration, with the world, unable to stand still, but unwilling to go forward along the road that the logic of a technological civilization points out—Communism.
>
> This is Communism's moral sanction, which is twofold. Its vision points the way to the future; its faith labors to turn the future into present reality. It says to every man who joins it: the vision is a practical problem of history; the way to achieve it is a practical problem of politics, which is the present tense of history. Have you the moral strength to take upon yourself

the crimes of history so that man at last may close his chronicle of age-old, senseless suffering, and replace it with purpose and a plan? The answer a man makes to this question is the difference between the Communist and those miscellaneous socialists, liberals, fellow travelers, unclassified progressives and men of good will, all of whom share a similar vision, but do not share the faith because they will not take upon themselves the penalties of the faith. The answer is the root of that sense of moral superiority which makes Communists, though caught in crime, berate their opponents with withering self-righteousness.[8]

It is this faith in the centrality and capacity of human rationality and will, effectively embodied in science and technology, and in scientific theory—of which Marxism claims to be the social scientific representative—that makes a belief in communism possible and that allows the communist to undertake, excuse, and/or deny a host of crimes committed against humanity in its name.

That being said, what brings a communist to "break" with it? How does the communist escape this "iron cage," a phrase that Max Weber, a sociologist and critic of Marxism, used in a slightly different but related context?[9] The answer, as Chambers saw it, amounted to a choice between "God or Man, Soul or Mind, Freedom or Communism."

While Chambers doesn't explain exactly what this choice means, I will try to flesh it out here. The choice is very much like the one I made just over two years ago.

What does it mean to choose between God and man, between soul and mind, between freedom and communism?

I believe Chambers meant that Marxism maintains a faith in the human capacity to determine the course of events to a degree that he later came to regard as inflated at best and delusional at worst. One need not posit the existence of God to

---

8 Chambers, Whittaker. *Witness* (Cold War Classics). Regnery History. Kindle Edition.
9 Weber, Max. *The Protestant Ethic and the Spirit of Capitalism.* Scribner, 1930, p. 181.

grasp the problems with the extreme hubris that Marxism entails. The overweening belief in the power and near infallibility of rationality implies that humans possess the capacity to control factors that are barely understood, including our very selves, as well as the unforeseen consequences of many poorly understood phenomena beyond ourselves. For example, it assumes a thorough knowledge of human nature—of the brain, of its creative potential, and its potential for destruction. Or, more accurately, it implies a disbelief that human nature exists in the first place. After all, Marx posited the utter plasticity of "human nature," a nature without a nature as it were, and thus endowed humans with the ability to shape themselves according to whatever preconceived image given only by themselves.[10] Except among leftist believers in this extreme environmental determinism, such unlimited human malleability has been rejected, thanks to modern genetics. And much more remains to be known.

The Marxist vision also implies that humans know everything that we need to know about our niche, about our productive capacities, and about the possible modes of human production—despite purposefully excluding the adventuresome gambles and gambols of individuals, the aleatory conditions of markets, and the workings of whatever creativity can happen only beyond the control of the state.

The Marxist hubris suggests that human rationality is essentially godlike, capable of controlling itself and everything that it comes into contact with, capable of choreographing events as if in possession of a blueprint that is valid for all time, as well as having the capacity to follow said blueprint without fail.

One can be an atheist and still accept the criticism suggested here. In his *Theses on Feuerbach*, Marx ended by writing: "The philosophers have only interpreted the world, in various ways; the point is to change it."[11] In 1845, this was quite a pre-

---

10   Tabak, M. *Dialectics of Human Nature in Marx's Philosophy*. Palgrave Macmillan US, 2012.

11   Marx, Karl. "Theses on Feuerbach." *Theses on Feuerbach*, 1845. Marxists. org. https://www.marxists.org/archive/marx/works/1845/theses/theses.htm.

mature conclusion, and it remains premature to this day. At the time, very little was known about the animal in question (*homo sapiens sapiens*). We lacked the science to know what on earth we were dealing with. Little or nothing was known about evolutionary history, evolutionary psychology, epigenetics, and so on. Knowledge that might be provided by the social sciences, including sociology, cultural anthropology, and psychology, was sorely lacking. It would take much more knowledge to venture a plan adequate for all of futurity, and even with this knowledge a strict plan would remain woefully incomplete and terribly dangerous to follow. Without the appropriate knowledge, we lack the slightest chance of successfully creating a planned economy and society. We do have historical evidence, however, about how such plans have worked out. The translations of Marxism into historical reality have proven disastrous beyond anything attempted thitherto, or since.

Chambers discusses how some communists (miraculously) resolved to leave communism. He tells how, without warning or prior indication, a pro-Soviet German communist, apparently visiting the USSR, reached a breaking point. According to his embarrassed daughter: "'He was immensely pro-Soviet,' she said, 'and then—you will laugh at me—but you must not laugh at my father—and then—one night—in Moscow—he heard screams. That's all. Simply one night he heard screams.'"[12]

And who emitted such screams? Chambers reminds us:

> They come from husbands torn forever from their wives in midnight arrests. They come, muffled, from the execution cellars of the secret police, from the torture chambers of the Lubianka, from all the citadels of terror now stretching from Berlin to Canton. They come from those freight cars loaded with men, women and children, the enemies of the Communist State, locked in, packed in, left on remote sidings to freeze to death at night in the Russian winter. They come from minds driven mad by the horrors of mass starvation ordered and enforced as a policy of the Communist State. They come from the starved skeletons, worked to death, or

12 Chambers, *Witness*.

flogged to death (as an example to others) in the freezing filth of sub-arctic labor camps. They come from children whose parents are suddenly, inexplicably, taken away from them— parents they will never see again.[13]

In other words, the screams were expelled from those who represented potential impediments to the rationality of communist planning. Such screams sometimes managed to break through the mental barriers of communist believers precisely because the screams starkly contrasted with the Marxist, communist vision these believers had accepted. The screams sometimes broke the spell of communist belief because they slipped past the armed guards of the mind, past the ideological iron curtain, managing to reach unwary, unhampered, and relatively free mental processes that lay beneath rational control and the unremitting rehearsals of Marxist creedal commitments. Those who screamed had either failed to get the memo, disbelieved the memo, or to their surprise and horror, discovered that the memo had changed meanings without notice. Those who really heard the screams realized that despite or because of the memo's paltry and insubstantial existence, its arbitrary and often nonsensical import, and its flimsy indictments, the memo nevertheless bore indelible and overwhelming witness against their neighbors, trumping their very humanity.

Nothing remotely as dramatic as hearing such screams happened to me. It was 2016 and I didn't live in a communist society, nor had I been an underground member of the official Communist Party, USA, as Chambers had been. I had been a communist for at least ten years and, at a time when communism's popularity was curiously on the rise, I was a member of a loosely affiliated group of left communists. I wrote a number of essays for this group and other communist publications.

I broke with left communism and communism *en toto* after my criticisms of social justice ideology and identity politics had been assailed and I was denounced, not only by social justice warriors, but by all variety of leftists, by left communists, and by

---

13 Ibid.

most other communists as well. I didn't hear the screams of victims but nevertheless I had a vision of the horrors of communist dictatorship. My "comrades" showed me the totalitarian character that lay just beneath the thin veneer of egalitarianism that they otherwise proclaimed and the virtuous-sounding rhetoric that they usually mouthed.

I suppose I did hear screams of a kind. I heard screaming that was aimed at me and the shrieking convinced me of the contracted wickedness of my fellow travelers. I have been criticized for leaving communism primarily in response not to communist ideals but to those who held them. There is some truth to this accusation, although it is only partially correct. As it turned out, I realized that the actual behavior of people is more telling than the lofty abstractions that they avow. But I soon regarded the abstractions differently and realized that they concealed more than they revealed.

The abstractions concealed the force required to actualize them. But once the required force is witnessed—heard in the screams, anticipated by the imagination, and registered beneath the deliberative rationality that refuses its acknowledgement—the abstractions lose their grip. It is then that they show their full character and reveal that which they must reduce or eliminate to arrive at that which they promise. The tradeoff is far greater, far more expensive than any committed communist can or will ever admit. And there is no use trying to convince the communist with argumentation, evidence, or even pathos that the equitable price of a workers' paradise cannot be millions of lives. The consciousness of the committed communist is locked against any and all polemics, evidence, or emotional appeal. Their release can only come upon hearing the screams themselves. They must witness the tragedy of the past to recognize the farce of the present.

CHAPTER EIGHT

Shaming & Shunning[1]

I: The People Who Do It, & Its Likely Effects

I CAN TELL YOU A LITTLE about shaming and shunning— what types of people initiate it, the way it builds, and how it is maintained. I can also speak to the kinds of responses the shamed and shunned are liable to make. The effects of shaming and shunning are indeed variable but predictable.

In my case, I gave an interview with the *Washington Square News,* NYU's student newspaper;[2] one particular "colleague" of mine found my views intolerable. She railed and wrote a social-justice-jargon-laden response, replete with the plug-n-play rhetoric so rife in social justice circles, including "gas-lighting" and other nonsensical Legos-like prefabricated phraseology. You can find this phraseology[3] easily on the

---

1 Originally published as "Shaming & Shunning: The People Who Do It, & Its Likely Effects (Part I)" and "Shaming & Shunning, Part II: 'You Must Be a Rightwing Nut-job'" by *CLG News,* https://www.legitgov.org. August 16 and 30, 2017. Reproduced here by permission.

2 Siu. Diamond Naga. "Q&A with a Deplorable NYU Professor." *Washington Square News.* October 24, 2016. https://nyunews.com/2016/10/24/qa-with-a-deplorable-nyu-professor/.

3 Liberal Studies Diversity, Equity and Inclusion Working Group. "Letter to the Editor: Liberal Studies Rejects @antipcnyuprof's Faulty Claims." *Wash-*

web; no thought is required to construct a social-justice-in-flected manifesto or argument as the language pieces stand ready-made for easy assembly, much like IKEA furniture. (No disrespect to IKEA furniture or its buyers is intended.)

She then apparently imposed on the other members of the committee on which she "served," "The Liberal Studies 'Diversity, Equity and Inclusion' Working Group." She rallied the committee members and induced them to sign onto her screed. Thus, she managed to have an official Liberal Studies Program committee and thus an official NYU committee condemn me. This set the stage for an all-out, collective shunning by my faculty "colleagues" in Liberal Studies at NYU.

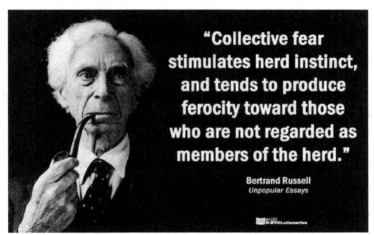

Bertrand Russell, from *Unpopular Essays*

The pattern is clear: led by a religious zealot or two, shunning begins with the zealot's finger-pointing and shaming of the soon-to-be-outcast individual. It relies on a mob mentality and the induction of the desired behavior toward the accused by herd-compliance and mimicry. The followers, some true believers, others merely cowards, soon fall in line. As word spreads throughout the community, it quickly reaches a critical mass,

ington Square News. October 26, 2016. https://nyunews.com/2016/10/26/ letter-to-the-editor-liberal-studies-rejects-antipcnyuprofs-faulty-claims/.

and thus an entire group—in this case, one of supposed "intellectuals," "independent thinkers," and "individuals" armed with mob-resistant educations—acts as one, a herd in motion, and thus treatment of a person as if he was the equivalent of a moral leper is attained. Members of the Jehovah's Witnesses could not have been more compliant than these supposed independent thinkers in their shunning routines.

I know exactly who initiated the shunning in my own case, as well as her underlying motivations. This is someone who, as a reader at a supposed poetry and short fiction performance, instead used the opportunity to deliver a series of vitriolic emails that she had sent to the curators of a film series about their supposed "racism"—an obscure, recognizable-to-social-justice-zealot-only kind of "racism," akin to a "micro-aggression," but even more incoherent and imperceptible to all but the most hypersensitive, insult-seeking persons alive.

After getting past my disappointment that she would read polemical emails rather than literature, I tried to give her my full attention and to suspend skepticism to a degree, to dispose of doubt and thus to give her the benefit of its lack. Yet, I strained to follow her "reasoning," although the underlying ethos seemed to be clear. A snowflake totalitarian, she had a predilection to be offended and would stop at nothing in her pursuit to find offenses and offenders. She then weaponized her offense-taking and turned it on the culprits. Meanwhile, the curators had sent perfectly reasonable responses and apologies (she read these aloud as well), but clearly nothing would ever satisfy her unquenchable thirst for "justice," her demand to be vindicated, her overweening desire to express herself through self-righteous indignation.

I realized then and there that this person, the reader of those emails, was someone utterly consumed with rage, that her entire life revolved around demanding recognition of, and for, her righteousness. I remarked to myself that this was an eternally unhappy person and that I should stay clear of her, because she is likely to be dangerous. My premonition could not have been more spot on.

II: "You Must Be a Rightwing Nut-job."

One of the many difficulties that attends a mass attack by hordes of cyber-critics is getting around to answering them. I would never try to respond to every critic, for, as the late O.W. Crane often admonished me, "If you stop for every barking dog, your path will never end." Yet I have wanted to address at least the most egregious cases and also to answer one or two of the predominate types. Mind you, I am not hereby issuing any apologies or attempting to regain any love or appreciation from my critics. I, myself, don't care what they think, frankly. What I do care about involves how others may be misled by utter misrepresentations, falsehoods, defamation, and in some cases, libel. I simply do not want bald, bizarre, and sometimes libelous defamations of character floating around in the simulacrum—without providing Google an opportunity to de-list my responses, that is.

A rather non-specific characterization implicit in leftist attacks of my position has been that I am "guilty by association." The left believes avowedly and unreservedly in guilt by association, and perhaps not unreasonably. After all, mass politics is a matter of association. Likewise, one's associations, as leftists see it, are crucial, and one has a responsibility on account of them. Indeed, one can be "charged" with apostasy on the basis of so-called associations, and associations alone.

The standard-issue leftist critic does not seem to grasp that my criticism of PC and "social justice" authoritarianism represented and continues to represent—to an even greater extent—a criticism of mass politics *en se*. I'll leave that aside for the moment and simply address the apparent "charge:" because I am followed by rightwing and right-leaning, Trump supporters and others of whom leftists disapprove, and because I remain "friends" with people of these persuasions on Facebook, without attacking them, I am thereby "guilty."

First, I reject the very self-arrogating claim implicit or explicit in the attacks of such presumptuous arbiters of behavior and expression. I keep a short-hand response handy that at least literally elides vulgarity—IDGAF! (I don't give a f***!).

But seriously, at some point, one must reference the characteristics of these hurlers of ad hominem epithets and throw ad hominem epithets right back in their faces. The "actually-existing" left not only attacks those on the right. Leftists also attack those who won't attack the right as they do. And they will do so with nearly if not the same level of vituperation, vehemence, and violence that they direct at the actual right, if not more.

According to the new New Left, toleration equals association. I reject this premise entirely—because I am first and foremost a believer in what leftists once prized: self-determination, or, to use an unfashionable word, liberty.

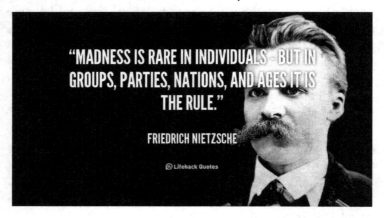

"MADNESS IS RARE IN INDIVIDUALS - BUT IN GROUPS, PARTIES, NATIONS, AND AGES IT IS THE RULE."

FRIEDRICH NIETZSCHE

Ⓒ Lifehack Quotes

Meanwhile, the assumption represents the very sort of authoritarianism that I deplore, and the main reason that I criticized PC/SJW authoritarianism in the first place. Why would I accept leftists' attempts to control and "bully" me now?

I have retained friends and followers on Twitter and Facebook—of many political persuasions. The only requirement is that they do not troll or otherwise attempt to torture me for what I do or do not say. I issue no ideological or political litmus tests, other than one. If a person or group of people cannot tolerate what I say, then they should leave me alone. If they persist in harassing me, I will show them the door. No, this is not a contradiction on my part; it is not tantamount to censorship. You can say whatever you want within constitutional limits—which are very broad, by the way. That doesn't mean I have to listen to what you say. Leftists seem to be under the mistaken impression that the speech of others carries the compulsion on the part of audiences to attend to it. No wonder they try so desperately and violently to no-platform expression that they don't like—or, in many cases, do not understand.

My sharp "anti-SJW turn" hinged and continues to hinge on this very point. The "tipping point" was the afternoon in the fall of 2016 when I posted an article on Facebook about the University of Michigan student who, when given a carte blanche pronoun preference opportunity, selected "His Majesty."[4] I simply posted a link to the story.

The hysterical response marked my social justice tipping point. I decided "never again." I would no longer accede to the demands of social justice ideologues, or restrain my words, actions, or thoughts according to demands stemming from the social justice creed. And, as I noted in *Springtime for Snowflakes*,[5] I am a fierce critic of contemporary transgenderism—that is, of the belief structures that underwrite transgender ideology. But my criticisms of transgenderism do not thereby make me a transphobe. A leap like this requires a category mistake of the sloppiest kind. I believe transgender theory or transgenderism represents a seriously mistaken creed, philosophically and otherwise. It is a mistaken ideology that happens to be attended by pernicious consequences. Such criticism no more makes me transphobic than criticizing Scientology makes the critic, a priori, a hater of individual Scientologists.

To return to the main path of my argument; my public criticisms of social justice ideology and politically correct au-

---

4 Bever, Lindsey. "Students Were Told to Select Gender Pronouns. One Chose 'His Majesty' to Protest 'Absurdity.'" *The Washington Post.* March 31, 2019. https://www.washingtonpost.com/news/education/wp/2016/10/07/a-university-told-students-to-select-their-gender-pronouns-one-chose-his-majesty/.

5 Rectenwald, Michael. *Springtime for Snowflakes: "Social Justice" and Its Postmodern Parentage.* Nashville, TN; London, UK: New English Review Press, 2018. https://amzn.to/2toA1YE.

thoritarianism have resonated with large swaths of the political right. I gained a sizeable new audience and support network through Twitter, Facebook and via hundreds of supportive emails—from the traditional right. I also drew backing from "cultural libertarians," as Paul Joseph Watson dubbed this newly emergent "counterculture." It should come as no surprise that many Trumpists backed me, especially given Trump's regular (although non-specific) criticisms of political correctness.

Criticism of political correctness was supposed to be the exclusive province of the rightwing. For most observers, it was almost inconceivable that an anti-P.C. critic could come from another political quarter. Unsurprisingly, then, the majority of people who discovered my case, including some reporters, simply assumed that I was a conservative. As one Twitter troll put it: "You're anti-P.C.? You must be a rightwing nut-job." But as I have explained on numerous occasions in several interviews and essays, I was not a Trump supporter then. I was never a right-winger, or an alt-right-winger. I was never a conservative of any variety. I wasn't even a classical John Stuart Mill liberal.

In fact, for several years, I had identified as a left or libertarian communist. For many reasons, I no longer identify as such and reject collectivist politics *en toto*. But at this point, that is, at the moment of my earliest criticisms of ID politics and social justice authoritarianism, my politics were decidedly and publicly declared to be to the left (and considerably critical of the authoritarianism) of Bolshevism!

I published essays in socialist journals on several topics, including analyses of identity politics, intersectionality theory, political economy, postmodern theory and "the crisis of capitalism," and the prospects for socialism in the context of transhumanism. I became respected as a Marxist thinker and essayist.

As the financial crisis of 2008 struck, around the fall of 2008 and into the spring of 2009, I had flirted with a Trotskyist sect. Despite some areas of agreement, especially regarding Obama, I soon found their authoritarianism and doctrinaire, hair-splitting line to be absurdist. In any case, after I shared with leadership a paper I had written in my field regarding the historical (theoretical and familial) evolutionary ancestors of Charles Darwin, the group ironically and idiotically declared my thinking to have been irremediably tainted by postmodern theory, and thus rejected my application to join the party. They had no idea what they were talking about. They thought that taking account of social context in the history of science and rightly noting that Darwinian evolutionary theory is not teleological represents "postmodernist thought." Ludicrous! I remain grateful that they spared me who-knows-how-many-otherwise-wasted years peddling a crusty and defunct Trotskyite line as if it were the indisputable gospel truth.

I later became affiliated with a loosely organized left or libertarian communist group, a group whose views I had believed more closely resembled my own perspective. The ultimate liberation, as I read Marx to suggest, will not involve the liberation of a class or other groups, but rather the liberation of individuals to become themselves, to be full expressions of their own singularities.

It wasn't only strangers who took me for rightwing or conservative. So too did many who actually knew better. I attribute a lot of the backlash to the anti-Trump mania and the reactionary fervor that gripped liberals and leftists of nearly all stripes, and still does. This "resistance," as I suggested elsewhere, has long ago been co-opted, if it ever had any legitimacy in the first place.[6] It's an Astroturf movement whose prefabricated ideology is matched by the rapidity with which it produces cliché slogans and slick signage. But previously unaffiliated and warring left and liberal factions, even the "social justice" warriors and communists that had hitherto been utterly dismissive of each other, now consolidated and circled the wagons. Anyone who failed to signal complete fidelity to "the resistance" risked being savaged. I wouldn't and thus I was.

After my first appearance on Fox Business News, such rabid ideologues ambushed me. The social-justice-sympathetic

---

6 Rectenwald, Michael. "The Inauguration of Trump and the Early Opposition to Trumpism." *CLG News*. January 23, 2017. https://www.legitgov.org/Inauguration-Trump-and-Early-Opposition-Trumpism.

members of the left communist group to which I "belonged" denounced me in a series of group emails. Several members conducted a preposterous cyber show trial, bringing charges against me on a number of alleged transgressions. From what I could tell, my offences included appearing on Fox News, sounding remotely like a member of an opposing political tribe, receiving positive coverage in right-leaning media, and criticizing leftist milieus just as Trump became President.

I denied that these self-appointed judges held any moral authority over me and declared their arbitrations null and void. Meanwhile, the elders of the group (supposed friends of mine) had remained silent, allowing the abuse to go on unabated for a day. When they finally chimed in, they called for my official expulsion. I told them not to bother as I wanted nothing further to do with them; I quit. In their collectivist zeal, they later stripped my name from three essays that I'd written for publication on their website and assigned their authorship to someone else entirely. Upon discovering this fraudulence, I publicly berated them for plagiarism. A prominent member of the American Association of University Professors noticed my complaint and investigated the alleged breach of intellectual integrity. Verifying my authorship of the essays, he condemned the group's actions in a popular blog. Only then did the benevolent dictators return my name to the essays' mastheads.

Friends and acquaintances from other communities also turned on me with a vengeance, joining in the group-think repudiation. After my appearance on "The O'Reilly Factor" on Fox News, the Twitter attack was so fierce, vitriolic, and sustained that my associate Lori Price and I spent a whole night blocking and muting tweeters.

Even to this day, former friends and acquaintances continue defaming me and misrepresenting my views, while ascribing intentionality to my actions and their outcomes as if I had masterminded some sinister plot. They ascribe to me an ambition to become "famous" at any cost, a willingness to sacrifice principle for popularity. But nothing could be further from the truth. In fact, I risked my career and reputation to express what I actually thought, thoughts I have since developed further.

An essay published by the socialist Ross Wolfe and written by the socialist Juraj Katalenac provides an example of this kind of mendacious, reckless, and libelous imputation to me of political malice and naked opportunist ambition. As much as I loathe providing it exposure, I will quote from the essay, which is entitled "Intellectual Imperialism."[7] [Since retitled "'American thought': From theoretical barbarism to intellectual decadence."]

But first, I must note the stunning hypocrisy embedded in the title and essay. It suggests a criticism of intellectual imperialism—as if the author does not hope and work for a day when his thought might become "hegemonic,"" when his ideas might spread as far and wide as possible and "colonize" whatever ideological and mental space they can penetrate, while carrying the author's name with them.

In any case, Katalenic merely repeats and extrapolates from a vulgarized and completely errant version of events propagated by U.S. leftists. Katalenic's reiteration of the same, tired and bald-faced lies taken from "American Thought" makes the essay all the more ironic. Katalenac reproduces the very vulgarized "American Thought" that he decries, precisely while complaining about it:

> Social networks are crucial for spreading of 'American thought' not only because they promote simplified expression, but also they are simplifying language itself which suits this narrative of theoretical simplification and impoverishment. Also, social networks allow certain academics, who have not published anything genuine or important in their lives and that cannot even grasp the basics of their own academic disciplines, to gain attention and a following just by saying "shocking things" on the Internet. I am talking about cases such as George Ciccariello-Maher's tweets about 'white

---

7 "'American Thought': From Theoretical Barbarism to Intellectual Decadence." *Communists in Situ*. August 30, 2017. https://cominsitu.wordpress.com/2017/08/30/american-thought-from-theoretical-barbarism-to-intellectual-decadence/.

genocide' or Michael Rectenwald's stunt to get tenured employment at New York University. Narcissistic need for constant attention is certainly one of the most important missions of "American thought," but unlike academia of the past it is unable to fulfill its basic social purpose: to educate and to develop theory. Even though, one could point out that they are still developing theory that serves the agenda of the ruling class in this present capitalist epoch with its identitarian and individualist discourse. Also, this narcissism is present in activist circles too. Some of the worst examples of this were the various "thinkpieces" surrounding the recent murder of Heather Heyer.

I responded in the comment section below the post, stating that Katalenac's pot shot is both factually errant but also tonally condescending and beneath contempt. Further, the statement betrays a blatant and transparent *ressentiment*.

Katalenac gave me far too much credit. If this had been a planned operation, I would have had to be a mastermind. But it wasn't planned and Katalenac makes two wrong statements about it.

First, I did not get "tenured employment" at NYU. I did receive a promotion from Assistant Professor to (full) Professor. And I got a raise. But there is no tenure in the program for which I taught, so that was not an option, and I didn't receive it.

Second, I had applied for the promotion in April 2016, over six months before my kerfuffle over PC/social justice authoritarianism. My application portfolio was unparalleled among the other applicants in my program. I had published three books in one year, and seven while employed at NYU. None of the other applicants came remotely close to that. I had published in top Cambridge University Press periodicals and anthologies. I had the idea for the first international conference (on secularism) hosted by our program. The proposal was accepted. I chaired it and ran the whole thing. It was a major success. Scholars from around the world presented. I produced an anthology on the basis of the conference.

So, while on the one hand Katalenic gives me credit for being some sinister and successful schemer—as if I had planned this entire scenario and successfully predicted how it would turn out—on the other, Katalenic is clueless about the actual conditions of my promotion, and the fact that of nineteen other applicants, my application was unparalleled in terms of accomplishments, and that included my excellent teaching evaluations.

Katalenic should have gotten the facts straight before spouting off erratically. These kinds of ideologically induced and libelous lapses are "unfortunate."

Katalenac's remarks merely represent one of the most explicit statements to the same, spurious effect. Many others drew similar conclusions with no knowledge of context, or me, my career history, or anything. These include a post on *Libcom.org*, suggesting that I was "doing a Christopher Hitchens." The post is followed by comments from others, who, without the slightest knowledge about me or the institutional context in which I had worked, made the same baseless libelous claims—even, like other leftists, endorsing the version of events surrounding my case as given by the institutional behemoth, NYU—NYU, whose "ethical standards" have been well-documented—not only by the *New York Times*[8] but also by me[9] and others.[10]

But the worst treatment came from the NYU Liberal Studies community—to which I had contributed a great deal, and for which I had striven for years to be a well-regarded member. Soon after the open letter appeared (two days after my interview), I recognized a virtual universal shunning by my facul-

---

8 Kaminer, Ariel, and Alain Delaquérière. "N.Y.U. Gives Its Stars Loans for Summer Homes." *The New York Times*, The New York Times. June 18, 2013. https://www.nytimes.com/2013/06/18/nyregion/nyu-gives-stars-loans-for-summer-homes.html.

9 Brunwasser, Joan. "Apartheid at NYU? Prof. Michael Rectenwald Is Afraid So." *OpEdNews*. June 20, 2013. https://www.opednews.com/articles/Apartheid-at-NYU-Prof-Mi-by-Joan-Brunwasser-130620-534.html.

10 "The Art of the Gouge: How NYU Squeezes Billions from Our Students—and Where That Money Goes." *Naked Capitalism*. https://www.nakedcapitalism.com/wp-content/uploads/2015/05/The-art-of-the-gouge-Part-1.pdf.

ty colleagues. One after another, colleagues unfriended and blocked me on Facebook. The few that didn't simply avoided me entirely, until I saved them the trouble and unfriended them. Most stinging were the betrayals of those who once relied on my generosity, some whose careers I had supported and considerably advanced.

Despite the harsh treatment doled out to me by the social justice left and the warm reception I received from the right, I did not become a "right-winger," or even what would be considered a conservative. But after the social-justice-infiltrated left showed me its gnarly fangs and drove me out, I could no longer identify as a leftist. Yet I also resisted the libertarian label, at first—even though the denotation of the term addressed many of my concerns. [I have since declared myself a civil libertarian.]

Part of the problem is that our conventional political vocabulary has been adulterated beyond recognition—utterly ruined. In any case, I no longer felt at home in any political grouping. I was and remain committed to and believe that the ultimate liberation is liberation of and into the singularity of the individual, the emergence of the one's autonomy to be who one is and may become.

CHAPTER NINE

The Bias of Bias-Reducing Methods: Bias Training, Bias Reporting, and Bias Warnings Do More Harm Than Good[1]

RECENT ATTEMPTS to address bias and stereotypes— including bias training in the workplace, bias reporting hotlines on campuses, and warnings about bias and racism in movies—are not only ineffective, they make matters worse.

Bias training creates workplace tensions where they didn't exist, while also reducing employment opportunities for those it aims to protect.[2] The encouragement of bias reporting on college campuses restricts free speech,[3] encourages hoaxes,[4] and

---

1 Originally published by *RT.com*. November 23, 2019. Reproduced here by permission.

2 Lipman, Joanne. "Diversity Training Fails American Companies." *Time*, Time. January 25, 2018. https://time.com/5118035/diversity-training-infuriates-men-fails-women/.

3 Soave, Robby. "First Amendment Group Sues the University of Illinois Over Bias Reporting System, Restrictions on Political Speech." *Reason. com*, Reason. May 30, 2019. https://reason.com/2019/05/30/first-amendment-group-sues-the-university-of-illinois-over-bias-reporting-system-restrictions-on-political-speech/.

4 Grasgreen, Allie. "Hate Crime Hoaxes Present Burdens, Lessons for College Campuses." *Inside Higher Education*. January 31, 2012. https://www.insidehighered.com/news/2012/07/31/hate-crime-hoaxes-present-bur-

"institutionalizes surveillance."[5] Movie warnings posted by entertainment companies condescend to their viewers, treating them like bigots and racists foaming at the mouth at the prospect of seeing outdated depictions of racial and other stereotypes.[6]

Bias Training

With revenues of approximately of $8 billion per year, the bias training industry is big business. Nevertheless, the enterprise has been considered highly ineffective, even dangerous.[7]

The notion of implicit bias gained currency with the introduction of the Implicit Association Test that supposedly measures the prevalence of "implicit bias."[8] But the test has failed to predict racist or other bigoted behavior.[9] Its predictive failure has led scholars to doubt whether implicit bias can even be measured, let alone be correlated with behavior.[10]

It is little wonder, then, that workplace bias training has produced such miserable results. Bias training has not only exacerbated workplace tensions, it has even reduced the employment opportunities of those it sought to protect. "That's right," remarks *Time* columnist Joanne Lipman, drawing on studies by Harvard organizational sociology professor Frank Dobbin and

dens-lessons-college-campuses.

5   "2017 Report on Bias Reporting Systems." *FIRE.* https://www.thefire.org/research/publications/bias-response-team-report-2017/report-on-bias-reporting-systems-2017/.

6   Kruiser, Stephen. "Disney Plus Issues Stupid Wokeness Warning About Old Movies." *PJ Media.* November 13, 2019. https://pjmedia.com/lifestyle/disney-plus-issues-stupid-wokeness-warning-about-old-movies/.

7   Lipman, "Diversity Training Fails American Companies."

8   Project Implicit. https://implicit.harvard.edu/implicit/.

9   Harvard University News Office/Delacorte Press. "Psychology's Favorite Tool for Measuring Racism Isn't Up to the Job." *The Cut.* January 11, 2017. https://www.thecut.com/2017/01/psychologys-racism-measuring-tool-isnt-up-to-the-job.html.

10   Bartlett, Tom. "Can We Really Measure Implicit Bias? Maybe Not." *Chronicle.com.* January 5, 2017. https://www.chronicle.com/article/Can-We-Really-Measure-Implicit/238807.

others; "companies that introduced diversity training would actually employ more women and black men today if they had never had diversity training at all."[11]

Bias Reporting Hotlines

Responding to a supposedly steep rise in hate crimes and incidences of alleged bias on campuses, at least 260 colleges and universities across the US have instituted bias reporting hotlines, with such reports reviewed by response teams (BRTs) established to adjudicate reported cases of "bias incidences" perpetrated on minorities.[12] But bias reporting hotlines have caused problems of their own, including posing threats to constitutionally-protected speech, apparently encouraging a spate of "racist" hoaxes and, with BRTs operating behind closed doors and without transparency, producing a chilling effect on campuses.[13] Bias reporting hotlines and BRTs, as well as the prevalence of no-platforming by activists,[14] have combined to create free speech crises in American academe.

Warnings on Films

The film industry, most recently Disney, has also gotten in on the action, posting warnings on old films indicating that the movies include "outdated cultural depictions" of minorities.[15] With the introduction of its new streaming service,

---

11 Lipman, "Diversity Training Fails American Companies."

12 Knowles, Shelby, et al. "Bias-Response Teams Criticized for Sanitizing Campuses of Dissent." *Center for Public Integrity*. August 27, 2018. https://publicintegrity.org/politics/bias-response-teams-criticized-for-sanitizing-campuses-of-dissent/.

13 Soave, Robby. "The University of Oregon's Thought Police Investigate Students for Saying Anything." *Reason.com*, Reason. May 10, 2016. https://reason.com/2016/05/10/the-university-of-oregons-thought-police/.

14 Rawlinson, Kevin. "Trigger Warnings OK but No-Platforming May Be Illegal, Universities Warned." *The Guardian*, Guardian News and Media. February 2, 2019. https://www.theguardian.com/education/2019/feb/02/government-tells-universities-to-protect-free-speech-on-campus.

15 Adams, Alexander. "Disney Recuts Own Classics: Why Do Corporate Gatekeepers Think We Will Turn Racist If They Don't Censor Content?" *RT*

Disney-Plus, several old Disney movie cartoons warn viewers of these outdated depictions, which some critics found insufficient.[16] But even Disney's warning is pedantic and insulting to viewers, who must now be cudgeled by their PC overlords before watching a cartoon.

The Bottom Line

The problem with such bias-reducing methods is not that bias, stereotypes, bigotry, or racism do not exist, but rather that such institutional means for supposedly counteracting them actually produce more of what they intend to eradicate. In berating the would-be racist or bigot in advance, they produce resentment for the minority populations that they pretend to protect. Nothing is more effective for generating racism than anti-racism programming.

That's because these anti-bias, anti-racism, anti-bigotry mechanisms and methods are always behind the real trends in culture and society and are likewise redundant. The message they convey to the supposed racist or bigot is that he or she must nevertheless be monitored, reported-on, and reminded of what a racist he or she really is, even if only unconsciously. Is it any wonder that resentment for such liberal elitism has blossomed in the US?

International, 13 Nov. 2019, www.rt.com/op-ed/473361-disney-remake-racism-censor/.

16 Staff, TooFab. "Disney 'Weak Sauce' Warnings About Old 'Racist' Movies Slammed on Twitter." *Toofab*, TooFab. Nov 14, 2019. https://toofab.com/2019/11/14/disney-plus-warnings-about-old-racist-movies-slammed-on-twitter/.

CHAPTER TEN

A Genealogy of Social Justice Morals

**Presented as part of "The New Thought Police" Panel of the
New Left Forum. June 14, 2017.[1]**

Introduction

AS A GROWING BODY of scholars and public intellectuals
suggest, nothing less than a moral revolution is underway in liberal society, broadly construed. The old rules of
speech and behavior are giving way to a new package of moral and political imperatives. As illustrated regularly on college
campuses and beyond, the advocates of this new moral creed
aim to enforce adherence to their beliefs with the ferocity of religious zealots. The political and quasi-religious creed is known
as "social justice," and the rationale for its enforcement is to protect and promote the members of marginalized identity groups.
Far from being limited to a few student activists and keyboard
warriors, the social justice creed has been adopted by a majority of North American university administrations and codified
in university policies. And social justice has also traveled far
afield of academia, exerting a growing influence on social media, mass media, corporate America, and other elements of the
broader culture.

---

1 "The New Thought Police." Panel of the *New Left Forum*. John Jay College,
NYC. June 3, 2017. https://www.youtube.com/watch?v=zvLzHfINqeo.

I should make clear that the contemporary "social justice" movement does not simply or clearly represent a commitment to social justice in the abstract. The movement should not be mistaken for such older social justice engagements as the Catholic Workers movement or Tikkun. Nor is today's social justice a child of the Civil Rights movement. While sharing some vocabulary with these apparent ancestors, this new creed actually has very little in common with them. Instead, contemporary social justice has quite different origins and represents a different and quite particular set of beliefs. And it takes entirely different tactical approaches.

Social justice ideology is premised largely on intersectionality theory and includes the belief prongs of identity politics, contemporary gender theory and politics (including transgender identity), queer theory and its politics, the notions of white privilege, "cisgender" privilege, ability privilege, heteronormativity, rape culture, micro-aggressions, discursive violence, and cultural appropriation, among others. The tactics, practices, and mechanisms of social justice ideologues include call-out culture, self-criticism, privilege-checking, public shaming routines, "no-platforming" of speakers, safe spaces, a ritualized vocabulary for dismissing and condemning opponents, sloganeering, chanting over others, and violence or the threat of violence.

English departments served as the primary incubators of today's social justice ideology, although most social justice warriors are unaware of this fact. They also appear to have no idea as to the political and theoretical roots of their beliefs and tactics, which I point out briefly in this essay. Contemporary social justice can be traced to left authoritarianism in Europe and elsewhere, and to the totalitarian regimes of the Soviet Union and Communist China.

In this essay, I will argue that with its surveillance mechanisms, shaming techniques, mob routines, bewildering anti-free-speech attitudes, and violent anti-intellectualism, the new social justice ideology is not a means for realizing social justice at all—if in fact anything could be. Rather, for the institutions that adopt it, the doctrine conveniently provides a thin ethical gloss for increasingly illiberal policies in a neoliberal era. On behalf of those whom it champions, social justice operates as a negative egalitarianism, primarily working to remove the privileges of some as opposed to enhancing the rights of others. Far from bringing about liberation, social justice increases repression and thus reduces overall freedom. Meanwhile, those under its sway presume to make social wrongs evaporate with the mere pronouncement of the correct shibboleths. The postmodernist epistemological conviction that language constructs reality itself permits an eradication of materiality. As such, social justice ideology promises nothing more than linguistic emancipation, while actually serving as a means of oppression in its own right. Thus, the social justice creed is precisely an ideology in the Marxist sense. That is, the social justice belief system presents a false, upside-down image of reality, while offering no effective means for changing it for the better.

Understanding the historical contexts of the movement is essential for deciding how to respond to it. In this essay, I will describe the illiberal nature of the new creed by briefly tracing its historical roots.

*   *   *

"Social justice warriors" are the children and the students of the 1960s and '70s student activists become parents and professors. This story thus embeds a generational narrative, bookended by the free speech movement of the sixties and the anti-free-speech movement of today. I will address the most salient question: how did we get here from there? Unlike most treatments of social justice, here I offer a criticism from the perspective of a civil libertarian, including suggestions for how and why liberalism and the left could and should liberate themselves from this pernicious ideological invader.

Despite its ubiquity, one would be hard-pressed to find a study that subjects social justice ideology and its panoply of apparatuses to scholarly, historical examination. While countless editorials and numerous books have appeared, no one has adequately explained the theoretical and historical roots of these developments. Nor has anyone provided a theoretical framework with which to understand them. Such a treatment of this movement is long overdue.

For several years before my fallout with the social justice ideologues, I was highly critical of identity politics and political correctness, offering Marxist analyses of these trends.[2] My audience abruptly grew, and my critique took a sharper, more strident turn when I decided to attack the trend using public satire. Under the now-notorious Twitter handle @antipcnyuprof [since changed to @TheAntiPCProf], I lambasted the PC policing in academia and the broader culture. I critiqued higher education for adopting and enforcing social justice ideology and the coercive and self-limiting mechanisms it entails—including bias reporting hotlines, safe spaces, trigger warnings, and the no-platforming of speakers. Though mounted in the name of "diversity, equity and inclusion," such practices, I argued, serve only to police, disempower, and discipline, enforcing intellectual and political conformity. (See "Trigger Warnings, Safe Spaces, Bias Reporting: The New Micro-techniques of Surveillance and Control" in this volume.) Social justice, I argued, represents the ideological basis of a brave new world of indoctrination and control, offering nothing like the liberation promised by the traditional left.

After the publication of my interview with the *Washington Square News* and the outing of the @antipcnyuprof as myself,[3] my critique drew a nearly instant response in an open letter issued by "the Liberal Studies Diversity, Equity and Inclusion Working Group," whose Orwellian appellation was matched by

---

2 See, for example, Rectenwald, Michael. "What's Wrong with Identity Politics (and Intersectionality Theory)? A Response to Mark Fisher's 'Exiting the Vampire Castle' (And Its Critics)." *The North Star* (no longer publishing). December 2, 2013. Republished on MichaelRectenwald.com. https://www.michaelrectenwald.com/essays/whats-wrong-with-identit-politics.

3 Siu. Diamond Naga. "Q&A with a Deplorable NYU Professor." *Washington Square News*. October 24, 2016. https://nyunews.com/2016/10/24/qa-with-a-deplorable-nyu-professor/.

the double-speak of its pronouncements.[4] After denouncing me for "the structure of [my] thinking" (ideology), the committee chastised me for straying from accepted liberal PC orthodoxy, and literally declared me "guilty"—of expressing the wrong kinds of thoughts. On the very same day that their open letter appeared, I was summoned to the dean's office, and met by him and the hitherto unannounced head of Human Resources. The upshot of the meeting was a "voluntary" leave of absence, supposedly owing to concerns for my mental health. During this paid medical leave, I was promoted to full professor, which led some in the media to declare that I had been vindicated in my battle with the PC police. The promotion and the kerfuffle were unrelated, but a negative decision certainly would have presented grounds for a discrimination case.

My run-in with the PC police and subsequent developments have been covered widely in the media. I have written on the topic for several venues, including the *Washington Post, American Conservative, Quillette,* and others. I have been interviewed on dozens of media outlets, including One America News Network, PBS, Fox Business News, and *The O'Reilly Factor,* becoming one of Bill O'Reilly's very last Fox News guests. Yet such programs and their hosts often misleadingly framed my appearances, and either misunderstood or deliberately misrepresented my arguments and political perspective. In this essay, I intend to set the record straight—while offering an historical analysis of social justice in order to show that it is anything but emancipatory.

In a recent conversation about campus illiberalism and my role in assailing it, Jonathan Haidt—NYU social psychologist, author of *The Righteous Mind,* and founder of Heterodox Academy—told me that the social justice movement is nothing less than a new species of religious fundamentalism and that the fervor of its believers matches, if not outstrips, that of the re-

---

4 Liberal Studies Diversity, Equity and Inclusion Working Group. "Letter to the Editor: Liberal Studies Rejects @antipcnyuprof's Faulty Claims." *Washington Square News.* October 26, 2016. https://nyunews.com/2016/10/26/letter-to-the-editor-liberal-studies-rejects-antipcnyuprofs-faulty-claims/.

ligious right of the 1980s. My conversation with Haidt led me to recall my scholarship on nineteenth-century British Secularism, especially the legal persecution and social censure that the early Secularists endured at the hands of religious bigots and legal prosecutors. While the persecution for my defection has paled in comparison, an analogy was clear. In the frenzied, religious environment of early twenty-first-century PC culture, I was a new kind of secularist, and I advocated a new secularism.

What Is "Social Justice" and How Does it Operate?

Social justice should now be understood as a dominant ideology, that is, as an ideology that serves the interests of power, whatever it accomplishes for those it supposedly champions. From this understanding, it follows that one should undertake the kind of ideological and historical analyses usually employed by the academic left and reserved for the study of almost exclusively rightist doctrines. Such analyses, I argue, should now be turned back on the academic and social justice left.

Social justice is also more than an ideology. It is also a set of tools and way of being and behaving in the world that corresponds somewhat to an ethical system. Yet it lacks the coherence of a fully elaborated ethics like Utilitarianism, for example. Each of the strands of the social justice matrix has its own storied history, which I will examine briefly. Many of the beliefs of social justice ideologues, which now form the basis of academic and non-academic policies, are implicit, and held as nearly inscrutable. Thus, social justice comes closer to a religious creed than it does to a formal ethical system.

The significance of this understanding is that any attempts to counter or negotiate with social justice ideology are likely to be met with hostility and reproach. Indeed, social justice ideologues and apologists are quick to condemn critics as racists, homophobes, transphobes, fascists, or even Nazis—regardless of their avowed political orientations.

The Maoist Roots of Privilege-Checking and Callout Culture

I began tracing social justice to particular moments and movements from the late 1960s and later. My search for plausible precursors to the privilege-checking and callout culture of social justice milieus led to post-1968 French feminists, who read Mao's *Little Red Book* and imbibed a Maoist ethos, incorporating ideological purging elements of the Cultural Revolution, such as "struggle sessions" and "autocritique," or self-criticism. In Chinese struggle sessions, the guilty party, accused of selfishness, ignorance, and the embrace of bourgeois ideology, was pilloried with verbal and often physical assaults by her comrades, until she broke down and confessed her characterological and ideological flaws, and then pledged self-reform, or faced imprisonment and possible death. Meanwhile, autocritique began with the guilty party, who subjected herself to brutal verbal self-inspection and derogation before the jury of her peers.

As for "safe spaces," Moira Kenney in *Mapping Gay L.A.* traced the concept to gay and lesbian bars of the 1960s in Los Angeles and elsewhere, from which it made its way into feminist circles.[5] As such, they became spaces free of men and "patriarchal" thought and expression. In colleges and universities, they serve to protect students and others from ideas deemed triggering or otherwise harmful. I argue that in the context of higher education, safe spaces constitute a means of self-imposed cultural containment, not unlike that decried by Ralph Ellison,[6] writing in reply to the socialist critic, Irving Howe,[7] whom, he wrote, sought to consign him to a corked "jug" of cultural isolation not unlike that of the Jim Crow south.

These practices, modified of course and transmuted mostly

---

5 Kenney, Moira. *Mapping Gay L.A.; The Intersection of Place and Politics.* Temple University Press, 2001.

6 Wellington, Darryl Lorenzo. "Fighting at Cross-Purposes: Irving Howe vs. Ralph Ellison." *Dissent.* Fall 2005. https://www.dissentmagazine.org/article/fighting-at-cross-purposes-irving-howe-vs-ralph-ellison.

7 Howe, Irving. "Black Boys and Native Sons." *Dissent.* Autumn 1963. http://writing.upenn.edu/~afilreis/50s/howe-blackboys.html.

into an exclusive rhetorical character, have infiltrated not only academia but also social media, where the practices of privilege-checking, callout, and dogpiling are often exercised with a particular ferocity. Given that these practices have been undertaken in face-to-face settings and often to more substantive and horrific conclusions, the vindictiveness shown by social justice ideologues cannot be explained away by the relative anonymity and distance afforded by the Internet. Although the digital realm does provide some cover, social justice carries on even in face-to-face encounters, and has advocates within universities who practice these routines, with the implicit endorsement of university administrations.

The Liberal and Marxist Progenitors of "No-Platforming"

I turn now to the practice of "no-platforming," or the refusal on the part of students and other activists to allow guest speakers to have a platform or a stage to voice their views. I have tracked the history of this practice on campuses and elsewhere and find its provenance in the theoretical discussions of two main thinkers: the Marxist, Frankfurt School theorist, Herbert Marcuse (1898 -1979), and the liberal philosopher of science and society, Karl Popper (1902-1994).

In his "Repressive Tolerance," Marcuse argued against "pure tolerance"—for the refusal to allow speakers and other promulgators of intolerance to have a platform for promoting their views.[8] Thus, "tolerance" required the abolition of views deemed intolerant. Some speech and expression must be stopped, and the left is correct and even obligated to stop it. A similar though less illiberal position, known as the Paradox of Tolerance, was developed by the philosopher Karl Popper.

Marcuse's stance represents a slippery slope, establishing as it does a tribunal of censorship consisting of ideologically charged activist milieus. It effectively means that illiberalism

---

8 Marcuse, Herbert. "Repressive Tolerance," from Wolff, Robert Paul, Barrington Moore, Jr., and Herbert Marcuse. *A Critique of Pure Tolerance.* Boston: Beacon Press, 1969, pp. 95-137.

must be a characteristic of "liberal" society. This principally represents a contradiction and fails to consider the strong possibility that, sooner or later, the continually narrowing Overton window[9] will close on the speech of the very people who sought to bar the speech of others. In any case, one must wonder: just who is fit to be arbiter, and what makes them—and not others—the interpretative conscience of society, suited to ban expression they deplore? In our contemporary moment, the strange irony is that these arbiters aim to foreclose lines of inquiry they have never even directly encountered or considered. But if they had, the irony would be even greater. The arbiters have survived, so why wouldn't others? Marcuse's advocacy of social and legal intolerance toward supposed intolerance reproduces the very repression that he lamented and hoped to prevent. And one wonders just how he managed to arrive at such conclusions as early as 1965. Not that he was prescient; as a prominent communist theorist, had he already completely forgotten the McCarthy hearings?

Postmodernism, neoliberalism, and the Birth of Trigger Warnings and Microaggressions

Underlying the concern for offensive language in social justice ideology is also the belief that language can materially harm others. Language is also considered to effectively displace materiality. To explain this belief, I have turned to the postmodern and other recent theories of language. Drawing on Frederick Jameson's critical assessment of structuralism in *The Prison-House of Language* (1975),[10] I have begun a treatment of the precursors to postmodernist language theory in structuralist linguistics. I then move to consider notions of discursive power as theorized by French historian and philosopher, Michel Foucault. It seeks another source in Jacques Derrida's De-

---

9 Junior, Christi. "The Overton Window: What It Is & Why It's So Important." *The Ralph Retort*. July 22, 2016. https://theralphretort.com/overton-window-important-7022016/.

10 Jameson, Fredric. *The Prison-House of Language: A Critical Account of Structuralism and Russian Formalism*. Princeton University Press, 2015.

construction. Trigger warnings and micro-aggressions are only explicable in connection with these continental, structuralist, post-structuralist and deconstructionist understandings of language as material power and as constructing material reality.

I have begun to compare these continental language theories with the understanding of language that underwrites classical liberal theory and law, including the U.S. Constitution's understanding of expression and its protection. The contradictions between classical liberalism's presuppositions about language and the explicit claims of postmodernist language theory go a long way in making sense of the ongoing conflicts between free speech advocates and social justice ideologues, and administrators who enact social-justice-inflected policies.

The New Left and Intersectionality Theory

Certainly, much of the social justice arsenal and ethos has been inflected by intersectional feminism. Intersectionality provides the architectural blueprint for the kind of "subaltern" status-seeking that we encounter in social justice ideology and groups. Developed in the 1970s and '80s, intersectionality seeks to describe how power intersects identities along various axes, including those of race, gender, sexuality, sexual preference, ability, and more. It aims to locate the articulations of power as it traverses various subordinated peoples in different, multiple ways. Suggestive of a radical critique of patriarchy, capitalism, and white supremacy, which its adherents see as distinct yet interconnected forms of domination, it complicates any sense of gender, sex, class, or race as homogenous wholes. And it calls into question any hierarchy of one categorical determination over others.

Yet in practice, intersectionality serves to isolate multiple and seemingly endless identity standpoints, without sufficiently articulating them with one another. The upshot in political practice, as Christina Hoff Sommers argues, is an endless splitting of categories,[11] with the members of each category vying

---

11 Hoff Sommers, Christina. "Intersectional Feminism: What is it?" *Factual Feminist*. March 30, 2016. https://www.youtube.com/watch?v=cY-

for more-subaltern-than-thou status. Intersectionality is no doubt the source of what has been derogatorily referred to as "the Oppression Olympics" by unsympathetic observers, some of whom may have once competed in the games themselves.[12]

Conclusion: Recommendations for Reform: A Post-Secular University

I now return to the understanding of social justice as a religious creed and consider possible means for reforming institutions that have adopted it, as well as for undermining its influence in the broader culture. Given that social justice ideology can be considered a religion, any successful change will necessarily involve a secular alternative. This chapter considers the possibilities for a new kind of secularism in the university, from where, it is hoped, broader social change may emanate.

To consider the question of a newly secular university, I return to my work on historical Secularism. Contrary to received notions, as originally conceived and founded by George Jacob Holyoake in 1851 in Britain, Secularism did not signify the absence or negation of religion. Rather, the secular indicated a substantive category in its own right, a complement to the religious. Holyoake imagined and fostered the co-existence of secular and religious elements subsisting under a common umbrella known as Secularism. For Holyoake, the secular and religious were figured as complementary and co-constituting aspects of what we might now call an overarching secularity, but which Holyoake called Secularism. Secularism was introduced not as a counter to religion, per se, but rather to atheism.

In conclusion, I argue that what is needed in the university is not a negative secularism like that undertaken by the subsequent leader of the Secularist movement, Charles Bradlaugh. Bradlaugh believed that Secularism represented the abolition of religion and the belief in atheism. Holyoake's Secularism, on the

---

pELqKZ02Q.

12 Ridgway, Shannon. "Oppression Olympics: The Games We Shouldn't Be Playing." *Everyday Feminism Magazine*. November 4, 2012. https://everydayfeminism.com/2012/11/oppression-olympics/.

other hand, is compatible with contemporary notions of what is now called "post-secularism." An ambiguous and contested term, post-secularism may signify a skepticism or antagonism toward the hard secularism of a Bradlaugh, in recognition of the persistence or resurgence of religion. It refers to an attempt to overcome the antinomy of secularism/religion, such that both are granted recognition under a common umbrella. Post-secularism recognizes the persistence of religion and marks an acknowledgement of a religious and secular pluralism. It also recognizes the ethical resources and community-building efficacy of religious bodies and countenances the function of religion in constructing and defending cultural identities.

The recommendations of this conclusion are for the reconceptualization of the university and the broader culture in post-secular terms. That is, reform should not involve an attempt to eradicate the social justice creed, or to drive its believers to the margins, where they believe, falsely, that they already reside. If history is any indication, it shows that attempts to eradicate religion have not only failed but also backfired, ending by strengthening that which they sought to abolish. The contemporary religiosity of Russia is one such example, a state where religion had been legally abolished and under which the state was officially atheist. Instead of recommending such an approach, I argue that successful reform will necessarily allow social justice beliefs to remain within a broader matrix of possible creeds, including secular and other religious ones. The post-secular dispensation calls for balancing religious and secular perspectives within the same political, public, and educational spheres.

Only by admitting social justice belief as one of many other possibilities will the university and the broader culture successfully absorb this creed without becoming hostage to it. Yet the university can no longer make the social justice creed the basis for university policy. It must institute new post-secular policies and adopt what would amount to post-secular language and concepts. That is, the university and the broader culture must transcend while nevertheless including social justice within its ambit. Social justice must become a belief subordinated to a higher-level secularity under which it is one of many options, but not the official arbiter of behavior, language use, morality, pedagogy or policy.

CHAPTER ELEVEN

Why Political Correctness is Incorrect[1]

THE TERM "politically correct" is one of the most incendiary phrases of contemporary political jargon. Advocates for values deemed politically correct—antiracism, anti-misogyny, anti-transphobia, and so on—suggest that being politically correct is simply that: correct. Why would anyone want to be anything else—unless, that is, they are motivated by bigotry, or something worse? This position appears reasonable enough, and it might even be indisputable—if it didn't seek to obscure an underlying impulse—for political correction. Under regimes of political correctness, political correction is the typical response for those voicing "incorrect" opinions. Indeed, imposing "correct" ideas by the "necessary" means is precisely the crux of the problem.

A discussion of PC is well-served by tracking this political label to its earliest appearance. Official Soviet sources show that the term *politicheskaya korrektnost* (political correctness) was used as early as 1921, to positively describe "correct" thinking. As expected, its author was none other than the primary architect of the Bolshevik revolution, Vladimir Lenin. Lenin's promotion and later enforcement of political correctness followed from his notion of *partiĭnost*, or party spirit, which also stood

---

1 Originally published in the *International Business Times*. January 25, 2018. Reproduced here by permission.

for "party truth," or the correct interpretation of the world and everything in it. After the revolution, political correctness was enforced by the Soviet terror.[2] During the Cultural Revolution, Mao's Red Guard later adopted and adapted "autocritique," a technique for the enforcement of political correctness, while adding "struggle sessions" for good measure.

I mention the Soviet and Sino-Communist sources of political correctness not to invoke a Red Scare but rather to note that the contemporary "social justice" movement is marked by the same impulses. Former Soviet and Maoist Chinese citizens recall systems under which verbal spontaneity and skepticism could be fatal. During our soft cultural revolution, those accused of ideological deviation, such as Google's former employee, James Damore, while neither tortured or killed, are sent to the metaphorical gulags of public censure and unemployment.

In adopting social-justice-based policies and mechanisms, North American colleges and universities are unwittingly drawing on totalitarian resources of enforcement. The ranks of administrators swell, and college tuitions increase, due largely to the outsized administrations devoted to special "student needs." Most college administrations now include Bias Response Teams, tribunals that adjudicate, behind closed doors, reports of "microaggressions" and "bias infractions" at over 230 colleges and universities nationwide. Bias hotlines, safe spaces, trigger warnings, and no-platforming or shutting down of speakers yield the right to curtail free expression and open inquiry to social justice advocates and social-justice-dominated college administrators.

In academia, the mere questioning of social justice ideology and its mechanisms can land one in hot water, as it did in my case. I began by anonymously tweeting criticisms of social justice trends and was soon noticed by a reporter from the NYU student newspaper. I agreed to an interview and allowed the paper to reveal my identity as the operator behind the Twitter handle @antipcnyuprof.

---

2   Ellis, Frank. "Political Correctness and the Ideological Struggle: From Lenin and Mao to Marcuse and Foucault." *The Journal of Social, Political and Economic Studies.* Vol. 27, No. 4, Winter 2002, pp. 409-444.

The response was swift and severe. I was met with a strong rebuke from the Orwellian-named "Liberal Studies Diversity, Equity and Inclusion Working Group," which literally declared me "guilty" for "the structure of my thinking." The same day, I was called before my dean and the head of Human Resources, both of whom strongly suggested that I take a paid medical leave of absence. My tweets and interview were seen by an unnamed staff member as "a cry for help." In other words, as in the Soviet Union, airing views at variance with the official ideology was treated as mental illness.

After returning from the leave, I was hailed with a series of blistering emails from a handful of faculty colleagues. As they pelted me with racist and sexist slurs, they ironically called me a "racist," "sexist," "misogynist," and "Satan" himself. Incidentally, I had never mentioned a single individual or identity group in any of my discussions of the issues.

The fallout from my anti-PC Twitter "misdeeds" and the backlash over subsequent media exposure proved the point of the entire exercise. As they responded to my criticisms, the social justice ideologues demonstrated their authoritarian character. With their notoriously vituperative, pack-and-attack mentality, they acted as if they could punish and defame me with impunity.

Finally, by effectively ceding control to the social justice ideologues in their midst, just as the administrators at Evergreen State College would later do in the case of Bret Weinstein, NYU's administration revealed that social justice ideology is now official doctrine in the university.

Political correctness is wrong not primarily due to the values it espouses, but because it amounts to coercion or "social tyranny," as John Stuart Mill argued in *On Liberty*. Enforcing an orthodoxy like social justice infringes individual rights, while producing a chilling effect. Specially protecting dogma and those who advocate it is antithetical to open inquiry and free expression, the hallmarks of the university. We must act now to preserve this institution—not only for its own sake, but for the broader society that depends on it for trusted knowledge and an informed citizenry.

CHAPTER TWELVE

A Critique of "Social Justice" Ideology: Thinking through Marx and Nietzsche[1]

I N AN EARLIER ESSAY, I offered a brief sketch of the genealogy of social justice mechanisms and beliefs (see "A
Genealogy of 'Social Justice' Morals" in this volume). To date,
however, I have yet to examine the philosophical premises of
the creed, or formally to offer a theoretical framework or set of
frameworks for critiquing and refuting it. This essay represents
a first effort at doing both.

First, I will briefly trace a Soviet and a few postmodernist
contributions to social justice ideology. Then, I will turn my
attention to two major thinkers—Karl Marx and Friedrich Nietzsche—in order to find ways that the two thinkers may be
adduced to provide resources for understanding and critically
assessing the social justice ideology.

My decision to treat these two thinkers is based on more
than a mere hunch. I once figured Nietzsche as an unambigu-
ous anti-social-justice figure. Yet I also recognize that Nietzsche
is a well-known source for postmodern theory, and thus, indirectly, for some aspects of social justice ideology. Postmodernism adopted Nietzsche's view that power and knowledge are

---

1 Originally published by *CLG News*. https://www.legitgov.org. July 20,
2017.

inextricable, that values are historically contingent and socially constructed, that truth is a function of the most plausible narrative explanations as inflected by power, and so forth. Likewise, Nietzsche's relation to social justice ideology is not only a matter of applying the slave morality, *ressentiment*, and critiques of egalitarianism to social justice ideology. However, as I do not have the space to consider the consonances between postmodernism/social justice and Nietzsche, I will limit my discussion in this respect to a Nietzschean critique of social justice.

Many contemporary critics of social justice ideology see Marxism as the obvious progenitor of the creed. Some even mistakenly equate Marxism, postmodernism, and social justice. Yet substituting special identity groups for social classes does not establish a perfect analogy between social justice ideology and socialism. Too many postmodern theoretical antecedents have mediated the relationship between social justice and the Marxist-based left. Furthermore, Marxism and postmodernism are far from compatible. As such, social justice ideology and Marxism bear only a faint philosophical family resemblance. Yet, fruitfully, any resemblance they do bear is best understood in terms of a Nietzschean critique.

Postmodernism and Social Justice Ideology

The social justice notion that each person has their own truth based on their particular type of subordination has its origin in "standpoint epistemology." First introduced by the Hungarian Soviet theorist Georg Lukács in his book *History and Class Consciousness* (1923), standpoint epistemology is the notion that particular social outlooks lend greater access to knowledge of reality.[2] Lukács argued that the unique position of the working class within the social structure accorded the class a privileged vantage point for discerning objective truth. In her book, *The Science Question in Feminism* (1986), feminist Sandra Harding adopted Lukács's proletarian standpoint epistemology

---

2 Lukács Georg. *History and Class Consciousness Studies in Marxist Dialectics*. MIT Press, 1971.

and adapted it for a "feminist standpoint epistemology."[3] Having been relegated to being caretakers of men, children, and themselves, women experience a deepened and unified sense of "hand, heart, and head" activity, and thus appreciate a deepened "sensuous, concrete, relational" access to the world. Their standpoint accords them an enhanced cognitive and perceptual grasp of objectivity.

The notion of standpoint epistemology was then siphoned through other identity filters and inflected by postmodernism. In the hands of postmodernists, it came to suggest an absolute epistemological relativism, the belief that truth was a function of the standpoint of any particular persons, but particularly subordinated ones. Further, each group or individual had their own exclusive access to their *own* truth, and no one else could possibly understand their truth. This is the form it takes in social justice ideology. I call it an epistemological solipsism.

Social constructivism is a major prong of the postmodern outlook. According to postmodern theory, a social construct is a socially, culturally, and historically contingent construal of collective, conscious, and less-than-conscious human perceptions, cognitions, beliefs, and ideations. Social constructs include the construal of identities, groups, beliefs, sensibilities, tastes, sexual attractiveness, and theories themselves, among many other phenomena. Social constructivism holds that even such categories as "nature," as well as the most enduring methodology we have for studying it, namely science, are also social constructs.

Social constructivism comes in several flavors. I'll discuss only the most radical type here, namely, "radical constructivism." Developed within the postmodern quarters of the anti-science postmodern academic left and within the interdisciplinary field known as "Science Studies,"[4] radical constructivism is the

---

3 Harding, Sandra G. *The Science Question in Feminism*. Cornell University Press, 1993.

4 "Science Studies," also known as "Science and Technology Studies" or "Science, Technology and Society" (STS) is a dialogue ranging across many academic disciplinary boundaries. It includes the History and Philosophy of Science (HPS), the Sociology of Science, the Sociology of Scientific Knowledge (SSK), and such cross-disciplinary fields as the cultural studies

position that the material world does not significantly constrain our perceptions of it. It does not impose any significant constraints on our theories about it either. Likewise, in science, one theory is as good or almost as good as any other. The relationship between a scientific theory and its "natural object" is arbitrary or nearly arbitrary. This is a form of what philosophers call "social idealism," the belief that our ideas about the world are not only in our heads, but mostly, if not exclusively, made up by us. Something is surely "out there," but whatever it is, it does not necessarily bear any relationship to our ideas about it, or vice versa.[5]

---

of science, feminist critiques of science, Marxist analysis of science, and anthropological studies of science, amongst others. The postmodern wing of Science Studies became implicated in the "Science Wars," a controversy involving humanities and social science critics, who were badgered by such defenders of science as biologist Paul R. Gross, mathematician Norman Levitt, and physicists Jean Bricmont and Alan Sokal. The "Sokal Affair" or "Sokal Hoax" capped the controversy. When Sokal submitted a satirical article to the respected critical theory journal *Social Text*, the editors were duped and published it. The essay, entitled "Transgressing the Boundaries: Towards a Transformative Hermeneutics of Quantum Gravity," argued that quantum gravity is a social and linguistic construct. It was gratuitously littered with postmodern jargon and amounted to an obscurantism emblematic not only of postmodernist Science Studies essays and books, but of postmodernist theory in general.

5   Hess, David J. *Science Studies: An Advanced Introduction.* New York University Press, 2001, pp. 44-45. Hess writes: "Philosophers tend to use the term 'constructivism' somewhat differently to refer to the idea that scientists do not discover the world but impose a structure on it or in some sense 'make' the world. In its extreme version, constructivism amounts to more than an instrumentalist account of theories; it refers to a social idealism in which there is no material reality that constrains or structures sensory observations. Furthermore, regarding the problem of theory choice, this extreme version would hold that the world does not in any serious way constrain theory choice; in this sense the world is made or constructed rather than discovered. Some philosophers argue that the constructivism of social studies of science necessarily implies social idealism and epistemological relativism, but I suggest that there is no necessary connection between the two. There may be some social scientists who would accept the philosophical position of social idealism and epistemological relativism, and if they exist I would suggest calling their philosophical position 'radical constructivism.' Certainly some sociologists of scientific knowledge have made statements that suggest

Contemporary gender theory derives indirectly from the same provenance as such ideas. The transgender belief is that gender—or even, as the story currently goes, "sexual difference" itself—is a social construction. Gender identity is determined not by genetics, anatomy, hormones, or physiology. Such words are anathema and can only be used ironically or with derision in a Gender Studies classroom. Gender is determined by *beliefs* about sometimes inconveniently non-conforming phenomena, and ultimately, by names and words. This is social idealism through and through. Such social idealism had been made *au courant* by postmodernist versions of Science Studies and postmodern theory in general, from the late 1970s onward. Contemporary transgender theory would be inconceivable without these postmodern precursors.

Transgenderism is a subset of a broader social justice ideology, and radical constructivism underlies nearly all social justice claims. In the terms set by social justice ideology, language constitutes reality, rather than merely attempting to represent it. Reality is formed from a linguistic putty that social justice believers mold into whatever entities they can imagine or construe. Social justice ideology is thus a "practical postmodernism"—although the phrase necessarily strikes reasonable people as an oxymoron. How can postmodernism be "practical?" they ask. By being put into practice. By the same token, social justice ideologues are practical postmodernists. How can postmodernists be "practical?" By putting postmodernism into action. And this is exactly what they have done.

Marx and Nietzsche

Before turning to Marxian and Nietzschean critiques of social justice ideology, a comparison between the two thinkers is in order. First and foremost, Karl Marx and Friedrich Nietzsche should be understood as fundamentally antithetical with respect to at least one crucial issue—egalitarianism.

Scholars have debated whether or not Marxism amounts to an ethical system. The most convincing arguments suggest that

they accept radical constructivism or they did at one point."

it does not. As Bertell Ollman notes in *Alienation: Marx's Conception of Man in Capitalist Society* (1971):

> ... all ethical systems, that is all those ways of thinking which are generally accepted as such, have a basis for judgment which lies outside that which is to be judged. This results in a suspended commitment until the 'facts' have been gathered and their relation to the standard for judgment clarified. The evaluation, when it comes, is a matter of conscious choice.[6]

One of the problems with understanding Marxism as an ethical system is that for Marx no "outside of the system" exists and thus no previously existing standard can be applied to the elements within the system. Further, the elements already embed values, which are inextricable from the facts as such. That is, under Marx's analysis of capitalism, no value-free facts exist that can be evaluated in terms of externally derived values.

Karl Marx and Friedrich Nietzsche

Yet, despite the lack of an explicit ethics in Marx's work, his economic and philosophical arguments are inexplicable without reference to at least one value-laden premise: the working class is not *naturally* inferior to the capitalist class. Nothing intrinsic to the working class makes its exploitation inevitable or justifiable. Since the working class is not comprised of *naturally* inferior beings, its predicament must be explained in other terms. Marx explained the class's predicament in terms of its socio-economic positioning, which guarantees its subordination and exploitation. Further, its structurally determined positioning and the contradictions this entails make the class a world-historical agent, the only agent capable of eradicating class society altogether. This is hardly the portrait of an enfeebled and intrinsically deficient mass.

Thus, Marx must be regarded as essentially an egalitarian. Further, as Marx sees it, capitalist exploitation and its lottery-like conditions for workers render equality moot. According to Marx, liberal, abstract egalitarianism, or egalitarianism *de jure*, is a sham.

Nietzsche, on the other hand, scorned egalitarianism *en toto*, both in the abstract and in its concrete expressions. Nietzsche suggested that egalitarianism represented a moral valuation proffered on behalf of the weak by a monotheistic priestly caste—which by his time had included socialist intellectuals—in order to level the social order.

Egalitarianism enabled the trammeling of the natural superiors of the masses, and thus potentially foreclosed the emergence of the utmost in human individuality and possibility, as represented by the *Übermensch*, Nietzsche's natural aristocrat.

Nietzsche's most clear objections to egalitarianism are put forth in *Beyond Good and Evil* (1886) in the section, "What is Noble?"

> Every enhancement so far in the type 'man' has been the work of an aristocratic society – and that is how it will be, again and again, since this sort of society believes in a long ladder of rank order and value distinctions between men, and in some sense needs slavery. Without the pathos of distance as it grows out of the ingrained differences between stations, out of the way the ruling caste maintains an overview and keeps looking down on subservient types and tools, and out of this

caste's equally continuous exercise in obeying and command-
ing, in keeping away and below – without this pathos, that
other, more mysterious pathos could not have grown at all,
that demand for new expansions of distance within the soul
itself, the development of states that are increasingly high,
rare, distant, tautly drawn and comprehensive, and in short,
the enhancement of the type 'man,' the constant 'self-over-
coming of man' (to use a moral formula in a supra-moral
sense) …

Mutually refraining from injury, violence, and exploitation,
placing your will on par with the other's: in a certain, crude
sense, these practices can become good manners between individuals when the right conditions are present (namely, that
the individuals have genuinely similar quantities of force and
measures of value, and belong together within a single body).
But as soon as this principle is taken any further, and maybe
even held to be the fundamental principle of society, it immediately shows itself for what it is: the will to negate life,
the principle of disintegration and decay. Here we must think
things through thoroughly, and ward off any sentimental
weakness: life itself is essentially a process of appropriating,
injuring, overpowering the alien and the weaker, oppressing,
being harsh, imposing your own form, incorporating, and at
least, the very least exploiting, – but what is the point of always using words that have been stamped with slanderous
intentions from time immemorial?[7]

Nietzsche's remarks regarding the masses might seem to
suggest that the *Übermenschen* should exert control over and
directly aim to exploit the masses—a totalitarianism of the natural aristocracy as such. But was Nietzsche really a totalitarian?[8] Totalitarian recommendations are not explicit in his writ-

---

7 Nietzsche, Friedrich. *Beyond Good and Evil: Prelude to a Philosophy of the
Future*. Cambridge University Press, 2002, pp. 151-153.

8 In 1989, I posed this very question to my first literary mentor, Allen
Ginsberg. "A bohemian scribbler" was the sum of Allen's answer—suggesting
that Nietzsche should be best understood as just another rebellious ranter,
even one comparable to the Beats, one who rejected the dominant, bourgeois
culture and had a flair for the dramatic.

ing. In fact, even if he had suggested that the masses should be dominated, he dismissed specific measures for dominating them. Such measures had been rendered unnecessary. As "herd animals," the masses submitted to mediocrity, thus effectively remaining under subjection without the need for superordinate efforts on the part of their overlords. Their subordination had been accomplished by the slave morality. Due to their historically determined mass personhood, the question of mass social control had been rendered moot—except in terms of the domination of the social order by the masses. Yet Nietzsche did not fear a socialist uprising.[9] He did suggest, however, that egalitarianism made exceptions to the mediocre legions of the masses— and the emergence of *Übermenschen*—less likely.

For Nietzsche, the problem with egalitarianism was that it depended upon squelching greatness, and likewise upon denying the actualization of true individual human excellence. Egalitarianism, as Nietzsche saw it, was necessarily subtractive in character, based upon a morality of denial. Social leveling occurred not by elevating the majority but by suppressing the great, even by denying their possible existence. The weak masses had been encouraged by the priestly caste to believe in a subtractive, negative egalitarianism, using a religious or religiously derived morality, by which they imposed a "bad conscience" on the exceptional.

For Nietzsche, socialism represented a direct descendent of Christianity, and Christianity a direct descendent of Judaism. All three were premised upon what began primarily as imag-

---

9 Nietzsche's attitude toward the masses may be summarized as follows: "Who cares why people have been turned into sheep by their own weakness … The very fact that they allowed themselves to be turned into sheep is proof enough of the fact that they deserve to be sheep and therefore always will be sheep. To try to get the sheep to make a virtue out of their sheepishness through telling them that their weakness is a strength and that they can all liberate themselves through one form of *ressentiment* or another, through Christianity or class struggle, was a waste of time. Borrowing from Aristotle, his view was that there were natural slaves and natural masters and the existence of slaves and masters proved this." Thompson, Peter. "'The Übermensch is the Proletariat'. Marx + Nietzsche = ?," *Journal of Contemporary Central and Eastern Europe* 10:2, 2002, pp. 201-19, at p. 209.

inary inversions or reversals of the social hierarchy, which the priestly caste then imposed on the social order. According to this inversion ideology, the lower orders, the subordinated, the subaltern, were actually the true superiors: "... the socialists' conception of the highest society is the lowest in the order of rank..."[10]

The superiority of the subordinated was generally asserted in terms of moral value or worth, or on the notion that subordinated status itself actually signified superiority in its own right:

> Only those who suffer are good, only the poor, the powerless, the lowly are good; the suffering, the deprived, the sick, the ugly, are the only pious people, the only ones saved, salvation is for them alone, whereas you rich, the noble and powerful, you are eternally wicked, cruel, lustful, insatiate, godless, you will also be eternally wretched, cursed and damned![11]

Socialism represented the *ressentiment* of the lower orders for those who dominated them. As Nietzsche saw it, a morality of *ressentiment* had become the ruling moral system. By encouraging the maintenance of the weak, the sick, or the otherwise incapable, as Rainer Maria Rilke put it his short story "Der Apostel" (1896), the morality of *ressentiment* "had made the whole world an infirmary."[12] To appropriate and adapt a contemporary social justice term, it did this by encouraging and enabling a *dis*-ableism. It held in the highest regard the most degraded elements of humanity, as Nietzsche (and Rilke) figured them. For Nietzsche, class politics involved *ressentiment* and derived directly from the slave morality of Judaism and Christianity.

Despite these fundamentally irreconcilable differences be-

---

10 Nietzsche, Friedrich Wilhelm, et al. *The Will to Power: A New Translation*. Vintage Books, 1968, p. 32. Originally published 1901.

11 Nietzsche, Friedrich Wilhelm, et al. *On the Genealogy of Morality and Other Writings*. Cambridge University Press, 2017, p. 17. Originally published 1887.

12 Rilke, Rainier Maria. "Der Apostel" ("The Apostle"). 1896. https://www.bookrix.com/_ebook-rainer-maria-rilke-der-apostel/.

tween Marx and Nietzsche, we may nevertheless descry areas of overlap, and even some rationale for Marxists to draw on Nietzsche for the class struggle. Historically, attempts have been made to appropriate Nietzschean notions by leftists, some of them Marxists—before, that is, the Soviet project was established, and then again after its dissolution. One of these notions is the will to power itself.[13] Some Marxists have found in Nietzsche a validation and support for the unabashed assumption of power and its use in order to overthrow class society.

Another potential overlap is Nietzsche's notion of the slave morality. Nietzsche's characterization of a morality that praised lowliness and extolled the virtues of humility and obedience may be reconciled with the Marxist conception of ruling-class ideology, which serves to justify the subordination of the vast majority by a minority, drawing on the same notions of humility, obedience, and long-suffering.

Yet another attractive notion for Marxist readers of Nietzsche is the latter's notion of the transvaluation of values: the overcoming of conventional morality, followed by a period of nihilism, and then the most difficult task of leaving nihilism in establishing a new value system. The transvaluation of values might be translated into the Marxist project of overcoming ruling-class ideology and replacing it with a socialist understanding of the world, although Nietzsche understood this as the province of individuals alone.

Marx and Nietzsche also shared atheism. But their atheisms served different purposes and were arrived at and valued for different reasons. For Marx, religion was a ruling-class ideology, a "superstructural" means for dominating the proletariat, subduing them psychically and thus helping to render the use of force less necessary. However, Marx's atheism has sometimes been misunderstood. For Marx, the primary political work was not the intellectual task of eradicating religious belief. Rather, Marx figured religion as an almost necessary anodyne under capitalist social relations. It would disappear completely only

---

13 See Taylor, Seth. *Left-Wing Nietzscheans: The Politics of German Expressionism 1910-1920.* De Gruyter, 1990.

with socialism, not merely with demonstrations of its falsity. Marx's most famous passage about religion, too often truncated, makes clear that for him religion was not the problem, *per se*:

> Religious suffering is at the same time an expression of real suffering and a protest against real suffering. Religion is the sign of the oppressed creature, the sentiment of a heartless world, and the soul of soulless conditions. It is the opium of the people.[14]

For Marx, religion existed because people were oppressed. Religion served as a displacement of equity, bounty, and justice onto a realm outside of the human realm, precisely because the human realm lacked these qualities. Likewise, the socialist—unlike such left Hegelians as Feuerbach, whom Marx criticized fiercely—should not primarily aim to eradicate belief in the supernatural. Instead, the socialist should struggle to eradicate the conditions that make belief in the supernatural necessary.

On the other hand, as Nietzsche saw it, religion, especially Christianity and Judaism, were products of the priestly caste, not the aristocracy. Judeo-Christian religiosity originally represented the *ressentiment* of the priestly caste for the aristocracy and was an expression of their will to power. Meanwhile, atheism had been made possible by science and modernity. God, or God's functions, had been rendered obsolete. But Nietzsche also suggested that most so-called atheists merely substituted a new godliness for a newly dead one. Scratching the surface of their atheism revealed yet another form of religiosity. Socialism was one such form of atheism, as Nietzsche saw it. After all, socialism retained a Christian-like eschatology and merely substituted a new savior, the working class—or the vanguard in Bolshevism—for the Christ. Further, socialists perpetrated a very similar sense of hallowed social values that subordinated the

---

14 Marx, Karl. "Critique of Hegel's Philosophy of Right." *Marx's Critique of Hegel's Philosophy of Right, 1843-4.* https://www.marxists.org/archive/marx/works/1843/critique-hpr/index.htm.

great to their inferiors—through a subtractive egalitarianism, a morality of denial, and *ressentiment* for worldly superiors.

Toward Marxist and Nietzschean Critiques of Social Justice Ideology

We see the *modus operandi* for which Nietzsche savaged Judaism, Christianity, and socialism also operative within contemporary social justice ideology. The social justice left's attempts to overthrow the hierarchy are premised precisely on inversion or reversal; the supposedly subordinated is taken to be ethically and morally superior to the socially dominant. The subordinated is accorded a superior epistemological standpoint from which to put forth assertions. Finally, the subordinated's low status becomes the very basis for its (newly acquired) high status. Those supposed to be without privilege within the existing social hierarchy are accorded the most esteem and privilege under social justice.

As such, social justice ideology does not represent egalitarianism but rather a reversal or inversion of hierarchy. Hierarchy is kept in place; only the order of rank is inverted. It is no wonder then that social justice activists and other participants compete vigorously for the status of "most subordinated"—in the games derogatorily referred to as "the Oppression Olympics"—because the lowest position puts one on the top of the totem pole in social-justice-dominated spaces. These spaces now include the major institutions of academia, mass media, social media, and others.

The social justice phrase "check your privilege" is best understood, then, in connection with this inverted hierarchy. It should be interpreted as follows: Note where you stand on the (inverted) social justice hierarchy and act accordingly. Defer to all those ranked above you. Acknowledge their superior access to knowledge, experience, or what have you. Never suggest that you have knowledge or experience that they do not have. And finally, speak only if/when granted permission by your social justice superiors.

We saw these social justice rules recently play out at Evergreen State College in Washington state, where social justice student activists inverted the social hierarchy, took command of the college, and exerted their will-to-power over professors and the college president. They were able to silence professor Bret Weinstein and president George Bridges—"Shut up, Bret!" and "Shut up, George!" they yelled—even after the two had been asked questions.

Nietzsche saw such inversion ideologies as means by which the weaker, less accomplished or otherwise dominated or degraded exerted their will-to-power. Unlike the forthright expressions of the natural aristocracy, these attempts, which were successful in the cases of Judaism and Christianity, involved surreptitious, devious and necessarily veiled power gambits— stealthy assertions of the will-to-power:

> The beginning of the slaves' revolt in morality occurs when *ressentiment* itself turns creative and gives birth to values: the *ressentiment* of those beings who, denied the proper response of action, compensate for it only with imaginary revenge. Whereas all noble morality grows out of a triumphant saying 'yes' to itself, slave morality says 'no' on principle to everything that is 'outside', 'other', 'non-self': and this 'no' is its creative deed. This reversal of the evaluating glance – this essential orientation to the outside instead of back onto itself – is a feature of *ressentiment*: in order to come about, slave morality first has to have an opposing, external world, it needs, physiologically speaking, external stimuli in order to act at all, – its action is basically a reaction … His soul squints, his mind loves hide-outs, secret paths, and back doors; everything that is hidden seems to him his own world, his security, his comfort; he is expert in silence, in long memory, in waiting …[15]

Surprisingly, perhaps, the early Marx also criticized such subversive tactics as a part of leveling ambitions:

> Universal envy setting itself up as a power is the concealed form of greed which merely asserts itself and satisfies itself in

---

15 Nietzsche, *On the Genealogy of Morality and Other Writings*, pp. 10, 20.

another way. The thoughts of every private property owner as such are at least turned against those richer than they as an envious desire to level down. This envious desire is precisely the essence of competition. Crude communism is only the completion of the envy and levelling down to a preconceived minimum. It has a particular and limited standard. How little this abolition of private property constitutes a real appropriation is proved by the abstract negation of the whole world of culture and civilization, a regression to the unnatural simplicity of the poor man without any needs who has not even arrived at the stage of private property, let alone got beyond it.[16]

Thus, like Nietzsche, Marx critiqued subtractive, negative egalitarianism, an egalitarianism premised on envy, a near equivalent of *ressentiment*. Such a subtractive egalitarianism did nothing to establish communism. Further, it posed a threat to culture and civilization themselves, without which humanity was no better off than non-productive beasts. (The above passage also implies a Marxist critique of primitivism.)

Unlike social justice ideology, for Marx, the leveling down or stripping social superiors of "underserved privilege" has nothing at all to do with achieving "justice" or "equity." Lacking any critical opposition to capitalism, the primary means by which the social order is structured, and involving no arguments or tactics for overthrowing capitalism, it is rendered impotent.

Social justice ideology is primarily concerned with morality, with an abstract justice and a hierarchical inversion, or at least a leveling, of individuals and groups. But if, as Marx argued, the proletarians, or the vast majority of the human race, are exploited, robbed of the fruits of their labor and essentially of their very lives, then collective action resulting from the recognition of collective self-interest, and not some attempt to realize an abstract "social justice," is the only effective means for realizing liberation.

Marx's answer for social quandaries and plaguing inequities did not involve the exposure of an ethical breach but rather a

---

16   Marx, Karl. *Karl Marx: Selected Writings*. 2nd ed., Oxford, 2000. "Economic and Philosophical Manuscripts". p. 96.

systemic analysis of capitalism's economic and social structure and the overcoming of these structures. In short, existing social relations—the class system—depend on a socially-organized labor force that operates within a privately-owned system of production. Only by overthrowing these social relations and eliminating this ownership system can equity be achieved.

Marx's object was universal human emancipation, which is not a mere matter of reducing the "privilege" of one's social superiors. In fact, such jockeying for social ranking would have been more appropriate within feudal society, although mostly impossible within it as well. In Marx's terms, inequity within capitalist society is not due to a surplus of privilege for some and a corresponding lack of privilege for others. Such honorific notions are abstractions involving mere ephemeral social signaling. If he was alive today, Marx would instantly note that even if the aims of social justice could be achieved, the most significant matters of material inequity, exploitation, poverty, and social domination would remain intact.

Conclusion

Whether one takes a Nietzschean or a Marxist view of the social justice creed, or, if such is possible, a combinatory position, we can see that social justice should be opposed and likely defeated by several major social contingents. Social justice ideology will (or should) be opposed by believers in true egalitarianism. Its inversion or reversal ideology is manifest in its ranking procedures and rituals, procedures and rituals under which those who have been at the top must take their places at the bottom. This is not a temporary condition for membership in the social justice movement. Only those egalitarians who believe that the inversion is a necessary and temporary measure, or otherwise do not recognize it as an inversion at all, will support the social justice movement. But hierarchical inversion will be a permanent feature of social justice, as the continuation of this inversion or reversal will be necessary for fueling the animus or *ressentiment* upon which the movement depends.

Social justice ideology will also be opposed by those satisfied with whatever social position or currency they enjoy, including even the manual laborer and the (sociologically speaking) middle-class householder. That is, it will not attract those who do not harbor *ressentiment* or live under the sway of a slave morality. The exceptions to this will be those who are guilt-tripped into acting against their own self-interests, duped into believing that they must submit to a new form of hierarchy or otherwise experience a life dominated by guilt without remission. We can expect minions of the liberal "middle class" and some even from even higher classes to submit to this ordeal – for whatever reasons, whether they be masochists, or idiots, or both.

Since social justice ideology depends on anti-realist postmodern epistemological doctrines, it will be opposed by scientists and science advocates—and by all believers in a real, material object world, however grasped. These will recognize that the postmodern-inflected social justice epistemology amounts to a denial of the material world as well as of the scientific means for knowing about it. The social justice charlatans will be exposed for what may amount to a giant Sokal Hoax perpetrated on the entire social order. I look forward to, continue to work for, and will welcome the day.

CHAPTER THIRTEEN

"Grievance Studies" Fields Encourage "Marginalized" Students & Faculty to Become Jacks of All Grievances, Masters of Nothing[1]

ENIAL OF TENURE to a Harvard "grievance studies" professor has led aggrieved students and fellow grievance faculty to protest. But grievance fields provide no scholarly criteria for tenure and can only lead to more grievances.

Lorgia García Peña,[2] currently an associate professor of romance languages and literatures at Harvard and the supposed centerpiece of Harvard college's fledging "Ethnic Studies" program, was denied tenure in late November 2019. Her popularity among Latinx and other minority students, who were baffled and shocked by the decision, has led to sit-ins and protests,[3]

---

1 Originally published as "Harvard hoisted by own petard as 'diversity' students protest decision to deny tenure to 'grievance studies' professor" by *RT.com*. January 4, 2020. Reproduced here by permission.

2 "Lorgia García Peña." *Home*. https://rll-faculty.fas.harvard.edu/garciapena/home.

3 McCafferty, Molly C. "Students Protest, Pen Open Letter In Response to Professor's Tenure Denial: News: The Harvard Crimson." *News | The Harvard Crimson*. December 3, 2019. https://www.thecrimson.com/article/2019/12/3/garcia-pena-tenure-denial-protest/.

and an open letter to university administrators demanding the reversal of the tenure denial.[4] The decision to deny Peña tenure also evoked the outrage of other grievance studies faculty around the U.S. and beyond,[5] some of whom have formed a coalition to promote Ethnic Studies.[6]

"Grievance studies"[7] is the satirical name given to fields devoted to various victim groups by the perpetrators of an elaborate publishing hoax[8] modeled after the Sokal Hoax of 1996.[9] As the editor Helen Pluckrose, and the academics James A. Lindsay and Peter Boghossian explained, their publication of farcical articles in journals devoted to "gender studies, masculinities studies, queer studies, sexuality studies, psychoanalysis, critical race theory, critical whiteness theory, fat studies, sociology, and educational philosophy" revealed "academe's leftist, victim-obsessed ideological slant and low publishing standards."[10] The trio roiled academia by securing the publication of 7 of 20 satirical papers submitted to grievance studies journals.

While ethnic and other grievance studies have been scoffed at and scorned inside the university and out, the *New York*

---

4 "Garcia Peña Tenure Denial Statement." *Google Docs*, Google, docs.google.com/document/d/1w4I-Vfk4jWzD2Xs6jiMOHdG1zH6anZ8JgL416qld-Wi8/edit.

5 Payne, Daniel. "Many in the Academic World Are Outraged over a Professor's Denial of Tenure. Why?" *The College Fix*. January 2, 2020. https://www.thecollegefix.com/many-in-the-academic-world-are-outraged-over-a-professors-denial-of-tenure-why/.

6 Gil, Alex. "Ethnic Studies Rise." *Ethnic Studies Rise*. https://ethnicrise.github.io.

7 "Grievance Studies Affair." *Wikipedia*, Wikimedia Foundation. January 7, 2020, https://en.wikipedia.org/wiki/Grievance_studies_affair.

8 Kafka, Alexander C. "'Sokal Squared': Is Huge Publishing Hoax 'Hilarious and Delightful' or an Ugly Example of Dishonesty and Bad Faith?" *The Chronicle of Higher Education*, The Chronicle of Higher Education. October 3, 2018. https://www.chronicle.com/article/Sokal-Squared-Is-Huge/244714.

9 Lingua Franca. *The Sokal Hoax: The Sham That Shook the Academy*. University of Nebraska Press, 2000.

10 Pluckrose, Helen. "Academic Grievance Studies and the Corruption of Scholarship." *Areo*. October 30, 2018. https://areomagazine.com/2018/10/02/academic-grievance-studies-and-the-corruption-of-scholarship/.

Times reports that student fans of professor Peña feel that Harvard exploits their ethnic identities to meet admissions "diversity" numbers, while their identities are taken for granted and their needs as marginalized students go unmet once they are on campus.[11] They argue that their pet professor provides recognition of their "stories" and "elevates their voices" as students from marginalized backgrounds.

But the expectation among such student constituencies that their social identities should be the center of their educational pursuits is the product of grievance studies programs themselves. When or if such students find that their identities cannot (and should not) be the constant focus of their classroom experiences and social encounters, the grievances they've learned to nurture in grievance fields are redoubled, making them even more aggrieved.

Meanwhile, the scholarship of Peña and other faculty in grievance studies fields can't be judged on anything like objective standards of excellence. That's because the fields are based on the supposed marginalization, exceptionalism, and peculiarity of the fields and those who study them, including both faculty and their students. The primary criterion for being a grievance studies "scholar" is membership in the oppressed and marginalized group being studied. Such groups are supposedly "underrepresented" in the academy—on the basis of "racism." But the standard of "inclusion" in a social identity group is not an academic standard.

Grievance fields are established as distinct from and at odds with the rest of the academy. Grievance studies scholars describe the rest of the academy as "a hotbed for racist, sexist theorizing, research, and practices since its inception."[12] Considering the accomplishments in other fields as due to white

---

11 Taylor, Kate. "Denying a Professor Tenure, Harvard Sparks a Debate Over Ethnic Studies." *The New York Times*, The New York Times. January 2, 2020. https://www.nytimes.com/2020/01/02/us/harvard-latinos-diversity-debate.html.

12 Davis, Jonita. "How a Denial of Tenure at Harvard Became a National Controversy." *Vox*, Vox. December 16, 2019. https://www.vox.com/identities/2019/12/16/21020572/harvard-ethnic-studies-department.

supremacy means that the standards in other fields are seen as reflecting white supremacism as well. As a result of rejecting the standards in other fields, dismissing rigor as sexist,[13] and deeming excellence as white supremacist, the "lack of legitimacy given to ethnic studies continues to plague not only the programs, but also the professors who created and maintain them."[14]

The effects of grievance studies, meanwhile, have far exceeded the boundaries of the grievance fields. They have fueled the "social justice" drive for diversity. As Heather MacDonald argues,[15] and as I have noted,[16] social justice is eroding academic standards across all of academia, including in the STEM fields. The derailment of academic institutions by a victimology ethos originating in grievance studies fields not only harms students by denying them knowledge but also undermines the broader society's faith in academic knowledge claims.

Harvard, not unlike the vast majority of US colleges and universities, has cooked its own goose where diversity and grievance studies are concerned. By placing the representation of social identity categories and social justice imperatives above the pursuit of knowledge, Harvard has hoisted a social justice standard above the standard of truth.

---

13 Patrick, John. "Engineering Professor: Academic Rigor Enforces 'White Male Heterosexual Privilege.'" *Washington Examiner*. December 13, 2017. https://www.washingtonexaminer.com/engineering-professor-academic-rigor-enforces-white-male-heterosexual-privilege

14 Ibid.

15 MacDonald, Heather. "How Social Justice Is Destroying Objectivity, Excellence, Due Process, Science - and Much More (Speech)." *The College Fix*. January 2, 2020. https://www.thecollegefix.com/bulletin-board/how-social-justice-is-destroying-objectivity-excellence-due-process-science-and-much-more-speech/?fbclid=IwAR3B9kwTXaWfEW8RfLgxC-dWHdo5a8snvYuCIrFhJ-2LvHch6lrpjjX54Or4.

16 Rectenwald, Michael. "'Social Justice' and Its Postmodern Parentage." *Academic Questions*, Vol. 31, No. 2. April 10, 2018, pp. 130–139.

CHAPTER FOURTEEN

(Re)Secularizing the University[1]

I HAVE UNWITTINGLY inserted myself into an ongoing and intensifying maelstrom[2] in which speakers are now routinely prevented from speaking by "anti-fascist," black bloc activists, who overturn cars and set them on fire,[3] pepper-spray speakers,[4] and then, if speakers manage to reach the microphone, chant them down with collective hecklers' vetoes.[5] At the same time, "social justice" activists and other students retreat to safe spaces—replete with crayons, coloring books and

---

1 Originally published by *The American Conservative*. March 14, 2017. Reproduced here by permission.

2 Rectenwald, Michael. "Here's What Happened When I Challenged the PC Campus Culture at NYU." *The Washington Post*. November 3, 2016. https://www.washingtonpost.com/posteverything/wp/2016/11/03/campus-pc-culture-is-so-rampant-that-nyu-is-paying-to-silence-me/.

3 Bodley, Michael and Nanette Asimov. "UC Berkeley cancels right-wing provocateur's talk amid violent protest." *SFGate*. February 2, 2017. https://www.sfgate.com/news/article/Protesters-storm-Milo-Yiannopoulos-event-at-UC-10901829.php.

4 Chasmar, Jessica. "Conservative speaker Gavin McInnes pepper-sprayed by NYU protesters." *The Washington Times*. February 3, 2017. https://www.washingtontimes.com/news/2017/feb/3/gavin-mcinnes-conservative-speaker-pepper-sprayed-/.

5 Krantz, Laura. "'Bell Curve' author attacked by protesters at Middlebury College." *Boston Globe*. March 4, 2017. https://www.bostonglobe.com/metro/2017/03/04/middlebury/hAfpA1Hquh7DIS1doiKbhJ/story.html.

therapy pets.[6] Such safe spaces are meant to protect students, not from the alarming violence of their compeers, but from the supposedly triggering, injurious expression of those protested.

Becoming a lightning rod in this raging and confused storm was not a point on the career trajectory that I had envisioned for myself when I agreed to give an interview to a reporter from NYU's student newspaper.[7] Nor does the figurative target plastered on my back by anti-fascists represent an enviable status symbol. Still, my personal and professional crisis has opened up a new research artery for me, and I have begun to examine some of the dearly-held beliefs, practices and apparatuses of the contemporary left—received opinions about viewpoint diversity and expression, the practices of shaming, the conviction that language itself can pose a real substantive threat to well-being, and the surveillance mechanisms universities are instituting— to locate their likely provenance, and to begin tracing their genealogies. (See "Trigger Warnings, Safe Spaces, Bias Reporting: The New Micro-techniques of Surveillance and Control" and "A Genealogy of Social Justice Morals," in this volume).

Looking first at viewpoint diversity (or the lack thereof) I was led to reconsider one of the most salient arguments regarding the question of toleration, written by the Frankfurt School theorist Herbert Marcuse. In his essay "Repressive Tolerance," included in the slim anthology *Against Pure Tolerance*, Marcuse essentially argued that some expression is so intolerant to others as to be completely intolerable.[8] "Pure tolerance" is unbearable in liberal society. Some speech and expression must be stopped, and the left is correct and even obliged to stop it.

6　Athey, Amber. "'Safe spaces' abound for students in 'emotional crisis' over Trump." *Campus Reform*. November 10, 2016. https://www.campusreform. org/?ID=8376.

7　Siu. Diamond Naga. "Q&A with a Deplorable NYU Professor." *Washington Square News*. October 24, 2016. https://nyunews.com/2016/10/24/qa-with-a-deplorable-nyu-professor/.

8　Marcuse, Herbert. "Repressive Tolerance," from Wolff, Robert Paul, Barrington Moore, Jr., and Herbert Marcuse, *A Critique of Pure Tolerance* (Boston: Beacon Press, 1969), pp. 95-137. https://www.marcuse.org/herbert/publications/1960s/1965-repressive-tolerance-fulltext.html.

A similar though less illiberal position was developed by the philosopher Karl Popper. Could no-platforming be the legacy of this thinking?

As my public statements should suggest, I think that Marcuse's stance represents a slippery slope, establishing as it does a tribunal of censorship consisting of ideologically charged activist milieus. It effectively means that *illiberalism* must be a characteristic of "liberal" society. This principally represents a contradiction and fails to consider the strong possibility that, sooner or later, the continually narrowing Overton window[9] will close on the speech of the very people who sought to bar the speech of others. In any case, one must wonder: just who is fit to be arbiter, and what makes them—and not others—the interpretative conscience of society, suited to ban expression they deplore? In our contemporary moment, the strange irony is that these arbiters aim to foreclose lines of inquiry they have never even directly encountered or considered. But if they had, the irony would be even greater. The arbiters have survived, so why wouldn't others? Marcuse's advocacy of social and legal intolerance toward supposed intolerance reproduces the very repression that he lamented and hoped to prevent. And one wonders just how he managed to arrive at such conclusions as early as 1965. Not that he was prescient; as a prominent communist theorist, had he already completely forgotten the McCarthy hearings?

Thinking of some of the other aspects of social justice ideology, I began looking for cognate elements in leftist history and theory. My search for plausible precursors to the privilege-checking and callout culture of social justice milieus led to post-1968 French feminists, who read Mao's *Little Red Book* and imbibed a Maoist ethos, incorporating ideological purging elements of the Cultural Revolution, such as "struggle sessions" and "autocritique," or self-criticism. In struggle sessions, the guilty party, accused of selfishness, ignorance, and the embrace of

---

9 Junior, Christi. "The Overton Window: What It Is & Why It's So Important." July 22, 2016. *The Ralph Retort.* https://theralphretort.com/overton-window-important-7022016/.

bourgeois ideology, was pilloried with verbal and often physical assaults by her comrades, until she broke down and confessed her characterological and ideological flaws, and then pledged self-reform, or faced imprisonment and possible death. Interestingly, the "Diversity, Equity, and Inclusion" working group in my program of Liberal Studies at NYU undertook a strictly rhetorical version of this exercise when they condemned me and my views on PC culture.[10] Meanwhile, autocritique began with the guilty party, who subjected herself to brutal verbal self-inspection and derogation before the jury of her peers. Perhaps this was the sort of confession the Orwellian working group had in mind, instead of my eventual reply.[11]

As for "safe spaces," Moira Kenney in *Mapping Gay L.A.* traced the concept to gay and lesbian bars of the 1960s in Los Angeles and elsewhere, from which it made its way into feminist circles.[12] As such, they became spaces free of men and patriarchal thought and expression. In colleges and universities, they serve to protect students and others from ideas deemed triggering or otherwise harmful. I have argued that in the context of higher education, safe spaces constitute a means of self-imposed cultural containment, not unlike that decried by Ralph Ellison,[13] writing in reply to the socialist critic, Irving Howe,[14] whom, he wrote, sought to consign him to a corked "jug" of cultural isolation not unlike that of the Jim Crow south. (See "A

---

10 Liberal Studies Diversity, Equity and Inclusion Working Group. "Letter to the Editor: Liberal Studies Rejects @antipcnyuprof's Faulty Claims." *Washington Square News*. October 26, 2016. https://nyunews.com/2016/10/26/letter-to-the-editor-liberal-studies-rejects-antipcnyuprofs-faulty-claims/.

11 Rectenwald, Michael. "Reply to LS Diversity, Equity and Inclusion Working Group." *Washington Square News*. February 6, 2017. https://nyunews.com/2017/02/06/reply-to-ls-diversity-equity-and-inclusion-working-group/.

12 Kenney, Moira. *Mapping Gay L.A.: The Intersection of Place and Politics.* Temple University Press, 2001.

13 Wellington, Darryl Lorenzo. "Fighting at Cross-Purposes: Irving Howe vs. Ralph Ellison." *Dissent*. Fall 2005. https://www.dissentmagazine.org/article/fighting-at-cross-purposes-irving-howe-vs-ralph-ellison.

14 Howe, Irving. "Black Boys and Native Sons." *Dissent*. Autumn 1963. http://writing.upenn.edu/~afilreis/50s/howe-blackboys.html.

Genealogy of Social Justice" in this volume.)

Certainly, much of the social-justice arsenal and ethos has been inflected by intersectional feminism[15] and funneled through the bewildering vortex of postmodern theory, including poststructuralism[16] and deconstruction.[17] Intersectionality provides the architectural blueprint for the kind of "subaltern" status-seeking that we encounter in social-justice ideology and groups. Developed in the 1970s and '80s, intersectionality seeks to describe how power intersects identities along various axes, including those of race, gender, sexuality, sexual preference, ability, and more. It aims to locate the articulations of power as it traverses various subordinated peoples in multifarious ways. Suggestive of a radical critique of patriarchy, capitalism, white supremacy—which its adherents take to be distinct but connected forms of domination—it complicates any sense of gender, sex, class, or race as homogenous wholes and it confuses any hierarchy of one categorical determination over others. Yet in practice, intersectionality serves to isolate multiple and seemingly endless identity standpoints, without sufficiently articulating them with one another. The upshot in political practice, as Christina Hoff Sommers argues, is an endless splitting of categories,[18] with the members of each category vying for more-subaltern-than-thou status. Intersectionality is no doubt the source of what has been derogatorily referred to as "the Oppression Olympics" by unsympathetic observers, some of whom may have once competed in the games themselves.[19]

---

15 See "Feminist Perspectives on Power." *Stanford Encyclopedia of Philosophy*. First published October 19, 2005; substantive revision July 7, 2016. https://plato.stanford.edu/entries/feminist-power/.

16 See "Post-structuralism." *New World Encyclopedia*. https://www.newworldencyclopedia.org/entry/Post-structuralism.

17 See "Jacques Derrida: 'Deconstruction.'" *Stanford Encyclopedia of Philosophy*. First published November 22, 2006; substantive revision July 30, 2019. https://plato.stanford.edu/entries/derrida/#Dec.

18 Hoff Sommers, Christina. "Intersectional Feminism: What is it?" *Factual Feminist*. March 30, 2016. https://www.youtube.com/watch?v=cY-pELqKZ02Q.

19 Ridgway, Shannon. "Oppression Olympics: The Games We Shouldn't Be

Poststructuralist theories of language including deconstruction, developed by Jacques Derrida, are foundational to the social-justice belief that language can either imprison or substantively injure those who encounter it. For Derrida, famously, there is nothing outside of the text. Given their power to imprison and oppress, texts, including written and oral expressions, become weapons wielded consciously or unconsciously by aggressors. Thus, the likely source of both the microaggression and the trigger warning.

I have been accused of safe-space-seeking and microaggression-reporting in my self-defenses against social justice activists and their fellow travelers. My primary retort is that social-justice activists, with their notoriously vituperative, often outrageous pack-and-attack mentality, create a need for that which they demand. Before returning to my teaching, I considered requesting a safe space, free from the hostility of colleagues. But I realized that the irony would be lost amid the accusations of hypocrisy.

While I have endured the shunning of most of my colleagues, the ejection from political groups, and the damnation of the left, I do have some support in academia and beyond. I am working with like-minded people to establish a consortium for challenging echo chambers and promoting the exchange of views to build consensus on fundamental principles. I have also turned to the advice of those working toward similar goals to develop cognate structures. One such ally is the NYU social psychologist and founder of Heterodox Academy,[20] Jonathan Haidt.

In a recent conversation, Jonathan explained that we find ourselves in the midst of a new moral order that is emerging on many campuses and vying for members. The old discursive and

---

Playing." *Everyday Feminism Magazine*. November 4, 2012. https://everyday-feminism.com/2012/11/oppression-olympics/.

20 "Heterodox Academy." https://heterodoxacademy.org/. [I have since reconsidered the function of Heterodox Academy and think that the project represents social justice lite, or a controlled opposition that arrogates to itself the role of mediating between social justice ideologues and their opponents, telling the latter what they are "allowed" to say to the former.]

behavioral rules no longer apply. He characterized this package of moral imperatives as equivalent, psychologically, to religious fundamentalism and suggested that its believers are passionately committed to their beliefs. Therefore, nothing I might say or write will change their minds. For those who belong to this new moral order, he continued, I am the equivalent of a devil. I had mistaken my interview in the student newspaper with acceptable criticism of institutions, yet my detractors regarded it as sacrilege.

After this meeting, I hearkened back to my studies of nineteenth-century British Secularism, recalling the legal persecution and social opprobrium that the early Secularists endured at the hands of religious bigots, cowardly conformists, and state apparatuses. I have experienced nothing remotely comparable, though there was a clear analogy. In early twenty-first-century academia, replete with its attendant religious dogma, I was a new kind of secularist.

Yet there was a wrinkle in this comparison in the form of the decisive split in the Secularist movement. I was vacillating between the two major Secularist camps: a conciliatory camp, like that of Secularism's founder and coiner of the word, George Jacob Holyoake, and a more staunchly oppositional posture as adopted by Secularism's bombastic, anti-clerical, Bible-bashing subsequent leader, Charles Bradlaugh.

Jonathan had suggested that I moderate my tone and use less incendiary, more academic, conditional language, the contemporary equivalent of Holyoake's approach. I had celebrated Holyoake's brand of Secularism in my book, *Nineteenth-Century British Secularism*,[21] and elsewhere. Yet, amidst this twenty-first-century academic religiosity, I had been cast by opponents and even some allies in the position of a Bradlaugh. Which posture would I adopt, or did I no longer have a choice?

My answer is both. So, while this essay is the precursor to

---

21 Rectenwald, Michael. *Nineteenth-Century British Secularism: Science, Religion and Literature*. Houndsmills, Basingstoke, Hampshire, UK; New York: Palgrave Macmillan (2016). http://www.palgrave.com/us/book/9781137463883.

what will be more measured and scholarly writing on the topic, do not expect my Twitter pronouncements to become less strident any time soon.

CHAPTER FIFTEEN

The Gender Jackpot[1]

I N THE FALL of 2016, as *Campus Reform* reported at the time, the University of Michigan instituted a policy allowing students a *carte blanche* pronoun preference opportunity.[2] Students were encouraged by the university administration to choose existing pronouns or to create new pronouns of their choice, without limitation, and to input them into the Wolverine student access portal. Students could then demand to be called by these pronouns in the classroom. No matter what pronouns a student chose, the university promised to honor their choices. That is, until one clever student, Grant Strobl, selected "His Majesty" as his chosen pronoun. His pronoun choice, a scandalous heresy according to the priesthood of political correctness, made the news and embarrassed university administrators—or should have.

Strobl's pronoun choice was a sendup of the university administrators' decision to enact such a policy, highlighting the lengths to which institutions of higher education have gone to appease the gender pluralists. "His Majesty" hilariously under-

1 Originally published by *Campus Reform*. December 5, 2019. Reproduced here by permission.

2 Athey, Amber. "UMich to Profs: Don't Say 'Ladies and Gentlemen,' 'Mom and Dad.'" *Campus Reform*. November 10, 2016. https://www.campusreform. org/?ID=8372.

scored the absurdity of gender and pronoun proliferation and the lunacy of institutional attempts to keep pace with it. Unsurprisingly, editorialists, including those at *The Michigan Daily*[3] (the University of Michigan's student newspaper) and *The Chronicle of Higher Education*, denounced his satirical trope.[4]

According to the New York City Commission on Human Rights, no less than 31 genders exist.[5] By other counts, the total is 63.[6] Still others put the number at 112.[7] By my count, Facebook now recognizes 57 genders, at least in the U.S. The number of Facebook genders is reportedly greater for users in the U.K.

Given that the number of genders differs across times, places, and cultures, it is clear that the gender categories are the result of the whimsy and will of the gender pluralists, who mean to foist their innovations on the majority at the latter's expense.

According to Planned Parenthood, children as young as 2 to 3 years-old are aware of their gender identities as well as how their gender identities may differ from the gender identity of others.[8] Planned Parenthood would have us believe that 2- and 3-year-old children not only grasp the complex and nearly incomprehensible concept of gender but also that the special ones

---

3 Thompson, Conor. "Op-Ed: An Open Letter to His Majesty." *The Michigan Daily*. October 13, 2016. https://www.michigandaily.com/section/viewpoints/op-ed-open-letter-grant-strobl.

4 Ferriss, Lucy. "Pronoun Challenge in Ann Arbor." *Lingua Franca Pronoun Challenge in Ann Arbor*. October 3, 2016. https://www.chronicle.com/blogs/linguafranca/2016/10/03/preferable-pronouns/.

5 De Blasio, Mayor, Bill, and Carmelyn P Malais, Commissioner/Chair. "Gender Identity/Expression." *NYC.gov*, NYC Commission on Human Rights. https://www1.nyc.gov/assets/cchr/downloads/pdf/publications/GenderID_Card2015.pdf.

6 Laughin, Jacob. "Here Are 63 Genders of The Hundreds of Genders: Virtual Space Amino." *Virtual Space Aminoapps.com*. AminoApps. June 6, 2016. https://aminoapps.com/c/virtual-space/page/blog/here-are-63-genders-of-the-hundreds-of-genders/J1Id_uPD0bGDNakkXVJa4YoNL2ZNlN.

7 Dude. "How Many Genders Are There In 2020?" *Dude Asks*. January 20, 2020. https://dudeasks.com/how-many-genders-are-there-in-2020/.

8 Planned Parenthood. "Sex, Gender, and Gender Identity." *Planned Parenthood*. https://www.plannedparenthood.org/learn/sexual-orientation-gender/gender-gender-identity.

among them, namely the gender-nonconforming and transgender toddlers, know that their own gender identities differ fundamentally from those of the gender conformists.

Yet even as gender-savvy toddlers supposedly recognize their gender identities and distinguish their identities from those of others, their parents and other adults are far from a consensus about gender and gender identities, even in terms of how many gender identities exist. Thus, the agency finds it necessary to teach adults about sex difference and gender identity, while remaining virtually mum about the gender non-transgressive toddlers, the so-called "cis-gendered"—except to admonish new parents to be wary of reinforcing such gender identities and stereotypes.[9] Such nondescript reprobates toddle into bleak gender-generic futures and continue to reproduce. This state of affairs requires that Planned Parenthood administer rapid transfusions of the current lexicon and parental protocols—before such vulgate speakers commit child abuse by inducing the trauma of the misgendered child.

To understand how we got into this morass, it is necessary to recall the fact that before the second half of the 20th century, the term "gender" represented a distinction within linguistics. Gender difference referred to the distinction between feminine and masculine nouns and adjectives. It was not associated with human sex difference—until 1955.

That's when the "sexologist" John Money introduced the term "gender roles" to describe the sets of behaviors and personality traits conventionally associated with human sex differences. Gender roles referred to the behavioral expectations and treatment typically expected from and doled out to males and females. Money also introduced "gender identity" to refer to a person's perception of his or her gender, including identity as a man or woman, boy or girl …

Soon, gender feminists described sex as a "skeletal coat

---

9 Planned Parenthood. "Gender Identity & Roles: Feminine Traits & Stereotypes." *Planned Parenthood.* https://www.plannedparenthood.org/learn/sexual-orientation-gender/gender-gender-identity/what-are-gender-roles-and-stereotypes.

rack" on which the accoutrements of *gender* hung like so many tailored coats, scarves, and hats. Unlike sex, gender was conceived as a "social construct"—the woven product of socialization and social environment, as opposed to nature. As a social product, gender might be refashioned along different lines by reconfiguring the socialization processes and by altering social relations.

The transgender movement later turned gender into a matter of individual whimsy, treating gender choice like an ice-cream flavor preference. The female-male sex binary has since been buffeted by a tidal wave of proliferating gender identities and pronouns. As new gender identities debuted, the ratio of genders to sexes continued to rise.

According to gender studies "scholars," by introducing the term gender and associating it, however loosely, with sex difference, John Money inaugurated a whole new field of research. I beg to differ. Departments of Gender Studies do not conduct legitimate research. They constitute a vast ministry of PC propaganda.

Because gender identity was introduced by John Money, I refer to our gender predicament as "the gender jackpot." That is, by suggesting that the terms gender and gender roles differ from sex and sex roles, Money initiated the multiplication of identities that has bewitched us ever since.

Thanks to Money, it is doubtful that we can force the gender genie back into the bottle—to add another metaphor to the mess. Because "the new" is generally considered an improvement, we are unlikely to return to "sex" and "sex roles," which served quite well to describe biological, behavioral, and identity differences. Nonetheless, despite the efforts of the PC police to punish those who defy their prescriptions, humans overwhelmingly fall at the distant poles of male and female. Further, in the minds of those among this overwhelming majority, the terms male/female have always been strongly linked with man/woman, and always will be.

CHAPTER SIXTEEN

"Have You Found the Place that Makes You Want to Swallow Its Rhetoric Whole?"[1]

T HE LINE ABOVE is drawn from a Facebook post entitled, "To Any Folks Who Ever Want to Date Me: an anthem for 2017 singles." Written by an apparently earnest young leftist activist feminist, the anthem begins with a list of verboten statements and actions that a prospective (non-social-justice-activist) mate may err in saying or doing. It then moves on to the preferable approaches that appropriate types might undertake, inclusive of the line that is the title of this piece:

> Do not dare to comment on my body. Do not stare. Do not tell me all the things you want to do to me. Do not force me to bear the weight of your assumptions. Do not waste both of our time with things so hollow as this. Do not make wishes on my freckles. Do not touch my waist. Do not tell me I am precious, or pretty. Do not seek to make me smaller. Do not ask me to fit.
>
> Instead, tell me a story. Tell me a secret. Tell me where you

---

1 Originally published in slightly different form by *Quillette.com*. May 6, 2017.

141

come from. Are you a communist? A socialist? Where is your activist home? Have you found the place that makes you want to swallow its rhetoric whole?

The question is so redolent—or dare I say pregnant—with hermeneutic possibilities that one hardly knows where to begin. But let's start with the obvious: the sublimation of sex. Having foreclosed remarks about the body no matter how flattering, having shut down the "male gaze," eliminating the possibility for feckless romanticism (including wishing upon freckles), anathematizing the touch however slight, and turning compliments into crimes, the young would-be lover lies well beyond the grasp of the standard-issue aspirant.

Only a particular type will do, only a particular type will know that only language and a particular kind of language will open the lock: a story, a secret, but preferably a confession of having swallowed whole the rhetoric of a particular leftist political tribe. This is the only way in—but to what? The seeker can gain admission to an apparent blind alley only by pledging sexual renunciation at the outset, as well as, as a replacement for sexuality, the wholesale inculcation of some socialist-communist creed, no doubt the more obscure and hopeless the better. One cannot but imagine sputum dripping from this obsequious supplicant's lips, while he, she, ze, they, or whatever, confesses fealty to a leftist doctrine and begs admission to the cult of the goddess. Sex has been fully sublimated into religio-political devotion.

Now, to turn to the other disturbing aspects of this passage: its further implications regarding the contemporary left. First, I wish to express my gratitude for its having been enunciated. It so clearly epitomizes the demand for uncritical acceptance of an ideology, especially given the use of the word "rhetoric"—the received connotation for which is added flourishes extraneous to content or substance and the denotation for which is the language of persuasion or propaganda—that one could not have asked for a better expression.

This is why the question became a sort of reverse meme

bandied about among my friends and me on social media. And, for some time, I had been arguing against just this kind of uncritical and anti-intellectual acceptance of received notions, especially in connection with the academic, "social justice" left, which relies on knee-jerk responses to supposed infringements of its values and identities. This is the poll parrot, phrase-repeating, slogan-mongering left that chants mindlessly to no-platform speech that illiberal leftists deem intolerable. It is the left of the successful Stanford admissions essay that repeats "#BlackLivesMatter" a hundred times. The left that swallows its own rhetoric whole.

This is the left that I inadvertently introduced to my ex-partner some eleven or twelve years ago, and which eventually became one of the primary obstacles to an ongoing relationship. She may not see it that way, but I do. What follows is a somewhat agonizing tale for me to narrate, yet one necessary to expel. I cannot chronicle the entire relationship with the astonishing Sadie, but some of the history is necessary for showing how the swallowing whole of a political rhetoric became the final obtrusion that ended what had been an extraordinary love.

* * *

We met under rather inconsequential circumstances in the spring of 2003. From the moment that I laid eyes on her I knew without a doubt that she was destined to be mine. I had no trepidation about this prospect. It lay like an eventuality about to unfurl before me, between us. I only had to participate and follow the somewhat obscure but nevertheless preordained narrative. While this may sound romantic to the point of delusion—and allow me to say that I am an otherwise cynical person—I firmly believed that the truth of our love existed well before our meeting, and still do. It was just there, waiting for us to discover it.

The group we were part of sat in a circle and we sat across from each other, she in cut-off jeans. For reasons that I do not fully understand, her knobby knees, and affected, humble-bragging confessions of artistic doubt were sure signs of this inevitability. I think now that the latter indicated vulnerability and the former a peculiar beauty that needed no apology or adornment. Somehow, both were clear signs of our fateful connection.

At the time, however, I was a father of three and in a marriage with Heather that had been troubled for several years. I had been working as a writer in an Artificial Intelligence lab of the Robotics Institute at Carnegie Mellon University, and was also a Ph.D. candidate in the English department at the same university. I was writing a dissertation on nineteenth-century British science cultures. I would wake at six, be at my office by seven, and work on the dissertation until the programmers arrived in the early afternoon. If the project manager had any work for me, I would put the dissertation on hold and switch to writing about the AI software under development.

As it happened, I was left alone to work on the dissertation uninterrupted—often for hours, days, and weeks on end. I finished the dissertation in two years. In a field in which the average total start-to-finish time for the Ph.D. is eight years, I was done in just over seven, submitting an oversized, 420-plus page dissertation seven years and one month after beginning the program. During my time in the Ph.D. program and the three years in an M.A. program before that, I had also worked full-time, often more than full-time, on top of the full-time classwork, and the reading, teaching, and writing.

Meanwhile, coming as it did in my early thirties, this change in careers (from advertising executive to budding academic) put considerable stress on the marriage. Not only did the time spent taking classes, then studying for exams, then writing the dissertation, eat into our time together, but also and especially, my obsession with the field proved to be driving us apart. Little did I know that this situation would be paralleled by another, similar one in the future. Heather worked in real estate and my rather arcane pursuits were quite remote from her interests. She wanted to continue the marital and family life that we had hitherto engaged in somewhat normally (although even earlier it had been troubled by other factors). But that life was slipping away from her and, as I delved further into my academic pursuits, it appeared more absurd to me by the day. By the time I met Sadie, I had been convinced for at least three years that the marriage was loveless and effectively over and I'd moved out and filed for divorce.

Sadie was a renowned, New York choreographer on a paid visiting artist-in-residence gig at the Andy Warhol Museum in Pittsburgh. Over our first dinner together, she expressed a so-phisticated interest in my field of study and even knew about some of its leading lights. I remember distinctly as she said, "cultural studies," enunciating the phrase laughingly but also with a peculiar emphasis indicative of knowing what she was talking about, then mentioning Foucault and other theorists with familiarity.

She was clearly impressed. As was I. There was something very immediate about the attraction, but it pointed to some-thing beyond the mere signaling. A confluence of interests and something else, a sense of profound familiarity, were clear to us both. Mostly importantly, perhaps, she was the only woman I had ever met who had bitten her fingernails to the point of disfigurement, much as I had mine. Her targets were thumbs, while mine were baby fingers. As we both saw it, this was the ultimate sign to seal our union. When, that first night after din-ner, she said, "goodbye Michael," I knew it would not be the last time that I would hear those words from her lips. Her careful naming of me was a kind of love making; she formed my name in her mouth and issued it forth with care, as if delivering me to me.

When we drove in my van to a bar in Monroeville to hear a friend's band play, she complained about the suburbs like an adolescent. And I chided her lightly for the immaturity.

After that night, I lost track of her. Her six-week art-ist-in-residence stint neared its end and her return to New York was imminent. For some reason, I made no plans with her, nor did I ask for her email address or phone number.

On the Sunday when I knew she was due to leave, I drove to Shadyside, the neighborhood where she'd stayed. I was des-perate to make it to the door before she disappeared. Racing in the van from Point Breeze, I heard a flapping, thumping sound. I changed the right-front tire in the middle of Fifth Avenue. But by the time the spare was on, it was late afternoon and my hands were covered in grease. I rushed to the door of the house. The romanticism of the situation was not lost on me. I was playing a part in a movie and this was the most heart-rending scene. I knocked. I rang the bell. I repeated, again and again. But no one answered. Sadie was gone.

The next morning, I sat in my office, still desolate. Had I really let her slip away?

By 9 AM, I received an email—from her: a chipper and fetching communique. It was on. We were on. My belief was vindicated. From that point, the communication between us was never to be risked again by indolence on my part, or by impudence on hers. It was constant, intense, and extremely exciting. It brought her back to Pittsburgh for visits in no time and took me to New York as well.

There are many salient episodes in the romance that I could recall—like when we were spiritually "married" during an Easter Sunday service at Grace Episcopal church on Broadway in Noho and we felt the kneading together of our souls. Or the time we went to a dance performance in Union Square that took place above us on ropes and we peered into the air together, then kissed. Or the time we took a bus from Soho to Tribeca and she laid her head lightly on my shoulder.

* * *

After living just over a year in Pittsburgh with me in my new house, Sadie decided to begin a year-long, low-residency M.F.A. in dance. In hindsight, I suppose she had visions of becoming an academic, like me. She left for Hollins University in Virginia and left me alone in Pittsburgh.

Then, amazingly, I got an academic job in Durham, NC. This was truly incredible because Sadie had to finish the remainder of her M.F.A. at the American Dance Festival, which was held at Duke University in Durham in the fall. So, we were back together, this time in a spacious loft adjacent to Duke's East Campus. Sadie told me later of having had a dream, while still living in New York, in which we walked together through an idyllic college campus, apparently in our new world together. The fortuitous confluence of our lives continued.

If this were not enough, after two years in Durham, Sadie went on the academic job market and asked me to look for a job in New York as well. She wanted to get back to her career as a choreographer in the downtown avant-garde scene. We both applied for jobs in and around New York. I landed a job at NYU and she won a position at Gettysburg College, just over three hours from New York. We both accepted our offers and thus began my town and country life, living in Sadie's rent-stabilized apartment on Mott Street in New York during the week, and commuting to South Central Pennsylvania on weekends, while living in Gettysburg over holiday breaks and summers. Thus, we had realized our dream of being mostly together and having academic jobs. I relished both the city and the provinces—and whatever time I could squeeze from Sadie's now extremely demanding schedule.

It didn't take long for me to begin resenting Sadie's job—not because she was making more money than me, that she was the director of a dance program, that she was on tenure-track while I was on a long-term renewable contract, but because her job became her new lover. I found myself travelling three-plus hours every Friday, only to sit and wait for her to finish some school activity: a rehearsal; a show; a meeting with students, parents, or prospective students; or an activity she seemed to find that she wasn't really obligated to take on.

I had completed ten years of graduate study culminating in the M.A. and Ph.D., while she had undertaken only a year-long, low-residency M.F.A. program. Even so, I was happy that Sadie had landed a tenure-track although I had the contract job. Yet the disparity of preparations and outcomes grated on me, albeit unconsciously at the time. Further, her college was lodged on a pastoral, idyllic campus, like the one she had dreamed about, while I had to negotiate security checks upon entering every over-crowded building on NYU's "campus." What's more, Sadie had received a sizeable loan from her father, and managed to buy a house only a few hundred yards from her office building. By contrast, having to move from her apartment after a landlord dispute, I began a desperate, nine-year-long struggle to secure decent housing in New York.

But the real rub was the time she spent on the job, which amounted to no less than eighty hours a week. As she reminded me time and again, hers was a residential campus; the students expected faculty involvement, not only during classes but also in numerous extracurricular activities, almost around the clock. I saw this solicitousness as disgusting handholding and insipid over-nurturance, and for Sadie, surrogate parenting. Being on tenure track, she was extremely conscientious about doing everything asked of her. She never said no. And as a member of a theatre and dance program, notoriously time-intensive fields, the opportunities for activities were endless. And to compound matters, Sadie's insecurities about teaching fed her obsessive-compulsive class preparations. Likewise, despite her somewhat feeble attempts to integrate me into her life, I was increasingly left out.

I recalled a recurring childhood dream. I am a small boy standing outside of a large supermarket on a fall afternoon. Hundreds of people bustle past in all directions, pushing shopping carts. I cry out to them, but they can't hear or else ignore me.

And everyone is my mother.

I realized that our relationship was failing us both, but for precisely obverse reasons. Sadie saw me as the menacing male trying to derail her career, like her father's supposed short shrift of her "That Girl"[2] ambitions and accompanying favoritism for

---

2   "That Girl" is an American sitcom that ran on ABC from 1966 to 1971. It starred Marlo Thomas as the title character Ann Marie, an aspiring (but only sporadically employed) actress, who moves from her hometown of Brewster, New York, to try to make it big in New York City. Ann has to take a number of offbeat "temp" jobs to support herself in between her various auditions and bit parts." "That Girl." *Wikipedia*, Wikimedia Foundation. February 2, 2020. https://en.wikipedia.org/wiki/That_Girl.

her brothers. I saw her as a replica of my mother, never having time for me.

One afternoon after we worked for hours apart, Sadie came downstairs from her office and announced, apropos of nothing, that she was "really a radical feminist." I scoffed at this assertion, saying that she merely thought she should be a radical feminist because every woman on campus thought they should be too, and that she wasn't really a radical feminist at all. So, as if to prove herself a radical feminist, she went on to rant about "dick culture," "white male dickheads," and later, during the political talk shows, "talking dickheads." It all seemed so very juvenile to me, much like her scorning of the suburbs had been. Sometimes, she would suddenly demand to know why I was looking at her face. You're talking, I would answer. That's where the words seem to be coming from. She insisted that I was inspecting her. I tried to explain that if I was lingering on her features for a half-second beyond the time permissible, I did so because I found her face exquisitely beautiful. But that was never satisfactory.

I decided to teach a year abroad at NYU's campus in London, feeling less than obligated to gain Sadie's approval, although I did ask for it, and she did grant it. It seemed as if she might even have been happy to get rid of me, although she would later complain that I'd taken the gig. But I ignored this in light of the prospects. I would have free, luxurious housing with great amenities, and a light teaching schedule with no service work to speak of. Thus, I would find the time and wherewithal to undertake archival research for a book project I'd been delaying work on for several years, and this work helped me turn the corner on the publication front. But I was lonely as hell.

* * *

I have not yet mentioned that I had sworn off drinking over fifteen years before taking the NYU job, but after returning from England I began to occupy my time with the help of another addiction: workaholism. Sadie and I would work, she upstairs and I downstairs, twelve to fifteen hours a day, without interacting. I used to joke that the secret of our success was that we agreed to ignore each other.

The good news was that as I joined Sadie in her careerist obsession, I grew much less concerned with waiting around for her. I focused on my writing, and the method for undertaking it became another obsession. The proof was in the pudding. Publications began to roll in. After landing several well-placed articles, I began to focus on books. By the academic year 2015-2016, I managed to have three books published within a nine-month span. Over the entire period that Sadie was at Gettysburg and I at NYU, I also managed to edit and substantially revise every document that she submitted for her job, including end-of-year review documents, program notes for dance concerts, grant applications, and nearly every installment in her tenure file.

* * *

I came to despise Sadie's priorities and values. Despite being an artist of some renown, she grew more and more obsessed with financial security and other rather pedestrian concerns. And I told her so. But this was not until she had berated me about money, seemingly without cessation. The daughter of a successful doctor, Sadie had never faced financial insecurity, yet she constantly felt financially insecure. The son of a home remodeler and the brother of eight siblings, I had known nothing but financial insecurity, yet rarely worried about money. I had always lived on the edge and was quite accustomed to it. Yet of the two, it was Sadie who always felt edgy.

The arguments led to expressions of bitterness about her circumstances. Who was she to criticize me about money? She'd never known financial hardship. Anyway, how was it that she had it made, while I, the far worthier academic, struggled without a break? I criticized her for being "nothing but a middle-class householder pretending to be an artist," and the like.

* * *

Thus, I arrive at the final hijacking of our relationship by social justice ideology. Over the course of several years, Sadie had imbibed the pseudo-feminist, identity-politics, victimhood tropes of campus and therapeutic feminist culture. Rather than joining me in my irreverence as she had once been wont to do, she now chastised me for being politically incorrect. She didn't use that phrase, but that's what her remarks amounted to. There was more of the male-gaze shaming. Why are you looking at my face, she would ask? And my answer was always the same. That's what people do when they talk to each other.

Above all, Sadie began to resort to the language of "abuse." But what she called abuse I called criticism. She had bought into the spurious snowflake totalitarian notion that any language use that one doesn't like represents a form of "violence." She wanted to no-platform my critical commentaries, while reporting me to the equivalent of the bias hotlines at her disposal. She wanted a safe space whose walls my contradictory views could not breach.

No doubt I was being demonized by several of her confidantes, for reasons unknown. Sadie had read websites and visited the Women's Center on campus, while also seeing a fainting-couch feminist[3] therapist. They subscribed to a narrative template of victimology and seized upon scenarios that might conform to and confirm it. Once the word "abuse" crept into her lexicon and between us, mediating every encounter, past and present, all hope for the relationship was gone. The word tainted me, her, and the relationship, irrevocably. She now identified herself as a victim of verbal abuse, and projecting this abuse into the distant past, berated herself for having accepted the purported abuse "for many years." This victimology narrative utterly reframed the history of our relationship.

---

3 Holmquist, Annie. "Scholar: 'Fainting Couch' Feminism Needs to Go." *Intellectual Takeout.* November 8, 2016. https://www.intellectualtakeout.org/blog/scholar-fainting-couch-feminism-needs-go.

* * *

In August of 2016, I was hospitalized in New York due to an allergic reaction to medication. On the phone, I heard Sadie say that she had no intention of visiting me. Crushed, but not entirely surprised, I noted that she was leaving me only now that she'd gotten tenure, which she had secured thanks in no small part to my extensive ghostwriting on her behalf. She said she wouldn't visit someone who had called her a fucking bitch. I hadn't called her a fucking bitch, but now I said that she was a fucking bitch for such a cold refusal, even if I had called her a fucking bitch. I'll talk to you later, she said. But those were her last words to me.

* * *

I ask, dear reader, have you found the place that makes you want to swallow its rhetoric whole? I have found no such place, but not because I haven't looked. Rather, I have seen too much to believe that such a place exists.

CHAPTER SEVENTEEN

After "Social Justice:" New Paradigms for the Humanities and Social Sciences

Presented at Case Western University as part of the English Department Colloquium series. February 1, 2019.[1]

THANK YOU for the very generous introduction, Martha [Woodmansee].[2] Of course, everyone else here knows that I don't deserve it. So, as part of the introduction that I do deserve, I'll remind the overflowing crowd that I'm an avowed and convicted thought criminal. My book, *Springtime for Snowflakes: "Social Justice" and Its Postmodern Parentage*, chronicles the capers undertaken during my latest academic career stage, when I became notorious for the @antipcnyuprof Twitter account and began tweeting trenchant, slightly ribald, and sometimes over-the-top criticisms of what I see as the domination of

---

1 Originally published by *New English Review*. February 2019.

2 "Martha Woodmansee." *Wikipedia*, Wikimedia Foundation. January 19, 2018. https://en.wikipedia.org/wiki/Martha_Woodmansee; "College of Arts and Sciences." Department of English, english.case.edu/emeriti/martha-woodmansee/; "FACULTY." Case Law School – Faculty. https://web.archive.org/web/20070426115830/http://www.law.case.edu/faculty/faculty_detail.asp?=0&id=149.

"social justice ideology" in the academy.

The book begins with the tension surrounding the disclosure of my identity in connection with this formerly anonymous Twitter handle. Then, after tallying the consequences to that point, the memoir travels back to find the thread that led me to graduate studies and a career as a professor in the first place. The retrospective narration is undertaken in order to locate and follow in my graduate school education the roots of what I began objecting to much later, at which point the narrative begins.

To be perfectly honest, I owe something for the plan and ultimate design of the book to the recommendations of Adam Bellow, an editor [previously] with his own imprint at St. Martin's Press and the son of the Nobel Prize winning novelist, Saul Bellow. A brilliant guy, who, having grown up in the Upper East Side among the intelligentsia with whom his father cavorted, is an unlikely conservative. Adam suggested that I write a memoir about my graduate school education. But I soon found that he wanted me to recount in literary prose what he regarded quite literally as "the history of your brainwashing" and later debriefing.

I wanted the book to appear with Adam's imprimatur, All Points Books.[3] So, I worked through seven months of revisions. But when the moment of truth arrived, Adam decided that the book wasn't doing it for him. It was too academic. He wanted a narration of my academic preparation, but not an academic rendering thereof. During the long process of revision after revision, I sensed that he resented academia and academics and seemed hell-bent on extracting from my academic autobiography a total send-up, an entirely jocular romp, and an ultimate dismissal of the entire enterprise as a farce—a genre that I had heard about but that I had never actually read.

Anyway, I didn't think of my graduate school education as a joke that I got twenty-five years later. I thought of it as a serious cultural and intellectual engagement with sometimes bewilder-

---

3   "Macmillan - All Points Books." Ampersand Inc. https://ampersandinc.ca/lines/macmillan-all-points-books/.

ing but always significant ideas and issues. Further, the requirement that I render the content and context of literary and cultural theory in jargon-free prose struck me as wrong-headed.
While I don't mean to go full Derrida here, I found that when
I attempted to extirpate all novel and arcane theoretical terms
and phrases from the text, I lost much of what made the experience distinctive. There were exceptions, of course, as I believe
the following passage attests. In it, I narrate the day that I first
set foot on the campus of Case Western, in the fall of 1993. I
hope it gives a sense of the book's content and texture—its attempts at dealing with ideas, people, events, and institutional
conditions, sometimes all at once:

> In mid-August, I met with my adviser, Professor Roger Salo-
> mon. An early septuagenarian, Professor Salomon matched
> most peoples' image of an English professor: tweed blazer
> with elbow patches over a wool sweater, thick-wale corduroy
> pants. He offered me a chair, not across from his desk, but be-
> side his own. I sensed the spiritual community that abided in
> his office, an ongoing séance between himself and the living,
> breathing books – a communication with great authors, who
> were supposedly dead. Salomon recommended that I start by
> taking only one course per semester for the first year. He felt
> confident that I might be very interested in a course called
> "Cultural Criticism," taught by Professor Martha Woodman-
> see. He read the course description aloud, which included the
> neologism "McDonaldization." The syllabus seemed to smirk
> with a sense of subversive glee at the prospect of roasting the
> field itself, with an attitude that might be described as a peppy
> nihilism. This was certainly not a path that Roger Solomon
> had taken or would ever have taken. The syllabus mocked the
> very values that he held dear. He knew that once put on the
> path trodden by Martha Woodmansee, I might never turn
> back. Yet noble soul that he was, he passed the torch, and me
> with it, to Martha Woodmansee.
>
> I tried to get a grip on Woodmansee before the start of the
> semester....The precise name for her own approach is called
> new historicism. New historicism holds that our only access
> to the past is through "texts," broadly construed as any carrier

of signification or meaning-making. But contrary to an "old historicism" as it were, texts don't exist in a vacuum handed down to us through literary history but rather in conversation with other texts, including "non-literary" texts, all of which are involved in ongoing discourses. Texts are not mere reflections of the past but interventions into ongoing conversations of their era – rhetorical structures that have to be read closely in order to discern and then excavate their meaning and import in connection with the conversations within which they intervened.[4]

The passage relates a common theme, the passing of the institutional baton or torch from one generation to the next, while offering a slight glimpse of some of the broad changes that had taken place within academia during the nine years that I spent working in advertising between the end of my undergraduate studies in 1983 and the beginning of my graduate work in 1993. We all know what this period in English Studies entailed: the "invasion" of theory, the canon wars, the struggles over multiculturalism, and so on and so forth.

I liked what I had written and took the book to another, smaller press, and this publisher, New English Review Press, accepted the manuscript without delay. Some may find the title offensive or off-putting. Allow me to explain. For various reasons, I really needed to sell books, and a memorable, even provocative title would help to attract buyers. It worked, although I'd like to think that content of the interior pages has something to do with the book's relative success. At several points since its official release in late July 2018, *Springtime for Snowflakes* has broken into the top 75 out of all 15 million books for sale on Amazon.com. I'm sure that the title has likely alienated potential readers, who, could they get past the title, might actually enjoy or at least appreciate it. But I understand. I did what I had to do, which was to write a compelling book and to find a memorable title. And they did what they had to do, which was

---

4 Rectenwald, Michael. *Springtime for Snowflakes: "Social Justice" and Its Postmodern Parentage: a Memoir.* New English Review Press, 2018, pp. 51-52.

nothing.

Allow me now to voice the main thrust of my criticism as delivered in the book. In parts of what follows, I will be revisiting the book, while in others I draw on more recent experience, including the circumstances surrounding this talk itself, because they illustrate so well my purpose for writing book in the first place.

First, I must address the elephant in the room—or rather the elephant not in the room. I know that my talk is actually being actively boycotted by a plurality of the members of the English department. Has anyone come up with more "inclusive," less "heteronormative," "masculinist" language for a such standard consumerist political activity? How about "people-cotted"? Rather, let's just call it "shunned."

I wrote *Springtime for Snowflakes* precisely to counter the assumption of an official, exclusive ideology within academia, one that precludes the expression of views at odds with it. I find in this development a failure of the left and a great bane to academic culture and the culture at large. As I see it, today's social justice left represents the early-21st century equivalent of the 1980s moral majority, no less bent on prohibition and censorship, only far more influential culturally. As I wrote in the Preface:

> Having gone so far as to officially adopt a particularly censorious subset of contemporary leftist ideology, colleges and universities have tragically abdicated their roles as politically impartial and intellectually independent institutions for the advancement and transmission of knowledge and wisdom.[5]

Meanwhile, since expressing views at odds with the official social justice ideology, I've learned a bit about shunning over the past two years, but I won't say how. I've learned that shunning is an ancestral behavioral pattern. Directed at the deviant individual, shunning is the means by which the herd ejects the stray and reinforces herd coalescence and mutual self-protec-

---

5 Ibid., p. xi.

tion. The herd is the Leviathan in the demos of the decentered Cathedral, the papacy with millions of popes, as I'll discuss later.

For individual herd members, meanwhile, herd compulsion is experienced as a yearning for collective protection and fear of the herd itself. This double compulsion ensures that compliance is the rule rather than the exception. And it almost all but guarantees that only deviants can see the herd's methods of superintendence, which are therefore incommunicable to herd members. Further, fear of the herd is based on the herd's history of terror, which all cognizant members have witnessed being applied to others, the deviants that everyone must avoid and avoid becoming.

Foucault was right about Panopticism and its coercive and productive power. It both produces and is produced by the subject under its subjection. But Foucault accorded too much of that power to structural determinants and not enough to the biopolitics of the herd, which makes power most effective and when intent on barring escape obviates the building of walls. Panopticism becomes even more light-weight. Herd mentality is both coercive and productive. Inscribed indelibly on the individual subject, it produces the subject as a herd being, while the herd is produced by the activation of the herd mentality of individuals.

Meanwhile, as Foucault argued, power works by engaging the active participation of the subject on which the power is imposed:

> He who is subjected to a field of visibility, and who knows it, assumes responsibility for the constraints of power; he makes them play spontaneously upon himself; he inscribes in himself the power relation in which he simultaneously plays both roles; he becomes the principle of his own subjection.[6]

---

6 Foucault, Michel. "Discipline & Punish - Panopticism." *Michel Foucault, Info.*, Michel Foucault, Info. https://foucault.info/documents/foucault.disciplineAndPunish.panOpticism/.

Under social justice ideology participation in the power of the academy involves the subject assuring herself—by virtue of avowing the dominant ideology to herself and others—of her indubitably superior social justice probity and intellectual capacities, which serve to obscure power's determinations over conscious choice. The banishment of deviants reinforces belief in one's own superiority and the rightness of the terms of one's belief. The deviant must not be considered "a real academic," must be dubbed beyond the pale—or, to use Pierre Bourdieu's notion of a "political field," must be figured as occupying an illegitimate position precluded by the field itself. The deviant must not be drawn as a courageous or gifted figure with peculiar insights. Rather, he is deemed infirmed, "idiotic," morally depraved, or so intellectually maladroit as to render him incapable of grasping the natural superiority of the herd's positions and pronouncements. The herd rewards conformists with such mutually self-and-other-congratulatory beliefs as these. And in addition to these carrots, the herd has its sticks as well. Historically, the alternative to conformity has been death.

The judgment of the progressive herd, meanwhile, is always right, because the herd's values are obvious, transparent, "natural," and clearly "on the right side of history"—or as French structuralist Marxist Louis Althusser wrote, they are ideological. As Althusser suggested, it is precisely when one imagines that one is outside of ideology (on the right side of history, etc.) that one is actually in ideology. Likewise, it is when one knows that one is in ideology, paradoxically, that one is not in ideology. Adherents to the dominant ideology may never see that they are in ideology as such (because the dominant ideology is the ideology of the dominant), and powerful forces are at work to ensure that the dominant ideology appears as anything but ideological, and instead as inevitable, "just so," obvious, right.

At this historical juncture, paradoxical as it must sound, I'm here to tell you that a new leftism is the dominant ideology—in the academy of course but also in the broader social order. In my last book, *Google Archipelago: The Digital Gulag and the Simulation of Freedom*, I call this dominant form of leftism, "corporate leftism."[7] At this point, although I've been working on the problem for two years, I can only conjecture about why leftism is dominant, while pointing to how.

As for the how: the primary means of ideological and thus also political production is the academy, and the primary owners of the means of ideological and political production are, as Marx referred to academics, the shopkeepers of intellectual life, the professoriate—you and people in your roles in colleges and universities everywhere. Although sometimes dubbed "the ivory tower," the academy is anything but a quaint exception to or ancillary adjunct of the "real world." Quite otherwise, academia is an ideological state apparatus (ISA), to use Althusser's term. I maintain that it is the dominant ideological state apparatus. Or, to borrow a more precise formulation, the academy is best understood as "the Cathedral," the contemporary equivalent of the medieval papacy in our "progressive," postmodern times.

The received notion of the academy's irrelevance is a guise that has allowed it to hide its ideological dominance in plain sight. Yet the Cathedral does generate the dominant ideology, although time is required for it to metastasize to the broader social body, and only after having been digested and excreted by the media, the interchange between the Cathedral and the unwashed.

I must say now that one "Mencius Moldbug," the abhorrent pseudonymous neoreactionary, is the author of the Cathedral theory.[8] His explanation of the academy-in-the-world is the best that I've encountered. Yes, I've encountered many others. My preference for the Cathedral theory has nothing to do with any allegiance to Moldbug's political orientation, which I don't even take seriously. He's a monarchist! It is based strictly on the

---

7 Rectenwald, Michael. *Google Archipelago: The Digital Gulag and the Simulation of Freedom*. New English Review Press, 2019.

8 See Moldbug, Mencius. "UR." Chapter 9: How to Uninstall a Cathedral | *An Open Letter to Open-Minded Progressives | Unqualified Reservations by Mencius Moldbug*. June 12, 2008. https://www.unqualified-reservations. org/2008/06/ol9-how-to-uninstall-cathedral/; and Moldburg, Mencius. "UR." . February 8, 2013. https://www.unqualified-reservations.org/2013/02/ charles-stross-discovers-cathedral/.

cohesiveness, simplicity, and explanatory power of the theory itself. By the way, I encountered Moldbug's Cathedral idea while still a Marxist, and only because I ignored the warning signs posted by academic and media gatekeepers, and instead read his actual writing. The role of such functionaries is to preclude all modes of explanation except those that are in accord with the dominant theoretical (and ideological) paradigm. I would say that alternatives are precluded "in advance"—if I wasn't for the fact that I'm speaking to a room empty of English Professors, whose very presence-in-absence provokes me to imagine that they are judging me. Actually, I am not imagining it. They are judging me. They just aren't here.

I think that Moldbug's political recommendations are extraneous and irrelevant to his analyses of the academy in particular, and rather than deeming his entire corpus inadmissible, as if reading him might turn me or anyone else into a neoreactionary overnight, I read what I found and found what I read illuminating. I do the same with Marx on occasion. Although I ceased being a Marxist well over two years ago [now four years ago], I continue to employ Marxist methods and modes of analysis, while scrupulously ignoring his recommendations—especially since the Marxist experiment has been run several times and in several places, with the same results—instead of the "universal human emancipation" promised, a monopoly of the state over the political, economic, cultural, educational and private spheres, limiting workers to choice of one employer, voters to a choice of one party, consumers to a choice of one brand, and the "democratic" process to a choice between tyranny and tyranny, to say nothing for now about political crimes. That the left maintains belief in the irrefragability of its political prescriptions despite the abysmal record of the left in power is a topic worthy of several volumes, volumes that will not be written under the auspices of the university, because the university would no more finance and reward such heresies than the medieval Church did in its heyday.

The analogy that Moldbug draws between monolithic Medieval Catholicism and monolithic postmodern liberalism is not exact. Moldbug compares the decentralized, postmodern Cathedral, with its millions of popes, with the univocal authority of the singular Pope within Medieval Catholicism. The postmodern Cathedral is a disorganized Church and most of its priestly caste members do not cooperate with each other. They do not constitute a conspiracy. The cohesion is provided by the dominant ideology, which both produces and is produced by the priestly caste within it. Like the Medieval Catholic Church, the postmodern Church also issues pronouncements *ex cathedra*. As long as they do not contradict the Church doctrine of progress, etc., such pronouncements are disseminated broadly and carry the authority of the papal seal.

My recommendation of neoreaction as an alternative paradigm was meant as a heuristic for examining and putting pressure on the dominant paradigm, not as a replacement of it. I should have made this clear. Similarly, integral theory and neo-modernism were suggested primarily for their heuristic value. Given that these three paradigms are very different in terms of their political valences (neoreaction is rightist; integral theory claims to transcend left-right binaries, and neo-modernism is an updated modernism based on lessons taken from postmodern theory), my politics should not have been inferred from my suggestion that they be considered.

Instead of neoreaction, had I mentioned in my abstract Heidegger's notion of "Being-in-the-World," I wonder whether it would have elicited similarly blistering emails that circulated about me, which found me guilty by association. Or does being a dead Nazi render a philosopher harmless? That's a real question. I don't understand the social justice rules, just as they say. But maybe that is because they don't make sense.

Even the three peddlers of the parodied "grievance studies" articles—James A. Lindsay, Peter Boghossian, and Helen Pluckrose—would not have been given the same treatment, although their serial "Sokal Hoax Squared"[9] has diminished the griev-

9 Kafka, Alexander C. "'Sokal Squared': Is Huge Publishing Hoax 'Hilarious and Delightful' or an Ugly Example of Dishonesty and Bad Faith?" *The Chronicle of Higher Education*, The Chronicle of Higher Education. October

ance studies fields and thereby may have lessened real grievances, thus doing a terrible disservice to the aggrieved *qua* the aggrieved.[10] Their Sokal hoax redux even included a paper that fobbed off on the editors of the esteemed feminist journal *Affilia* excerpts of Mein Kampf as feminist criticism.[11] Meanwhile, Peter Boghossian and Helen Pluckrose are friends of mine on Facebook, which makes me a Nazi. Retaining the line of argument and merely swapping the agents of Nazism with those of feminism, they proved Rush Limbaugh right. After all these years, we now know that Rush Limbaugh's "Femi-Nazis" are a reality.

Such a conflation is no worse than mistaking a civil and cultural libertarian NYU professor and scholar of nineteenth-century British freethought for an "alt-right provocateur." But never mind such fine distinctions! Reflexively smearing every critic of social justice ideology and the academic left with the alt-right label is not at all like failing to distinguish between Nazism and feminism! No, these two samples of inapt and inept false equivalence could not possibly be part of the same problem!

So, what is the problem?

At the moment postmodern theory lay dying in the academy, it bore a child, namely, "social justice." Social justice gestated within the university as postmodern theory ruled the roost. It was nursed during the Occupy movement and the Obama era. The financial crisis left its hapless followers in search of empowerment. It took root on the Internet on social media. But because its parent had taught it that the object world is not real, or else that the world at large was beyond one's purview, the child of postmodern theory could only change itself, as well as, so it imagined, those who bore signs of its oppressors. Although

3, 2018. https://www.chronicle.com/article/Sokal-Squared-Is-Huge/244714.

10 Pluckrose, Helen. "Academic Grievance Studies and the Corruption of Scholarship." *Areo*. October 30, 2018. https://areomagazine.com/2018/10/02/academic-grievance-studies-and-the-corruption-of-scholarship/.

11 Borschel-Dan, Amanda. "Duped Academic Journal Publishes Rewrite of 'Mein Kampf' as Feminist Manifesto." *The Times of Israel*. October 5, 2018. https://www.timesofisrael.com/duped-academic-journal-publishes-rewrite-of-mein-kampf-as-feminist-manifesto/.

political correctness has enjoyed a much longer, although intermittent sway over academia, social justice as such debuted in full regalia in higher education in the fall of 2016—when it emerged and occupied campuses to avenge its monster-mother's death and wreak havoc upon its enemies.

One of the great ironies of Western political history involves this term "social justice." Although a core idea within liberalism and socialism for at least 175 years, the background and origin of "social justice" is cultural and political conservatism. The irony of the "cultural appropriation" of social justice by liberalism and socialism has recently redoubled. Suggestive of a seemingly undeniably intangible good—that is, of just, fair social relations—social justice is now implicated in fierce and sometimes violent antagonisms, as well as the humiliating intellectual scandals I've mentioned. Social justice crystallizes in two words some of the most contentious issues roiling North American politics today.

The phrase "social justice" recalls movements of the recent past that used the same political terminology. But contemporary social justice bears little resemblance to the original social justice or even more recent movements that have gone by the same name. Contemporary social justice embodies postmodern theoretical notions as well as the latter's adoption of Maoist and Stalinist disciplinary methods. As I argue in *Springtime for Snowflakes*, contemporary "social justice" is an ideological and epistemological framework derived from New Left politics and postmodern theory. Examples of the postmodern theoretical provenance of social justice ideas are legion, but one extended example must suffice for today. It begins in arcane Soviet theory and ends up in the nonsense of "muh knowledge," that is, with everyone having his "own truth."

In *History and Class Consciousness* (1923), György Lukács introduced a form of epistemology that has had an outsized impact ever since its introduction. Lukács' idea, which he may have shared with Vladimir Lenin, has served as a source for the postmodern theoretical and social justice notion that each person has his own truth based on his particular type of subordination.

Lukács argued that the unique position of the working class within the social order and the relations of production provide the proletariat with a privileged vantage-point for discerning objective truth. He called the theory "proletarian standpoint epistemology." Lukács argued that reality under capitalism is a single objective reality.[12] (For the two of you left, who may be feeling asphyxiated by their mention, don't worry: "objectivity" and "reality" will later be shorn from standpoint epistemology.)

For Lukács, the proletarian occupies a position that affords him a peculiar relationship to objective reality. The objective world strikes the proletarian differently than it does the capitalist. Like the capitalist, the proletarian is a self-conscious subject. However, unlike the capitalist, the proletarian is also a commodity, an object for sale on the market. The proletarian's "self-consciousness of the commodity" (that is himself) contradicts his experience as a subject, a self-determining agent in history. This double vision, or double consciousness if you will, allows the working class an all-sided sense of the social order, which the bourgeoisie lacks.

While designating a position of subordination, Lukács simultaneously granted the working class a superior epistemological vantage point for access to objective reality. He thus effected the hierarchical inversion that Nietzsche notoriously lambasted as characteristic of Christianity and socialism. As he wrote in the *Genealogy of Morals*, under such inversion ideologies as Christianity, socialism, and, I would add, social justice ideology:

> Only those who suffer are good, only the poor, the powerless, the lowly are good; the suffering, the deprived, the sick, the ugly, are the only pious people, the only ones saved, salvation is for them alone, whereas you rich, the noble and powerful, you are eternally wicked, cruel, lustful, insatiate, godless, you will also be eternally wretched, cursed and damned![13]

---

12   Lukács Georg. *History and Class Consciousness Studies in Marxist Dialectics*. MIT Press, 1971.

13   Nietzsche, Friedrich Wilhelm, et al. *On the Genealogy of Morality and Other Writings*. Cambridge University Press, 2017, p. 17.

166 ᇰᇱ *Beyond Woke*

Lest quoting Nietzsche should confirm my "alt-right" identity at Case Western, which would come as a great surprise to
my former classmates here, as it was to me, I should say that
I regard reading Nietzsche merely as a necessary inoculation
against the contemporary social justice contagion. But I would
never adopt the lunacy of Nietzsche's philosophy in its entire-
ty. I can say the same about the loathsome neoreaction, which
amounts to the fantasies of roughly five people, who, unlike the
epigones of Marx, haven't killed anyone, let alone 94 million
people.

Meanwhile, in *The Science Question in Feminism* (1986),
Sandra Harding adopted Lukács's proletarian standpoint epistemology and adapted it to feminism. The particular standpoint
of women accords them an enhanced cognitive and perceptual
grasp of objectivity.[14]

The New Left then appropriated standpoint epistemology
and siphoned it through various postmodern identity filters.
Standpoint epistemology is the root of the contemporary social justice belief in the identity-knowledge nexus. Social justice holds that membership in a subordinated identity group
accords members exclusive access to particular knowledge,
their own knowledge, their own reality. Members of dominant
identity groups cannot access or understand the knowledge or
reality of subordinated others. Further, individual members of
subordinated identity groups have their *own individual* knowledge. For social justice believers, knowledge is finally personal,
individual, and impenetrable to others. Under the social justice worldview, everyone is locked in an impenetrable identity
chrysalis with access to a personal knowledge that no one else
can access. I call this social-justice-inflected belief prong, "epistemological solipsism."

In a recent *New York Times* op-ed entitled, "How Ta-Ne-
hisi Coates Gives Whiteness Power," Thomas Chatterton Williams discusses what I am calling epistemological solipsism,
which he calls "knowing-through-being" and "identity epis-

---

14 Harding, Sandra G. *The Science Question in Feminism*. Cornell University Press, 1993.

temology." Williams laments identity epistemology or know-ing-through-being because it limits knowledge to members of particular identity categories and it slides seamlessly into "identity ethics" or "morality-through-being." Morality-through-being is believed to follow from knowing-through-being as the subordinated assumes the moral high ground on the basis of a superior knowledge standpoint deriving from subordinated status. Morality-through-being or identity-ethics results in a moral ranking in which the lowest on the totem pole is deemed a moral superior by virtue of her (previous) subordination. Through the kind of hierarchical inversion that Friedrich Nietzsche saw in Christianity and socialism, low status becomes high status.

How did Lukács' proletariat standpoint epistemology become an epistemological solipsism resulting in the inverted moral hierarchy of the contemporary social justice movement? While Lukács argued that the proletariat's material standpoint yielded the class unique access to objective truth, by the time it reached contemporary social justice, standpoint epistemology had already been stripped of any pretense to objective truth by postmodern theory. According to postmodern theory, the very idea of "objective truth" is a master narrative. Under social justice ideology, objective truth is a legacy of patriarchal white supremacy.

In addition to its theoretical importance, standpoint epistemology has produced pedagogical offspring as well. A hallmark of social justice pedagogy is "progressive stacking," a method for ordering student class participation based on the inverted social justice hierarchy. This form of academic "priori-tarian-ism," or putting the worst-off first, became a topic of national controversy when a graduate student made a public declaration of the technique. It never seems to occur to the advocates of progressive stacking that such preferential treatment or prioritizing of supposed social subordinates might reify the very hierarchy that it is supposed to reverse, patronizing some while handicapping others based on a presupposed social superiority, however it may have been produced or reproduced.

In case I haven't made it obvious by now, I have mostly examined problems with social justice as a paradigm, while discussing only Moldbug's notion of the academy as the Cathedral. I found that in a talk of such length, I wouldn't be able to do justice to discussion of integral theory and neo-modernism.

As for the Cathedral theory of the academy, it helps to underscore the religious character of the dominant ideology, social justice ideology, and perhaps most of the paradigms that could, theoretically, replace it. Indeed, it is hard to imagine a paradigm for the humanities and social sciences that might elude ideology. Even those claiming to be based on strictly scientific bases will import ideological germs that in the context of the humanities will find hosts and multiply.

This is not to suggest that one paradigm is as good as another. The grounding of social justice in identity and identity politics is as shaky a foundation as one can imagine. The ontologies of social identity are mutable, uncertain, and sometimes utterly meaningless. Further, subordinated identity categories arguably should be dismantled rather than being used as anchors for knowledge claims. To what extent, one wonders, do the various "studies" devoted to this or that subordinated identity category actually contribute to the reification of the category and thus to the containment and subordination of members therein? This is what seems to be suggested by calling these identity-based studies "grievance studies." Where would they be without legitimate grievances and thus what incentive do they have to dismantle the categorical containment of the subjects whose interests they putatively represent and advocate for?

CHAPTER EIGHTEEN

Totalitarianism with Communist Characteristics, Corporate Socialism, and "Woke" Capitalism

Presented at the Free Enterprise Forum, Baylor University, February 13, 2020[1]

SEVERAL DECADES AGO, when China's growing reliance on the for-profit sectors of its economy could no longer be credibly denied by the Chinese Communist Party (CCP), its leadership approved the slogan "socialism with Chinese characteristics" to describe the Chinese economic system.[2] Formulated by Deng Xiaoping, the phrase became an essential figure of the CCP's attempt to rationalize Chinese capitalist development. According to the party, the growing "capitalization" of the Chinese economy was to be a temporary phase—lasting as long as a hundred years according to some party leaders, or long enough to make sure they were dead before it ended—on the way to a classless society of full communism. The party leaders claimed, and still maintain, that "socialism with Chinese char-

---

1 "Free Enterprise Forum with Michael Rectenwald." Baylor University | Graduate Programs | Free Enterprise Forum with Michael Rectenwald. https://www.baylor.edu/business/grad/event.php?event_id=126401.

2 Wilson, Ian. "Socialism with Chinese Characteristics: China and The Theory of the Initial Stage of Socialism." *Politics*. Vol. 24, no. 1, 21, September 2007, pp. 77–84.

acteristics" is a temporary phase of socialist development peculiar to China, necessary particularly in China's case because China was a "backward" agrarian country when communism was introduced—too early, it was implied. China needed a capitalist booster shot.

With the slogan, the party was able to argue that China had been an exception to the orthodox Marxist position that socialism arrives only after the development of capitalism—although Marx himself deviated from his own formula late in life. At the same time, the slogan allowed the CCP to confirm the orthodox Marxist position. China's socialist revolution came before developed industrial capitalism—an exception to orthodox Marxism. Capitalism was necessarily introduced into China's economic system later—a confirmation of orthodox Marxism.

Stripped of its socialist ideological pretensions, socialism with Chinese characteristics, or the Chinese system itself, really amounts to a socialist-communist state increasingly funded by capitalist economic development. One difference between the former Soviet Union and contemporary China is that when it became obvious that a socialist-communist economy had failed, the former gave up its socialist-communist economic pretenses while the latter did not. On the other hand, I am not sure whether or to what extent Russia overthrew its communist politicos, or, that is, to what extent Russia may be called "socialism with Russian characteristics."

Despite the remonstrances of Marxists to the contrary, socialism-communism always depends on capitalism to rescue it—and not the other way around. In the past, the socialist-communist prognostications of the always-incipient collapse of capitalism meant that socialism-communism would have to bail it out. Global warming is the new pretense for a socialist-communist bailout, never mind communism's egregious environmental record. The reality, as is so often the case, is the precise opposite of what socialists-communists suggest. The always-failing socialist-communist experiments have been reversible to date but they've always depended on the introduction or reintroduction of free market economics to address the catastrophes.

Whether the CCP leaders believe their own rhetoric or not, the ideological gymnastics on display are nevertheless spectacular. On its face, the slogan embeds and glosses over a ludicrously obvious contradiction in an attempt to sanctify or "re-communize" Chinese capitalist development as a precondition of full socialism-communism.

However, the Chinese slogan does capture an essential truth about communism, one that is either unrecognized or unacknowledged by the CCP and denied by Western Marxists. Contrary to the assertions of communist leaders and followers, and contrary to the claims of many who oppose it, socialism-communism is not essentially an economic but rather a political system.

Ever since revelations of the horrors of Soviet repression reached the West, Western Marxists began to use the term "state capitalism" to describe the former Soviet Union. Because China maintains state-directed capitalist sectors today, Western Marxists have suggested that the term applies even more demonstrably to present-day China. Western Marxists employ the term state capitalism to exclude the Soviet Union and China from the category of socialism-communism. They thereby reserve, in their own propaganda at least, the hallowed terms socialism and communism for the never-present, always-receding, and just-over-the-horizon ideal. The millennialism of Western Marxists—some of whom are in fact millennials—is breathtaking. But not as breathtaking as the exclusion of communism from the category of religion, a category whose contents Marxists also aim to eliminate.

Both Chinese and Western socialists-communists are wrong about China. The CCP leaders are wrong to the extent that they actually believe that true economic socialism-communism will evolve from capitalist development. Socialist-communist economics, if attempted, would fail again, leading to the eventual reintroduction, however reluctantly, of capitalist development. They are also wrong because China reached the ultimate stage of socialism-communism when socialists-communists gained control of society and the state. For reasons I will discuss soon, the Chinese system is a specimen of socialism-communism and remained so even after the introduction of capitalist development.

Western Marxists are wrong because China's "exploitation" of capitalist economic development does not preclude the possibility of Chinese communism—not in the future, and not now. It's not that China may yet evolve into full socialism-communism, but rather that China is already fully socialist-communist—as socialist-communist as any existing and surviving socialism-communism can be.

Contrary to its proponents, socialism-communism is not economic at base. It is not the abolition of private property and the establishment of economic equality, which are impossibilities in any case. At its most "advanced" stage, socialism-communism is the political takeover of the state by socialist-communist leaders under the pretext of the abolition of private property and establishment of economic equality. Socialism-communism is limited to "actually-existing"[3] types, such as the form Soviet Union and China, which represent the limit of socialist-communist "development." The establishment of a true economic socialism-communism was and will forever remain an impossibility. Therefore, socialism-communism must be understood as essentially limited to the political and ideological spheres, to "actually-existing" types.

Once in power, socialist-communist leaders recognize that given their control over resources, they have effectively become the new owners of the means of production (whereas, as Ludwig von Mises suggested, it would be more accurate to say that consumers effectively hold the power of economic disposal in

---

3 "Actually existing socialism" is a "[t]erm used in the former communist countries to describe them as they really were, rather than as the official theory required them to be. Its use was largely ironical, and more or less confined to the writings of dissidents." ("actually existing socialism." *Palgrave Macmillan Dictionary of Political Thought*. Roger Scruton. Macmillan Publishers Ltd, 3rd edition, 2007. Credo Reference. http://proxy.library.nyu. edu/login?url=https://search.credoreference.com/content/entry/macpt/actual¬ly_existing_socialism/0?institutionId=577

free markets[4]). This may have been their secret ambition all along, however much they fooled themselves into thinking otherwise. They also come to recognize—if they hadn't before taking power and simply lied about it—that economic equality is impossible. In attempting to implement a socialist-communist economy, they recognize that, in the absence of prices, large-scale industrial production requires supervisory decision-making and as the ultimate decision makers they are essentially the owners of the means of production. Likewise, decision-making is not democratic in the sense promised by socialist-communist ideologues. Decision-making must be centralized, or at least bureaucratized, to a great extent. Democratic decision-making is precluded by state-owned and controlled production, distribution, and consumption. Socialism-communism is a political system in which resource allocation is commanded by the state and thus effectively owned and controlled by the state leaders, the real ruling class. The latter retain control through ideology and force.

The limit of socialism-communism is a political arrangement. The economic pretensions will be jettisoned as capitalist development is introduced and cleverly rationalized, as in China. If such pretentions are maintained for long, they will wreck society, as in the former Soviet Union. In either case, the socialist-communist leadership will learn that wealth production requires the accumulation of privately held capital—whether they understand why or not.

Ludwig von Mises pointed to the reason for this necessity in his discussions of the calculation problem.[5] Without prices, the value of the factors of production are indeterminable; irrationality and systemic chaos must ensue. But prices depend on exchange. And exchange presupposes markets. And markets presuppose property relations. And property relations presuppose private property. And private property presupposes that persons possess property. Therefore, wealth production de-

---

4 Mises, Ludwig Von. *Socialism; an Economic and Sociological Analysis*. 3rd ed., Yale University Press, 1951, pp. 37-42.
5 Ibid., pp. 131-135.

pends on persons possessing private property.

But socialism-communism depends on political arrangements. And what are those political arrangements? In short, socialism-communism is totalitarianism, leftist totalitarianism, or "totalitarianism with communist characteristics." Unlike the Chinese slogan, and unlike the euphemistic "socialism" and "communism," this label makes clear and announces socialism-communism's true character.

Socialism-communism is totalitarian because it requires that the state decide on matters of production, distribution, and consumption. Contrary to Marx's assertion that the state will "wither away" under communism, the state must be maintained at all costs. It must be maintained because without it, a monopoly over production cannot be ensured. To maintain the state, all possible alternatives to the state as such must be excluded—repressed, shut down, and eventually destroyed. This requires the state's continuous use of force or the threat of force, although ideological indoctrination is cheaper and usually more efficient.

Further, socialism-communism is essentially a leftist totalitarianism that masquerades as something very much like its precise opposite. It is leftist due to what it promises: "economic democracy." But in the absence of prices, economic democracy is subverted and the jeremiads against economic inequality— the rhetoric of its usually unwitting political dupes, like Bernie Sanders and Alexandria Ocasio-Cortez today, for example— function as chimeras, diversionary tactics, loss leaders, ruses, the bait in an eventual bait-and-switch scheme. Even the socialist leaders, if they are true believers and not cynics, are on the other end of a bait and switch routine. They are forced into it as circumstances unravel. Economic equality means nothing in any "actually-existing" socialist-communist society—unless it means that almost everyone is equally poor.

It follows that anyone seeking to combat or ward off socialism-communism should understand exactly what they oppose. They would be mistaken to take socialist-communist ideologues at their word. The latter apparently don't know, or if they do know, won't let on, that what they recommend cannot exist.

Likewise, anti-socialists-communists shouldn't imagine that they fight against a classless, propertyless society. They should recognize that their real opponent is actually-existing socialism-communism—a political system buttressed by ideological and political force—and not a viable economic system. Economic socialism-communism will remain forever ideological.

Enter Corporate Socialism

A socialist sequel is coming to a theater near you. The same old characters are reappearing, while new ones have joined the cast. While the ideology and rhetoric sound nearly the same, they are being put to different ends. This time around, the old bromides and promises are in play and a similar but not identical bait and switch is being dangled. Socialism promises the protection of the underclass from the economically and politically "evil," the promotion of the economic interests of the underclass, a benign banning of "dangerous" persons from public forums and civic life, and a primary or exclusive concern for "the common good." China's "One Belt, One Road"[6] may hang the takers in Africa and other underdeveloped regions as if from an infrastructural noose. A different variety is on the docket in the developed world, including in the U.S.

The contemporary variant is "corporate socialism," or a two-tiered system of "actually-existing" socialism on the ground coupled with a parallel set of corporate monopolies on top. The difference between state socialism and corporate socialism is merely that a different constituency effectively controls the means of production. But both depend on monopoly—one the state and the other the corporate monopolization of the economy. And both depend on socialist-communist ideology of democratic socialism, or in a recent variant, "social justice" or "woke" ideology. Corporate socialism is the desired

---

6 Ma, Alexandra. "The US Is Scrambling to Invest More in Asia to Counter China's 'Belt and Road' Mega-Project. Here's What China's Plan to Connect the World through Infrastructure Is like." *Business Insider*. November 11, 2019. https://www.businessinsider.com/what-is-belt-and-road-china-infrastructure-project-2018-1.

end while democratic socialism and woke capitalism are among the means.

How could socialist ideology possibly become hegemonic, in the U.S. of all places, such that corporate socialism might be introduced, however gradually? Why and how could socialist ideology attain dominance in the world's "most capitalist" country?

First, as I've stated earlier, "actually-existing" socialism is essentially a political system, a system attained and maintained largely by means of an extremely alluring yet deceptive political ideology. In order to survive, socialism must conjoin with a for-profit economy. Leaving aside socialist ideology, corporate socialism is "corporate monopolism." When it includes socialist ideology, it becomes one variation of "actually-existing" socialism.

Second, the received notion that all corporate capitalists favor "rightwing" political ideology because "rightwing" political ideology best represents their interests is simply mistaken. This notion is itself ideological and has been falsified historically. In *Google Archipelago*, I discuss historical "corporate leftists" or "corporate socialists," and treat the contemporary variant. I'll review a specimen of historical corporate socialism in what follows.

Third, corporate socialists abjure and condemn free market economics and manage to rally a significant contingent of the population to oppose it as well. The corporate monopolists blame the free market for the evils that corporate monopolism itself produces. The free market is figured as the enemy of the people. The free market, with supposed evil of "competition," is equated with every evil derived from all forms of capitalism. A mass contingent is turned against the free market, which likewise paves the way for forms of corporate monopolism, including corporate socialism.

Fourth, socialist ideology continues to have purchase—pardon the apparent lexical incongruity—because it has not been required to atone for its criminal past. For several reasons, socialism-communism escaped the condemnation it deserved given its 20th-century scorecard of mass political incarceration and murder. Although it racked at least up 94 million dead, rather than receiving the deserved opprobrium, it passed through the 20th and into the 21st century like a defeated yet somehow dignified old man.

To review: one, corporate socialists are not free market advocates; they are monopolists. They favor a strong state and bolster it financially and ideologically so that the state can arbitrate and enforce their monopolistic desiderata. Two, corporate socialism depends on socialist-communist ideology and rhetoric "on the ground." It promotes socialist ideology to produce conditions conducive to its establishment and continuance.

I now want to make clear what I am not suggesting here. I am not suggesting that the U.S. is on the verge of becoming an economically socialist-communist country. I am not suggesting that Bernie Sanders or Alexandria Ocasio-Cortez are heralds of this possibility. I am not saying that the West is on the brink of becoming an extension of China, although Africa might become just that.

What I am saying is that the socialist-communist ideology—embraced by some and loathed by others—serves a function other than the function advertised. The ruling elites maintain no pretensions among themselves that actual economic socialism-communism can be established, nor do they want it. Nevertheless, they are promoting socialist ideology, and, as before, socialist ideology produces expectations for economic equality among the majority. The specter of socialism not only stirs the fantasies of subterranean socialist-communist milieus, holdouts from the communist left of yore, it also appeals to those less educated in socialist-communist theory, but who nevertheless constitute a disgruntled, mostly millennial, and millennialist set.

Woke Capitalism
The ideological needs of corporate socialism explain the in-

troduction and contemporary prevalence of "woke capitalism."[7] I've written about woke capitalism elsewhere, but I will summarize what I've written for the purposes of this talk, adding a few insights that I've had since.[8]

First, the word "woke." "Woke" is obviously a past tense and past participle of the verb "wake." It suggests "having become awake." But, by the 1960s, woke began to function as an adjective as well, gaining the figurative meaning in the African American community of "well-informed" or "up-to-date." By 1972, the once modest verbal past tense began to describe an elevated political consciousness. In 2017, the *Oxford English Dictionary* (OED) recognized the social-conscious awareness of woke and added the definition: "alert to racial or social discrimination and injustice."

Coined by *New York Times* columnist Ross Douthat, "woke capitalism" refers to a burgeoning wave of companies that apparently have become socially and politically conscious. Some major corporations now intervene in social and political issues and controversies, partaking in a new corporate activism. The newly "woke" corporations support activist groups and social movements, while adding their voices to political debates. Woke capitalism has endorsed #BlackLivesMatter, the #MeToo Movement, contemporary feminism, LGBTQ rights and concerns, and immigration activism, among other left-leaning movements and causes. Woke advertising has included Nike's ad campaign featuring Colin Kaepernick as an endorsement of #BlackLivesMatter, Gillette's "We Believe" ad, otherwise known as the "The Best A Man Can Get" or the "toxic masculinity" ad, and more recently the "MENstruation" ad from the feminine (not women's!) underwear company, Thinx. The ad, which suggests that "men can have periods too," made news when it

---

7   Douthat, Ross. "The Rise of Woke Capital." *The New York Times*. February 28, 2018. https://www.nytimes.com/2018/02/28/opinion/corporate-america-ac¬tivism.html.

8   See in particular Rectenwald, Michael. *Google Archipelago: The Digital Gulag and the Simulation of Freedom*. New English Review Press, 2019, Chapter 1, "Woke Capitalism, Corporate Leftism, and the Google Archipelago," pp. 41-53.

was rejected by CBS.[9] It had previously reported that Bravo, E!, Oxygen, BET, MTV, VH1, HGTV, the Food Network, TLC and NBC agreed to air the ad.[10]

Given the apparent incongruity between corporate capitalist objectives and leftwing politics as represented by wokeness or social justice, I have pondered the function of woke capitalism—whether it works, and if so, how, to what ends, and for whose benefit?

A few explanations for woke capitalism have been offered by business analysts in the establishment media. *Business Insider* columnist Josh Barro suggests that woke capitalism provides a form of political representation for consumers and workers.[11] Companies adopt woke capitalism to please their customers and employees, who are largely left leaning. When corporate rhetoric reflects the identity politics of customers, woke capitalists are rewarded with sales and brand loyalty. Despite the initial backlash, Nike's ad campaign featuring Colin Kaepernick—whose national anthem kneel-downs brought #BlackLivesMatter protest to the NFL and dramatically boosted Nike's sales—would seem to support Barro's theory.

Douthat of the *New York Times* offers a different explanation. He suggests that by appeasing various political contingents, woke capitalism works to ingratiate woke companies to liberal politicos who represent these contingents. Woke capitalism supports the liberal political elite's policies and agendas of identity politics, gender pluralism, transgenderism, lax immigration, sanctuary cities, and so on. In return for endorsing these and other woke positions, expressly woke corporations

---

9 Thinx. "MENstruation." *YouTube*, YouTube. October 3, 2019. https://www.youtube.com/watch?v=2UcwkL9zQDE.

10 Jardine, Alexandra. "The First TV Campaign for Thinx Imagines a World Where Guys Have Periods." *Ad Age*. October 3, 2019. https://adage.com/creativity/work/first-tv-campaign-thinx-imagines-world-where-guys-have-periods/2203976.

11 Barro, Josh. "There's a Simple Reason Companies Are Becoming More Publicly Left-Wing on Social Issues." *Business Insider*. March 1, 2018. https://www.businessinsider.com/why-companies-ditching-nra-delta-selling-guns-2018-2.

hope to be spared higher taxes, increased regulations, and anti-trust legislation aimed at monopolies.

These explanations, while plausible, leave unexplained the promotion of contemporary woke or social justice views by corporations, especially the effects that such promotions may have of making their consumer bases and employees more leftist rather than merely reflecting their existing views, a circumstance they would have to deal with at some point. Arguably, corporations would not espouse and thereby potentially spread political views merely to assuage consumer or political contingents, unless said views aligned with their own interests and especially not if they opposed said interests. One is led, therefore, to wonder what politics would best serve those interests and whether woke capitalism directly represents them.

To benefit global corporate interests, especially monopolies or near monopolies, a political creed would likely promote the free movement of labor and goods across national borders and thus would be internationalist rather than nationalist or nativist. It might seek to produce and promote new niche markets and thus it would benefit from a politics that encourages the continual splintering of identity categories. The global corporate monopolies or would-be monopolies would likely benefit from the creation of utterly new identity types, and thus might welcome and encourage gender pluralism, transgenderism, and other identity morphisms. Emphases on such identity pluralism would also prevent or disrupt the collective bargaining of organized labor. And the disruption of stable gender categories has the potential to erode and eventually contribute to the dismantling of the family, or the last bastion of influence between the social body the state-corporate power. Ultimately, the global capitalist corporation would benefit from a singular globalized governmental monopoly with one set of rules, and thus would promote a borderless internationalism under a global government, otherwise known as one-worldism.

Contemporary woke leftism hastens the dissolution of heretofore stable social ontologies, such as gender identities, the family, social hierarchies, historical memory, inherited culture,

Christianity, and the nation state. It also aims at a one-world monopoly of government. Thus, woke leftist politics align almost perfectly with the global interests of monopolistic corporations. Woke capitalism is the corporate expression of such politics.

The Prototypical Corporate Socialist

Corporate socialism has a fairly long history, with its first formal expressions dating to the late nineteenth century in the U.S. Over a series of surprising and controversial book-length contributions, the late historian and Hoover Institute Fellow Anthony C. Sutton argued that corporate socialists contributed both theoretically and materially to several twentieth-century political economies, including state socialism-communism in Russia and the former Soviet Union,[12] the New Deal in the U.S.,[13] fascism in Italy, and national socialism in Germany.[14] Sutton suggested that corporate socialists provided ideological as well as financial support for the Soviet Union, Italian fascism, Nazi Germany, and the political economy developed under Franklin Delano Roosevelt.

In *Wall Street and FDR*, Sutton discussed businessmen and financiers turned political economists whose books extolled the virtues of corporate socialism and opposed them to the "evils" of the free market.[15] Sutton characterizes these treatises as follows:

> Two themes are common in these Wall Street literary efforts. First, that individualism, individual effort, and individual initiative are out of date and that "destructive" competition, usually termed "blind competition" or "dog-eat-dog com-

---

12 Sutton, Antony C. *Wall Street and the Bolshevik Revolution: The Remarkable True Story of the American Capitalists Who Financed the Russian Communists*. Clairview, 2016.

13 Sutton, Antony C. *Wall Street and FDR: The True Story of How Franklin D. Roosevelt Colluded with Corporate America*. Clairview Books, 2013.

14 Sutton, Antony C. *Wall Street and the Rise of Hitler: The Astonishing True Story of the American Financiers Who Bankrolled the Nazis*. Clairview, 2010.

15 Sutton, *Wall Street and FDR*, Chapters 5 and 6.

petition" is outmoded, unwanted, and destructive of human ideals. Second, we can identify a theme that follows from this attack on individualism and competition to the effect that great advantages accrue from cooperation, that cooperation advances technology, and that cooperation prevents the "wastes of competition." It is then concluded by these financier philosophers that trade associations and ultimately economic planning—in other words, enforced "cooperation"—are a prime objective for responsible and enlightened modern businessmen.[16]

Leading Sutton's list of corporate socialist authors is Frederic Clemson Howe, who published his *Confessions of a Monopolist* in 1906.[17] Sutton took Howe to be the prototypical monopolist and the first to espouse corporate socialism in a book-length treatise, albeit in an autobiography. Yet as I have pointed out elsewhere, Frederic Howe was hardly a monopolist and *Confessions of a Monopolist* was not the autobiography of an actual monopolist but rather a piece of biting satire narrated by a fictional monopolist critical of monopolies and monopolists.[18] Nevertheless, Sutton does cite a handful of actual corporate socialists, authors whom, with Howe, he figures as having provided the theoretical basis of the New Deal. I would add that while they may also be considered to be among the progenitors of contemporary woke capitalism, none is the prototypical corporate socialist, an honor reserved for an earlier woke capitalist. Sutton's corporate socialist tribe includes Max and Paul Warburg, Bernard Baruch, Otto Kahn, Robert S. Brookings, and George W. Perkins.

The writings of these corporate socialist monopolists all sound the same themes: competition is wasteful, destructive,

---

16 Ibid., Chapter 5, section entitled "The Corporate Socialists Argue Their Case."

17 Howe, Frederic C. *Confessions of a Monopolist*. Public Publishing Co.,1906.

18 Rectenwald, Michael. "Libertarianism(s) versus Postmodernism and Social Justice Ideology." *AERC Papers and Proceedings 2019 Quarterly Journal of Austrian Economics*, Vol. 22, No. 2, 2019, pp. 122–138. at p. 131.

and evil; cooperation and planning are humane and essential for human welfare; big businesses have responsibilities to society and are more likely than small businesses to treat labor fairly; and perhaps most importantly, anti-trust laws prohibit necessary "cooperation" and eliminate its benefits.

Sutton either missed or overlooked the businessperson who may have been the first overt advocate of corporate socialist monopolism: King Camp Gillette. The founder of the American Safety Razor Company in 1901 who changed its name to the Gillette Safety Razor Company in 1902, Gillette published three books espousing corporate socialism: *The Human Drift* in 1894, *"World Corporation"* in 1910, and *The People's Corporation* in 1924.[19] He also financed and managed the contents of two others.[20]

Gillette's *Human Drift* railed against competition, which the razorblade maker believed was "the prolific source of ignorance and every form of crime, and that [which] increases the wealth of the few at the expense of the many...the present system of competition between individuals results in fraud, deception, and adulteration of almost every article we eat, drink, or wear."[21] Competition, he continued, resulted in "a waste of material and labor beyond calculation."[22]

Not to be outdone by later corporate socialist competitors, Gillette laid every evil known to man "at the door of this wonderful system of competition." Not only was competition the root of "selfishness, war between nations and individuals, mur-

---

19 Gillette, King Camp. *The Human Drift*. The Humboldt Publishing Company, 1894; Gillette, King Camp. *"World Corporation"*. New England News Company, 1910; Gillette, King Camp. *The People's Corporation*. Boni and Liveright, 1924.

20 Severy, Martin L. *Gillette's Social Redemption: A Review of Worldwide Conditions as They Exist Today Offering An Entirely New Suggestion For the Remedy of the Evils They Exhibit*. Herbert B. Turner & Company, 1907; Severy, Melvin L. *Gillette's Industrial Solution: An Account of The Evolution of The Existing Social System Together with a Presentation of an Entirely New Remedy for the Evils It Exhibits*. The Ball Publishing Company, 1908.

21 Gillette, *Human Drift*, p. 27.

22 Ibid., p. 34.

der, robbery, lying, prostitution, forgery, divorce, deception, brutality, ignorance, injustice, drunkenness, insanity, suicide, and every other crime" but "[b]esides crime, ninety per cent of all sickness is directly attributable to this senseless competition, such sickness being caused by worry, anxiety, and care, forced condition of living in crowded and filthy tenements, insufficient and coarse food, unsuitable and insufficient clothing, and forced condition of overwork and exposure."[23]

One wonders why Gillette ventured to put razorblades in the hands of such desperate people as these suffering under the yoke of dreaded competition. Perhaps his books were meant as preventative medicines meant to keep them from cutting their throats. Meanwhile, Gillette's animadversions against competition may explain the recent Gillette ad;[24] the original woke capitalist company believes that it has finally discovered the root of competition, and thus, of course, of all evil: toxic masculinity.

After inventing the safety razor and founding the company to produce and sell it, Gillette went on to write and publish *"World Corporation,"* in which he extended the "United Company" of *Human Drift* to the globalized "World Corporation"—a worldwide singular monopoly that would undertake all production while serving as a one-world government. As to the capitalist hiatus between his corporate socialist books, as Gillette's biographer put it, "[i]t was almost as if Karl Marx had paused between *The Communist Manifesto* and *Das Kapital* to develop a dissolving toothbrush or collapsible comb."[25]

In fact, despite their utterly different backgrounds and antithetical relationships to capital, Marx and Gillette both proposed thoroughgoing socialist systems, differing only in terms of the means of attaining them—political versus commercial, respectively. The two also had different attitudes toward capital and capitalists. Marx evinced a particular antipathy for the

---

23 Ibid., p. 35.

24 Gillette. 2019. "We Believe: The Best Men Can Be." *YouTube*. Accessed March 22, 2019. https://www.youtube.com/watch?v=koPmuEyP3a0.

25 Adams, Russell B. *King C. Gillette: The Man and His Wonderful Shaving Device*. Little, Brown, 1978, pp. 13-14.

bourgeoisie, while arguably entertaining aristocratic pretentions. Although he did earn money as a freelance journalist for
the *New York Tribune*, Marx owed whatever economic independence he enjoyed to the largesse of another businessman, the
factory owner Friedrich Engels, who served as both patron and
collaborator. One wonders whether, given the chance, Marx
could have rationalized a collaboration with someone like Gillette? Quite possibly, although Gillette's corporate socialism had
not yet fully emerged while Marx was alive.

While Gillette never mentioned Marx or Marxism in his
writing, passages in "World Corporation" closely echo the
Marxist understanding of history as class struggle:

> If you analyze the history of nations, you will find, no mat-
> ter what their form of government, all were internally di-
> vided into two distinct classes, Rich and Poor, Masters and
> Slaves...[26]

Like Marx, Gillette believed that the fundamental "opposition" between owners and servants must inevitably be resolved.
For Marx, the "contradiction" would be overcome with "the ex-
propriation of a few usurpers by the mass of the people"[27]—that
is, the "taking back" of all productive property from the capitalist class by the dispossessed. For Gillette, it would be surpassed
through the process of capitalist incorporation itself. Like Marx,
Gillette believed that capital accumulation tended inexorably
toward conglomeration and monopoly. The answer for Gillette
was to establish a "world corporation" and offer stockholding
to the masses, along with the continuous buying out of large
stockholders, until all stock was held in equal shares by the denizens of the world. The process would end in socialism:

> CORPORATIONS WILL CONTINUE TO FORM, ABSORB,
> EXPAND, AND GROW, AND NO POWER OF MAN CAN
> PREVENT IT. Promoters [of incorporation] are the true so-

---

26 Gillette, *"World Corporation"*, p. 102.

27 Marx, Karl. *Capital: Critique of Political Economy*. The Modern Library.
Vol. 1., p. 837.

cialists of this generation, the actual builders of a co-operative system which is eliminating competition, and in a practical business way reaching results which socialists have vainly tried to attain through legislation and agitation for centuries. To complete the industrial evolution, and establish a system of equity, only requires a belief in the truths herein stated— and the support of "WORLD CORPORATION."[28]

Just as Marx believed that socialism would eventually follow from capitalism, so too did Gillette hold that the socialization of the factors of production was inevitable. In fact, for both, such socialization of production had already been accomplished. The only problem remaining was ownership and control. For Gillette, the emergence of socialism depended not on the political organization of the working masses, as it did for Marx, but rather on the commercial organization of incorporation—the continual growth of corporations, and the mergers, acquisitions, and final subsuming of all commercial interests by a single corporate monopoly, eventually owned by "the People":

> Opposition to "WORLD CORPORATION" by individuals, by states, or by governments will be of no avail. Opposition in any case can only be of temporary effect, barriers will only centralize power and cause increased momentum when they give way.[29]

While clearly Gillette's World Corporation did not come to pass as such, his business practices did benefit from monopolistic tendencies. Gillette regularly took advantage of patents, and in 1917, with the outbreak of World War I, the company provided every soldier with a shaving kit, paid for by the U.S. government.

The Gillette Safety Razor Company may also be one of the first if not the first companies to have engaged in woke advertising. A 1905 full-color 3.5-by-5.5-inch postcard advertisement featured a "cherubic, beaming infant holding a razor, his face

---

28 Gillette, *"World Corporation"*, p. 9, emphasis in original.
29 Ibid., p. 62.

half-covered with shaving cream."[30]

Begin Early, Shave Yourself, Gillette Safety Razor, No Stropping No Honing

The text at the top of the postcard exhorted the shaver to "Begin Early, Shave Yourself." The ad subtly proposed a new kind of manhood (surprise!), in effect suggesting that "a man's personal freedom was compromised by the need to pay another man to shave him. At the same time, shaving could become a more telling expression of personal values if a man was potentially *responsible for shaving himself*."[31] Shaving oneself became an exhibition of self-reliance and freedom but more importantly for the Gillette company, the lesson was that from infancy on, men take care of themselves rather than putting the burden on their fellow men and, in short, reducing them to a kind of slavery.

Conclusion

The foregoing discussion certainly should convince the reader of the existence corporate socialism, at least as it was developed theoretically. It is important to note that corporate socialism has come closer to fruition than the theoretical socialism-communism developed by Marx. That's because the latter maintains private property in the factors of production—at least until their ownership is completely subsumed by "the people," which never happens. Today, woke capitalism uses socialist and social justice ideology to promote the kind of top-tier monopolization of production with the promise of "equality" for everyone else common to both "actually-existing" Marxist and corporate socialism.

CHAPTER NINETEEN

This Is the Big Reason Corporate America Has Gone Woke (plus 4 more)[1]

W HY HAVE THE BIGGEST and most profitable American corporations embraced leftist politics, as seen in their woke advertising and social justice activism? Hint: It's not because they've become non-profits and taken up philanthropy.

Judging by the Ted Talks of woke American CEOs, by the woke corporate advertising, and by the public relations campaigns promoting corporate "brand activism,"[2] one might reasonably conclude that the most successful, for-profit corporate giants in America have gone out of the money-making business to become centers of leftist political propaganda. And it's not only the most woke corporate behemoths that promote leftist political notions.[3] Go to a startup crowdfunding portal and

---

1 First published by *RT.com*. November 17, 2019.

2 Litsa, Tereza. "Brand Activism: Why More Campaigns Focus on Social Good." *ClickZ*. September 17, 2019. https://www.clickz.com/brand-activism-campaigns-focus-social-good/207888/.

3 Morefield, Scott. "America's Wokest Companies, And What They're Paying Their CEOs." *Townhall*, Townhall.com. August 10, 2019. https://townhall.com/columnists/scottmorefield/2019/08/10/americas-wokest-companies-and-what-theyre-paying-their-ceos-n2551464.

count how many times the word "democratizing" is used to describe the mission of the startups there, or how many startup investments are pitched with the supposedly progressive political outlook of the prospective investor in mind.[4]

What one encounters—from the boardrooms to the storyboards and beyond—is a nauseating, woke-up blend of equal parts Communist Manifesto, social justice handbook,[5] sanctimonious sermon, and used car sales pitch.

Just why has corporate America gone woke (while not yet broke)? Below, I run-down some of the possible explanations for woke capitalism or corporate leftism—from five to one—with five being the least compelling and one being the most:

5. The bosses are woke themselves. CEOs and other corporate executives went to business schools that weren't that far away from social science and humanities departments. Business professors became friends with humanities and social science professors, who are notoriously left leaning. Their leftism rubbed off on the business professors, who then spread it to their students, who went on to run corporate America.

4. To pander to their clients. Corporate leftism pleases the corporate customers with the most disposable income, those between 25 and 54, who likely live on the east and west coasts. This demographic includes millennials, whose politics are notoriously left leaning. Choosing these "coastal elites" over the deplorables in "flyover states" has been an easy decision. The deplorables have less money anyway and they can go to hell if they don't like corporate wokeness.

3. Being woke is easier than actually paying workers. Corporate wokeness acts as a placebo, a substitute for economic concessions by corporations. The statements of woke CEOs, the woke ads, the woke activism—these cost a lot less than higher wages and better benefits for workers, or lower prices for customers. Plus, the dummies seem to fall for it every time.

---

4 "Startup Investment Opportunities." *Republic*. https://republic.co/companies.

5 Cannon, Mae Elise. *Social Justice Handbook: Small Steps for a Better World*. IVP Books, 2009.

2. To keep the government wolf from the door. Woke capitalism appeases the political elite, putting corporations in the good favor of liberal lawmakers, in the hopes of favorable treatment from the latter. As liberals, these political operatives are more likely to impose burdensome regulations or to initiate anti-trust legislation that would pose big problems. Why not tell them what they want to hear?

1. Wokeness is itself part of globalist capitalism. Leftist politics are perfectly compatible with and supportive of the agendas of global corporate giants. Global corporations and leftist activists want the very same things:

• Globalism—or, in Marxist terms, "internationalism"— has always been a goal of the left and it has become a goal of multinational corporations. The latter extend their markets far and wide while the former think it advances the Marxist objective of "workers of the world unite!"

• Unrestricted immigration: Provides cheap labor for corporations and makes leftists feel politically edgy and morally superior for being anti-racists who welcome everyone—whatever their race, religion, gender or sexual orientation—including Mexican gang members running drugs and children?—into the country, but not to camp out in their living rooms.

• Transgenderism or polygenderism, the leading edge of leftist identity politics, is also good for business. It creates new niche markets for corporate products, keeps the workforce divided, and distracts leftists with daily arcana and absurdities.

• Getting rid of nations, stable gender, the family, Western culture and (why not?) Christianity—the hallmarks of leftist "progress" and avant-garde politicking—also advances global corporatist objectives, removing any remaining obstacles to global corporate dominance.

CHAPTER TWENTY

What is the *"Point de Capiton"* of Leftist Ideology?

"[I]t takes a great ideal to produce a great crime.'
—Martin Malia, *The Soviet Tragedy*

IDEOLOGY INCLUDES creedal commitments and narrative elements that vary depending on the ideology in question—as well as cognition-framing templates, or if you prefer matrix metaphors, consciousness-structuring codes. Some argue that the *sine qua non* of ideology is an organizing central element, the kernel around which the elements of ideology coalesce and are assembled into a whole.

In *The Sublime Object of Ideology*,[1] the Slovenian Marxist and Lacanian psychoanalytic theorist Slavoj Žižek, following the French psychoanalytic theorist Jacques Lacan, calls the central, organizing element *le point de capiton*, or the "quilting point," the "anchoring point," the element that holds an ideology together and around which a consistent perspective can be maintained.

To use a computing analogy, one might also think of this central organizing element as the .exe (Windows) or .app (Mac) file of a computer program—in the sense that the .exe or .app

---

1 Žižek, Slavoj. *The Sublime Object of Ideology*. Verso, 2019.

file, when activated, causes the elements of the program to run and the program to undertake other tasks, such as compiling new files from user inputs (like the program compiling this essay). The .exe or .app file is not analogous to the ideology itself. Rather, it enables ideology; ideology is analogous to the processes potentiated by the .exe or .app file.

Extending the computer analogy, we might understand the appearance of ideology in consciousness—that is, ideology as represented to the subject of ideology—in terms of the computer monitor or screen—the consciousness of the person experiencing and (re)producing the ideology and at once the one rendering to itself as visible a representation of the code behind or under the screen (the "real" computer and its operations, or reality), including a representation of the self-in-world. That is, as the computer screen makes visible and legible the real of computer code and its underlying operations, so ideology makes visible and legible the real of the world.

This is not to say, as postmodern theorists have suggested, that the world is a "social construct," simply the product of a society that co-produces and perceives it according to an implicit consensus—a radical philosophical and social idealism if there ever was one. Rather, ideology makes the real visible and legible to the subject as such—in a way that is characteristic of the particular ideology. Reality isn't constructed by ideology either *ex nihilo*, nor out of our collective (or individual) mind(s)—although those who hold such a view may be out of theirs.

Žižek insists as well on the role of ideology in representing the relationship between the visible and the invisible. My analogy accounts for that too. To most contemporary computer users, the underlying code remains invisible. Only Neo and computer programmers can see the code. (No, that doesn't make computer programmers immune to ideology—although Neo is. This is only an analogy.)

Žižek and others who treat ideology as an object of study make sure to insist that any particular ideology isn't merely one among other distortions of reality and that once these distortions are removed, one can finally arrive at a non-ideological,

reality-only construal. One cannot eliminate ideology, or ideologies, one by one, or all at once, to arrive at an undistorted
reality, the real. According to Žižek and many others, every
construal is ideological.

Given such an admission—and Žižek's view is by no means
singular among those who make ideology an object of study—
one might not expect that right-wing, conservative, libertarian,
and other non-leftist ideologies would be the only ideologies
worthy of analysis or exclusively subject to critique. One might
expect that leftist ideologies would be examined as well—and
on the same grounds and in the same terms as non-leftist ideologies.

But one would be wrong. One would be hard-pressed to
find such critical treatments of leftist ideology in academic
scholarship. After much searching, I have yet to find a single
mention of leftist ideology in connection with *le point de capiton* or ideological critique in general—as if leftist ideology is
somehow exempt from this supposedly "central" and "essential"
feature of all ideology, and its other features as well. As if leftist
ideology wasn't ... ideology.

Further, given the (debatable) belief that a non-ideological
position is impossible, we shouldn't expect to find conservative, libertarian, liberal, or other non-left ideologies treated as if
they were disorders, disruptions of the norm, social epidemics,
or the outbreaks of illnesses. But this is almost invariably how
non-leftist ideologies are represented in academic ideology critiques.

Why is this the case? I do not believe that the preponder-
ance of leftists in the social sciences and humanities is sufficient
to explain the asymmetrical treatment of ideology in the academy. It may be a necessary, but not a sufficient cause. Rather,
to understand the absence of critiques of leftist ideology by
academics, one should look to the signified in the critiques of
rightwing ideology—and especially at the characterizations of
the same in terms of disease, pestilence, sanitation, virus, and
so on and so forth. Although disease is no longer regarded in
moral terms (exceptions and contradictions exist, of course),

as Michel Foucault made manifest, the association of disease, especially infectious disease, with moral inferiority, deformity, and depravity has a long history and persists residually within modern (or if you're postmodern, postmodern) consciousness. Thus, the exclusive study of right-wing, conservative, libertarian, and other non-leftist ideology is explicable in terms of a moral distinction.

Rightist ideology is studied because it is "problematic," politically and morally evil. Leftist ideology is not examined because leftism purportedly poses no danger; it is not pernicious and is nothing to be concerned about. By default, the standard leftist regards leftist ideology as benign but also as obviously beneficial. The probity of leftist ideology is taken for granted. Leftist ideology is on "the right side of history." The implication is clear. Leftists do not believe that leftist ideology is ideological at all.

∗ ∗ ∗

This brings me to the ultimate question of this essay. Since, according to Žižek and others, a non-ideological perspective is impossible, and, as *le point de capiton* is the "kernel" of ideology, what is *le point de capiton* of leftist ideology, generally considered? That is, what is the common organizing principle of leftist ideologies?

But first, please don't admonish me by telling me that my category—"leftist ideology"—is too broad, unsophisticated, and meaningless. Academics regularly use such categories—only applied to their ideological others. The use of such phrases as "the right-wing," "right-wingers," and "right-wing ideology" is routine in academic scholarship. I've never seen any such usage criticized by another academic. So, to be symmetrical, academic leftists must permit my usage.

Yet, they will continue to object. How, and on what grounds? The answer goes straight to the heart of the matter and reveals *le point de capiton* of leftist ideology.

Intrinsic to leftist ideology is precisely the notion that no symmetry between right and left can be permitted—on the basis of the probity of leftist ideology and its obvious and indisputable political and moral superiority to rightist ideology. This should go without explanation, they think. And it does.

That is, *le point de capiton* of leftist ideology is the belief in its own, unique moral superiority and ultimate innocence.

How is this belief manifest? For one, leftist ideology presents itself—to itself and to others—as the default no-fault political belief system. While the crimes of right-wing political villainy are kept in circulation and replayed regularly—in classrooms, the media, casual conversation, and so on and so forth—the left's political crimes are swept under the carpet, ignored, or justified. Yes, in passing, once in a blue moon, someone—and maybe even a leftist critic undertaking an internalist critique—will acknowledge the 94 million murdered by communist regimes, or the eugenicist ideology of the U.S. Progressive Party—for example!

But the proponents of leftist ideology rarely bemoan these crimes. Very few on the right ever refer to them while protesting (and they don't protest much). Few, if any, of whatever political persuasion, do more than merely acknowledge them in passing and as if such criminality clearly had been the exception—or, presumably, due to a tacit acknowledgment of the purported noble ends—the specter of utopia as some have written—these crimes had been excused as if by divine dispensation, and ultimately amount to innocence. Believers in leftist ideology are the predestinarians—and the predestined—of the secular world.

I write as a former left communist of fifteen years, and by no means a right-winger or conservative. If you must label me, the most accurate political moniker would be "ex-leftist." If you demand more specificity—so that you can find a way to indict me—you may call me a "civil libertarian." Feel better?

How has the left apparently gotten away with the political criminality of its murderous past, you ask? You don't. That is, you don't ask. The answer is "beyond the scope of this essay." But a good start may be found in the foreword to *The Black Book of Communism* —you know, that piece of bourgeois propaganda with documentary evidence to support every substantive and numerical claim it makes. And then of course there is the lingering, but ever-receding, specter of utopia.

CHAPTER TWENTY-ONE

Google Marxism: Internet Ideology & the Academics Who Perpetuate It[1]

"**B**IG DIGITAL" consists of an array of business, political, and social interests, an ensemble of technology companies and Internet services, including but not limited to the Big Four: Alphabet (Google, YouTube, etc.) Amazon, Apple, and Facebook. Big Digital wields enormous economic and political power, presiding over Big Data, and serving as the chief arbiter of expression, with the power to effect the digital deletion of "dangerous" persons from its various platforms, as the gulag was the means to physically disappear dissidents and other thought criminals from "normal" life in the Soviet Union.[2]

In my book, *The Google Archipelago*, I recall the gulag archipelago of Alexander Solzhenitsyn's literary masterpiece, while referring to a singular system of interconnected digital producers or "islands." In comparing Google and the Gulag, each with its own set of archipelagos, I don't mean to suggest

---

1 Presented as the opening lecture of the Libertarian Scholars Conference hosted by the Mises Institute. Kings College, New York, NY. September 28, 2019.

2 Nolan, Lucas. "Facebook Falsely Brands Non-Violent Users 'Dangerous' to Justify Un-Personing." *Breitbart News*. May 3, 2019. https://www.breitbart. com/tech/2019/05/03/facebook-falsely-brands-non-violent-users-dangerous-to-justify-un-personing/.

that Google, an emblem for the digital giants of Big Data, and the Gulag, a massive prison system of the Soviet Union, can be understood as equally punitive or horrific. One was a vast network of arbitrary, brutal, elaborate, and tortuous penal camps "and special settlements...turned into an organized system of terror and exploitation of forced labor."[3] The other is a vast constellation of digital giants with enormous economic and governmental power, but no physical torture, incarceration, forced labor, or immediate prospects of facing a firing squad.

Yet, I certainly do mean to draw an analogy. As the Gulag Archipelago had once represented the most developed set of technological apparatuses for disciplinary and governmental power and control in the world, so the Google Archipelago represents the contemporary equivalent of these capacities, only considerably less corporeal in character to date, yet immeasurably magnified, diversified, and extended in scope.

The principals of what I call Big Digital—the purveyors of mega-data services, media, cable, and internet services, social media platforms, Artificial Intelligence (AI) agents, apps, and the developing Internet of Things (or Things of the Internet, as I describe the relation in what follows) are not only monopolies or would-be monopolies but also will either continue to be incorporated by the state, or become elements of a new corporate state power.

Even if only augmentations of existing state power, the apparatuses of Big Digital combine to produce the Google Archipelago, which stands to effect such an enormous sea change in governmental and economic power—inclusive of greatly enhanced and extended capabilities for supervision, surveillance, recording, tracking, facial-recognition, robot-swarming, monitoring, corralling, social-scoring, trammeling, punishing, ostracizing, un-personing or otherwise controlling populations to such an extent—that the non-corporal-punishment aspect of the Google Archipelago will come to be recognized as much

---

3 Khlevniuk, Oleg V. *The History of the Gulag: From Collectivization to the Great Terror*. Stalin Digital Archive. New Haven: Yale University Press, p. 10. Stalin Digital Archive. Web. June 1, 2019.

less significant than its total political impact.

In particular, the Google Archipelago is guided by a left authoritarianism. The significance of this corporate leftist authoritarianism will soon be made clear.

Given this characterization of the Google Archipelago, which is supported by evidence provided in my book, non-academics with a fervid or even modest interest in the phenomenon of Big Digital would find the academic digital media scholarship as akin to the scholasticism of monks quibbling about minor points of theology during the Inquisition. As for me, I knew the literature fairly well when I set out to write Google Archipelago, having taught digital media for fifteen years. The academic digital media scholars, whom I call "the digitalistas," are so blinkered by Marxist and "post-Marxist" approaches that they miss the most salient feature of the field they study—namely, its sharp and dangerous turn toward authoritarian leftism. This is an unfortunate circumstance because the problem with the Internet is leftist authoritarianism, of which Marxism is the main variety.

While one can find nary an academic article treating the blatant double standard of Big Digital in favor of leftists and liberal-leftists, the digitalistas jockey for position to proffer the most novel and anti-capitalist interpretations of the digital sphere. Scholars must find surreptitious surplus value extraction under every digital rock. The denizens of the Internet, or "netizens," are treated as "super-exploited" unpaid workers within a system of "digital capitalism." The digitalistas descry a super-exploitive and pernicious "digital capitalism," almost exclusively aiming to offer the best leftist explanation of the field. The greatest crime as the digitalistas see it involves facilitating and extending "neoliberalism" via the extraction of "free labor" from unwary netizens.

The digitalistas and other leftists see so-called "neoliberalism" as a kind of stealth campaign underwritten by anti-statist economists whose aim has always been the transfer of public goods and services into private hands, preferably at bargain-basement prices. As public services—like schools, fire

departments, the police department, and the highway system—
the tragedy of digital spaces is their commodification, another
sign that the capitalist order is asymptotically approaching the
libertarian's dream, and the socialist's nightmare, of complete
privatization.

Drawing on Alvin Toffler's notion of the "prosumer," a hy-
brid producer-consumer who supposedly labors, without pay,
while consuming, the digitalistas bemoan the transformation
of the digital commons into a digital labor camp. As they see it,
web searching amounts to exploited labor; the digital giants ex-
tract surplus value from the hapless web surfer, who mistakenly
thought that he, she, or ze was having a good time, only to have
his, her, or zir search histories sold. Of course, the validity of
the labor theory of value (LTV) on which "exploitation" rests is
mostly unexamined in these studies. If it is scrutinized, the LTV
is only amiss where the digital realm is concerned, and a new
basis for exploitation, such as "affective investments," is found.

According to the digitalistas, when users open Facebook
accounts, the "dumb fucks," as Mark Zuckerberg once referred
to his subscribers,[4] freely divulge valuable demographic information that Facebook then sells as data to advertisers. As such,
they are exploited. When they post status updates or comment
on the statuses of others, Facebook users produce, without pay,
the content that Facebook sells to advertisers, which means
they are exploited again. When conducting web searches, the
hapless and unwitting unwaged slave laborers of digital capitalism produce data that Google sells to advertisers jockeying
for ranking position—exploitation![5] With almost every online
activity, "[a] form of labor exploitation therefore occurs, albeit
one based on voluntary and noncoerced acts of labor."[6] Or, as

4 Vargas, Jose Antonio. "The Face of Facebook: Mark Zuckerberg Opens
Up." *The New Yorker*. September 13, 2010. https://www.newyorker.com/mag-
azine/2010/09/20/the-face-of-facebook.

5 Fuchs, "Google Capitalism;" Mager, Astrid. "Defining Algorithmic
Ideology: Using Ideology Critique to Scrutinize Corporate Search Engines."
*TripleC: Communication, Capitalism & Critique. Open Access Journal for a
Global Sustainable Information Society*, Vol. 12, No. 1, 2014, pp. 28–39.

6 Roberts, John Michael. "Co-Creative Prosumer Labor, Financial Knowl-

my favorite horror storyteller of the left, Michel Foucault puts it, albeit in the context of internalized surveillance, the unpaid digital laborer "becomes the principle of his own subjection."[7]

If you think that my characterization of digitalista Marxism is exaggerated, have a peek at an essay entitled "Capitalism, Patriarchy, Slavery, and Racism in the Age of Digital Capitalism and Digital Labour," by the Marxiest of all digitalistas, Christian Fuchs. In his essay, Fuchs draws parallels—although admitting differences—between four forms of unpaid labor, three of which are "productive"—meaning that they produce commodities for sale on the market. These include housework, reproductive labor, slavery, and posting on Facebook. The following two passages are by no means ripped out of context, and therefore my quotations do not "enact violence upon the text" (nor, I should hope, on the reader):

> Slave-labour, reproductive labour and unpaid Facebook labour have in common that they are unwaged, but by being integrated into capitalist society nonetheless they create surplus-value.[8]

> Whereas the wage-worker has a contractual and legally enforceable right to be paid a wage for the performed labour, slaves, houseworkers and Facebook workers do not have such a right, which enables their exploitation as unpaid workers.[9]

Mind you, by "Facebook workers," Fuchs means anyone who uses Facebook. That includes me, for one.

The capture of data as a result of the "labor" of web surfers is hardly the horror show that the digitalistas make it out to be.

---

edge Capitalism, and Marxist Value Theory." *The Information Society*, Vol. 32, No. 1, 2015, pp. 28–39; p. 28.

7 Foucault, Michel. *Discipline and Punish: The Birth of the Prison*. Vintage Books, 1995, p. 203.

8 Fuchs, Christian. "Capitalism, Patriarchy, Slavery, and Racism in the Age of Digital Capitalism and Digital Labour." *Critical Sociology*, Vol. 44, No. 4-5, 2017, pp. 677–702; p. 681.

9 Ibid., p. 692.

I've known dozens if not hundreds of Marxists who regularly spent ten to twelve hours a day complaining on Facebook about their exploitation as part of the working class. If their Facebook statuses contributed to the environment for ad sales, this hardly strikes reasonable people as a matter of grave concern. On the other hand, if the Google Archipelago does involve a partial privatization of state functions, then the most troubling aspect is not the smaller size of the state or the loss of state services but the flip side—*the governmentalization of private enterprise.* As an appendage of the state, if not, in fact, acting as surrogate for it, the Google Archipelago also involves the *expansion and magnification of state power.* The digital constellation increases the state's capacity for surveillance, information control, censorship, and the banishment or un-personing of *personae non gratae.*

Since leftist ideology is dominant in academia and the Internet, academic and other leftists cannot see the leftist authoritarianism in their object of study, any more than they can see it in their very midst. Their ideology is as invisible to them as the air they breathe, and thus they are unaware of its function. So, I remind them of what the French structuralist Marxist Louis Althusser argued in "Ideology and Ideological State Apparatuses"—captives of ideology are never able to recognize their own ideological convictions as ideological:

> ...what thus seems to take place outside ideology (to be precise, in the street), in reality takes place in ideology. What really takes place in ideology seems therefore to take place outside it. That is why those who are in ideology believe themselves by definition outside ideology ...ideology never says, 'I am ideological'.[10]

This allows the ideology to exert its power. If they were able to recognize their own perspective as ideological, they would

---

10   Althusser, Louis. "Ideology and Ideological State Apparatuses (Notes towards an Investigation)." *Ideology and Ideological State Apparatuses* by Louis Althusser 1969-70. https://www.marxists.org/reference/archive/althuss¬er/1970/ideology.htm.

thereby elude ideology. But since the victims of authoritarianism are their political enemies, the digitalistas appear to be unconcerned, as the Google Archipelago hastens the disappearance of places to exercise the right of free speech. Ironically, the disappearance of so-called "public space" was once a major concern of academic leftist media scholars. Even the phrase used to describe public space, "the commons," is a political, leftist metaphor that in the early days of the Internet was bandied about as the utopian ideal. But under the spell of ideology, the digitalistas miss the main features of the digital zeitgeist.

As such, the digitalistas produce decoys, false criticisms, and simulated radical critiques of the Google Archipelago. They substitute oppositional posturing and attempt to preclude other, more comprehensive explanations of the Google Archipelago. By suggesting that the problem is "capitalism"—which necessarily must be countered by some form of "socialism"—the digitalistas aim to appear as the ultimate radicals. Meanwhile, their scholarship serves precisely to obscure the authoritarian leftism of the Google Archipelago. Contrary to their self-conceptions, the digitalistas are ideologues. They are ideological appendages of the system itself. They serve, rather than undermine, the digital empire.

But what is the relationship between their political ideology and the monopolistic objectives of the Google Archipelago? And why is it important that the political ideology of the Google Archipelago is leftist and authoritarian? Finally, why do I call this political ideology Google Marxism? I address these questions next.

The Making, Manipulation, and Diversion of Digital Hive Minds

Much has been made of Google's historical ties to U.S. intelligence community (IC) and military research agencies. In the 1990s, the IC saw the Internet as an unprecedented source for harvesting actionable intelligence, while military research agencies recognized its potential for new data-driven warfare systems.[11] With only their human-based methods, the IC could not approach let alone make sense of the mass of data generated on the Internet.

Cultivating the information age from its infancy, the IC and military agencies invested in university research and entrepreneurial innovation to achieve their ends. Faced with an otherwise unintelligible dross of data, they farmed-out the information gathering and analysis of intelligence work, and the information warfare aspects of military strategy, to the advanced developers of information systems in and around Stanford and the wider Silicon Valley.

The Manhattan Project, satellite technology, the aeronautics industry, and the Internet were earlier examples of such collaborations. In fact, as David Shumway points out, although "[m]any people think that the dependence of the university on government and private support for research emerged only in the wake of World War II and the Cold War, … the dependence on external research funding began in earnest during World War I."[12] Yet prospects for Internet surveillance certainly foments distrust.[13] The Joint Enterprise Defense Initiative (JEDI) will prove no less collaborative.[14]

Ironically, those most likely to protest collaboration between state, corporate, and research institutions—namely, leftists—have been rendered inert by Big Digital, which agglom-

11 Ahmed, Nafeez. "How the CIA Made Google - INSURGE Intelligence." *Medium, INSURGE Intelligence.* November 13, 2015. https://medium.com/insurge-intelligence/how-the-cia-made-google-e836451a959e; Nesbit, Jeff, and Jeff Nesbit. "Google's True Origin Partly Lies in CIA and NSA Research Grants for Mass Surveillance." *Quartz,* Quartz. December 8, 2017. https://qz.com/1145669/googles-true-origin-partly-lies-in-cia-and-nsa-research-grants-for-mass-surveillance//.

12 Shumway, David. "The University, Neoliberalism, and the Humanities: A History." *Humanities,* Vol. 6, No. 4, 2017, pp. 83–92.

13 Ibid; Ahmed, Nafeez. "How the CIA Made Google."

14 [A] cloud computing platform that will eventually run much of the Pentagon's digital infrastructure—from data storage to image analytics to the translation of intercepted phone calls." Silverman, Jacob. "Tech's Military Dilemma." *The New Republic.* August 7, 2018. https://newrepublic.com/article/148870/techs-military-dilemma-silicon-valley.

erates and folds them into complicit and politically quiescent collectives. Big Digital has wooed and won over an otherwise obstreperous and oppositional political contingent by massifying and encouraging their group-self-conscious identification and constantly reflecting their values back to them. As if by Pavlovian conditioning, when leftists participate in a collective, they associate their participation with activism. Big Digital deceives the left into believing that it is engaging in activism, precisely as it plays the part of enthusiastic and unwitting shill for the agenda of the corporate, globalist, monopolist corporation. Jaron Lanier's term, "Digital Maoism," points to the resemblance between Maoist Cultural Revolutionary collectivism and the combined effects of digitalization and contemporary collectivism. But the leftism of the Google Archipelago is not only carried by humanoid leftists; it is functionally embedded within a whole spectrum of applications and features—including the structure of the Internet as such, the cloud, search engine algorithms, search result stacking software, web navigation tracking software, and many other applications. If or when leftist bias is not directly embedded in the software, it is superimposed by humanoid agents. And the sentinels of surveillance and control that populate social media sites, while not technologies or bots *per se*, may as well be; they act as predictably as any technology.

Collectivism is so central to leftism that I have sometimes wondered whether it represents the true end, rather than merely the means, of leftist politics. That is, rather than a means for applying mass political pressure to achieve particular goals, what if collectivism itself is the ultimate goal? If the true goal of leftism is collectivism, then collectivism may be an adaptive function developed for the protection of individuals who feel overpowered by dominant opponents.

The left derides anything standoffish or singular. Even Jaron Lanier's reference to a singular "hive mind" drew the ire of critics, who insisted that there are many and sundry hive minds.[15]

---

15 Tumlin, Markel, et al. "Collectivism vs. Individualism in a Wiki World: Librarians Respond to Jaron Laniers Essay 'Digital Maoism: The Hazards of the New Online Collectivism.'" *Serials Review*, Vol. 33, No. 1, 2007, pp.

But Lanier's point was not that there can be only one hive mind but rather that all hive minds, regardless of their differences, share the same set of hive-mind traits. The primary trait of the hive mind is group-self-consciousness. "We don't have to think, therefore we are right" is the collectivist equivalent of Cartesian self-affirmation.

As The People Who Know Everything, Google and YouTube must have a good reason for their exclusive policing of "right-wing extremism." It is likely one of the many tactics for building a massified constituency. YouTube's blogs and policies about eliminating "hate speech," for example, practically equate all hate speech with expressions of "supremacy."[16] While this may suggest a blissful ignorance of history—that four times as many innocent people have been killed in the name of "equality" than in the name of "supremacy"—one shouldn't discount the digital giants' omniscience. Certainly, the YouTube and Google hive mind knows.

But how is such asymmetry rationalized? What is the tacit explanation? Rightist ideology is policed because it is deemed "problematic" (politically and thus morally evil). Leftist ideology, on the other hand, is given a free pass because it obviously poses no danger. YouTube and other Big Digital principals represent leftism—to themselves and their constituencies—as the default no-fault political belief system. While the crimes of right-wing political villainy are kept in circulation and regularly denounced, the left's political crimes, despite its much larger number of victims, are swept under the carpet, ignored, or justified. YouTube regards leftist ideology not merely as obviously benign but also naturally beneficial. The probity of leftism is taken for granted. Leftists are on "the right side of history," even though their historical crimes are unparalleled.

What is accomplished by such whitewashing of leftism? In addition to producing and cementing its digital hive-minded

45–53.

16 "Our Ongoing Work to Tackle Hate." *Official YouTube Blog*. June 5, 2019. https://youtube.googleblog.com/2019/06/our-ongoing-work-to-tackle-hate. html.

collectives, by disappearing leftist criminality, Big Digital eludes criticism of its own authoritarian leftism. As I showed in a paper delivered at the Mises Institute in March of 2019,[17] just as the founder of the Gillette Razor Company, King Camp Gillette, couched his megalomania and dictatorial ambitions in a rhetoric of equality and altruism, so Big Digital's leftism has provided a mantle of virtue, transparent to some, to mask its dictatorial practices. As such, the principals of Big Digital have managed to divert attention and deflect criticism from their global monopolist and governmental ambitions.

Corporate Leftism

To benefit global monopolistic corporations, a political creed would likely promote the free movement of labor and goods across national borders and thus would be internationalist rather than nationalist or nativist. It might seek to produce and promote new niche markets and thus it would benefit from a politics that encourages the continual splintering of identity categories. Such splintering would also prevent or disrupt the collective bargaining of organized labor. The global capitalist corporation might benefit from the creation of utterly new identity types, and thus benefit from gender pluralism, transgenderism, and other identity morphisms. The disruption of stable gender categories will eventually dismantle the family, the last bastion of influence other than the state and major monopolistic powers. Ultimately, the global monopolistic corporation would benefit from a singular globalized monopoly of government with one set of rules, and thus would promote internationalism, otherwise known as global government or one-worldism. Meanwhile, contemporary leftism aims at the dissolution of heretofore stable social ontologies, such as gender identities, the family, social hierarchies, historical memory, inherited culture, Christianity, and the nation state. It aims at

---

17 Rectenwald, Michael. "Libertarianism(s) versus Postmodernism and 'Social Justice' Ideology." *Ludwig von Mises Memorial Lecture*. The Mises Institute. March 22, 2019. Published in The Quarterly Journal of Austrian Economics, Vol. 22, No. 2, Summer 2019, pp. 122-138.

a one-world monopoly of government. Thus, the politics that most closely aligns with the worldwide, global interests of monopolistic corporations is contemporary leftwing politics. The corporate adoption of leftist politics may be called "corporate leftism."[18]

Like "woke capitalism," corporate leftism—the leftism of corporations—will strike readers as an oxymoron. Leftism may seem entirely incompatible with corporate capitalism, especially given their historical relationship. Yet, the evidence of the corporate embrace and promotion of contemporary leftism, both past and present, is extensive.

Corporate leftism is a major feature of Big Digital. It is deeply embedded in the ethos and technologies of Big Digital, and has been for decades. Although Big Digital began as a sideshow, it has since taken centerstage and now presides over public and private life to such an extent that it rivals, if it doesn't surpass, the reach and apparent penetration of many governments combined. Big Digital effectively operates as what postmodern theorist Michel Foucault called a "governmentality," a means of governing the conduct of populations but also the technologies of governance and the rationality that underpins the technologies.[19] In the broadest sense, Big Digital is concerned with the collection and control of information, personal expression and its containment, and "privacy." But the governmentality of Big Digital also includes the "directing, constraining and framing [of] online behaviours."[20]

---

18 The first and one of the few uses of the phrase "corporate leftism" appeared in a *Time* article that ironically referred to the corporate leftism of Coors Brewing Co. The corporate leftism of the notoriously conservative company is explained as a public relations response to "its bad reputation with minorities and unions [that] nearly devastated Coors in the early 1980s" as well as "'changing expectations of a work force whose demographics have changed…'" (Cloud, John. "Why Coors Went Soft." *Time*. November 21, 1998, p. 70).

19 Michel Foucault introduced the term "governmentality" in a series of lectures from 1977 to 1979. By the rationality underpinning technologies of governance, Foucault meant the way that power rationalizes the relations of power to itself and to the governed.

20 The digital realm has been considered in terms of Foucault's notion of

As such, Big Digital may be a means by which the oversight and control functions that formerly were the province of national governments have been delegated to the market.[21] These governmental functions include not only commercial, cultural, corporate-political, and economic power but also the capability to shape the *political field* itself, or the bounded terrain that circumscribes what is allowable or possible and excludes what is not.[22] Big Digital sets the boundaries of acceptable discourse in digital spaces, allowing some positions and precluding others.

Although Big Digital does use censorship and bias to achieve governmental ends, the constraints are also technological and the technology itself is intrinsically political. Political ideology is not merely a subsidiary feature of Big Digital. Ideology is coded into its very DNA, which is replicated in every organizational offshoot and new technology. Big Digital's ideology circulates through the deep neural networks of cyberspace and other digital spheres. It is intrinsic to the foundations of the Internet, the cloud, algorithms,[23] apps, AI bots, social media services, web navigation tracking software systems, virtual assistants, and more. Google's beliefs and objectives regarding knowledge, as George Gilder argues, are political to the core:

---

a governmentality by Badouard, Romain, et al. "Beyond 'Points of Control': Logics of Digital Governmentality." *Internet Policy Review: Journal of Internet Regulation*, vol. 5, no. 3, September 3, 2016, pp. 1–13.

21 Slaughter, Steven. "Extended Neo-Liberalism: Governing Without the State." *Liberty Beyond Neo-Liberalism*, 2005, pp. 91–119.

22 The term "political field," defined by the French sociologist Pierre Bourdieu, refers to a particular kind of social terrain: a bounded space of struggle over political power that is structured by rules of access, where resources are differentially distributed among players and the set of legitimate positions on questions of government is constrained—that is, some political positions are beyond the boundaries of legitimate discourse. (Mudge, Stephanie Lee. "THE STATE OF THE ART: What Is Neo-Liberalism?" *Socio-Economic Review*, Vol. 6. August 26, 2008, pp. 703–731, at p. 707.

23 Mager, Astrid. "Defining Algorithmic Ideology: Using Ideology Critique to Scrutinize Corporate Search Engines." *TripleC: Communication, Capitalism & Critique*. Open Access Journal for a Global Sustainable Information Society, Vol. 12, No. 1, 2014, pp. 28–39.

The Google theory of knowledge and mind are not mere abstract exercises. They dictate Google's business model, which has progressed from "search" to "satisfy." Google's path to riches, for which it can show considerable evidence, is that with enough data and enough processors it can know better than we do what will satisfy our longings... If the path to knowledge is the infinitely fast processing of all data, if the mind—that engine by which we pursue the truth of things— is simply a logic machine, then the combination of algorithm and data can produce one and only one result. *Such a vision is not only deterministic but ultimately dictatorial.*[24]

Not only is the model intrinsically political, it embodies a particular kind of politics. Its aim is the centralized collection and storage of all of the world's data and its distribution through algorithms that steer users along particular paths. The Google system of centralized knowledge control resembles nothing as much as it does the centralized Soviet system of production and distribution, only digitalized and partially privatized. Moreover, the actually-existing, centralized, controlled and policed digital sphere of Big Digital has followed after a communalistic propaganda campaign, just as pre-Soviet socialist propaganda preceded the Soviet Union. As socialism-communism promised collective ownership and control of the means of production and distribution and ended in state monopolization of every sphere of life, the early Internet heralded an intellectual and cultural "commons," open to all and controlled by none. In the case of the Internet, the transformation was not strictly from an "information superhighway" to a series of toll roads but more importantly, from a leftist utopian notion of a digital commons to a version of digital centralization that, while privately-held, nevertheless functions like a state or, more accurately, an international private governmentality. Thus, to borrow and expand the meaning of George Gilder's phrase, the structure of ownership and control that Google commands may be called "Goo-

---

24 Gilder, George. *Life After Google: The Fall of Big Data and the Rise of the Blockchain Economy*. Gateway Editions. Emphasis mine.

gle Marxism."[25] Google Marxism, like "socialism with Chinese characteristics," manifests as state-supported monopoly capitalism, and "actually-existing socialism" for everyone else.

Google Marxism

Considered strictly in terms of ideology, Google Marxism works by collectivizing or socializing the masses for production, while also sufficiently individualizing them for particularized consumption and types of solitary production or non-productive lives. Google Marxism is much more than an ideology, however. It is a socioeconomic and political system, and as such, it represents the emergent global and digital version of corporate socialism, which is best represented as "socialism with Chinese characteristics"—a slogan the Chinese Communist Party (CCP) adopted to maintain a pretense of socialism despite its embrace of markets. Google Marxism is a profit-making and governance system undertaken by, and in the service of, corporate monopolists. But the monopolized top is paralleled by "socialism on-the-ground"—not only an economic stasis of reduced expectations but also a "socialism in theory," or the dominance of socialist ideology. In this respect, Google Marxism is simply a new instance of corporate socialism—but one that may continue to increasingly resemble China in terms of the denial of human rights and an overarching state of unfreedom.

Beyond its class-structural and sociopolitical character, in terms of its technological capabilities, Google Marxism in-the-making is unprecedented. Surely, it is tending toward centralized ownership, control, and distribution of all (digitalized) things. Yet the social relations of production—who does what—and class relations—who owns and controls what—will not be nearly as conspicuous to the naked eye as the continuously revolutionizing modes of production. In terms of technology or modes of production, Google Marxism is a new-and-vastly-im-

---

25   By "Google-Marxism," Gilder means that Google holds the same assumption that Marx held, that the contemporary mode of production is the ultimate mode and that likewise the only issues that remain to be solved are matters of distribution.

proved, up-and-coming version of corporate socialism. Google Marxism represents the first-ever possibility of a truly global economic system tending toward corporate socialism. Socialism has always had global pretensions. Only Google Marxism is capable of creating it, albeit in corporate socialist form. Google Marxism is the first system with the sufficient flexibility, scalability, connectivity, and, with the release of 5-G, the speed to enable the distance-defying, mass, and small-scale niche production and distribution possibilities to enable a truly globalized system. The necessary mode for eliminating the factors of time and distance and thus for a truly globalized system is digitization. All production will be converted into digital production. 3-D printing is presently the emblem of the digitization of production. But the new paradigm will not be limited to 3-D printing or the vaunted "smartification of everything," The Internet of Things (IoT).

Such phrases and acronyms hardly capture the extent of the profound transformation that is underway. Contrasting Google Marxism with the digital utopianism of 1990s makes this clear. In "A Declaration of the Independence of Cyberspace,"[26] John Perry Barlow, anarchist, civil libertarian, and songwriter for the Grateful Dead, described cyberspace as a new promised land, a prelapsarian digital Eden. Cyberspace was supposed to be a digital commons that the individual could explore at will, enjoying freedom from the constraints of property, government, the body, the differential treatment of persons based on identity and class markers, and the obstacles of space and time. The Internet promised freedom, equality, autonomy, selective interconnectivity, personalized and individualized production, and peer-to-peer social and economic exchange.

Barlow envisioned and worked to create an Internet specially designed for individual expression and liberation. But Google Marxism does not begin with, nor design, an Internet for the individual. Google Marxism begins with the Internet and

---

26 Barlow, John Perry. "A Declaration of the Independence of Cyberspace." *Electronic Frontier Foundation*. April 8, 2018. https://www.eff.org/cyberspace-independence.

makes individuals fit to inhabit it.

What about The Internet of Things? Under Google Marxism, all things are digitized and the place for everything digital is the Internet. As such, all things belong to the Internet. Google Marxism doesn't create The Internet of Things but rather The Things of the Internet (ToI). Yet the coming Internet is not best represented as ToI, because Google Marxism digitizes things, that is, converts things into packets of data. Data is information and "information wants to be free"—that is, free in Barlow's sense, self-determining, autonomous, not free as in cost-free. Google Marxism aims to free things, not to make things free. Google Marxism frees the things of the Internet by making the Internet ubiquitous, coextensive with the world at large. Thus, the best slogan for the Internet under Google Marxism is the Liberation of Things, or LoT. LoT can be understood as an inverse exodus. Rather than a people escaping a place of bondage, the place escapes itself. Rather than freeing individuals, the Internet is freed.

With Google Marxism and the production of the Google Archipelago, we will no longer "go online." We will not seek "freedom" in cyberspace—as if we ever did. Instead, cyberspace will have been freed, released from its silicon gulag. A vast digital world "exists and [will be] everywhere about us!" but it won't be "Heaven."[27] When information is freed—information about us, that is—it may imprison us. The Internet is not imprisoned, but it may become a prison, and once liberated, the world at large might become a digital gulag.

Under Google Marxism, the universe may "wake up," as futurist, inventor and now Google Director of Engineering Ray Kurzweil suggests. But the promised "singularity" won't amount to the birth of God, as Kurzweil implies.[28] It will more likely

---

27 Ginsberg, Allen. *"America." Howl and Other Poems*. City Lights, 1956, p.18. The fragment is from section II of "Howl." The full stanza reads: "They broke their backs lifting Moloch to Heaven! Pavements, trees, radios, tons! lifting the city to Heaven which exists and is everywhere about us!"

28 Kurzweil, Ray. "The Six Epochs". *Academic Writing, Real World Topics*. Michael Rectenwald and Lisa Carl. 1st ed., Broadview Press, Peterborough, Ont., 2015, p. 463.

come as a vast digital extension of the police force, or an open-air prison. After all, the liberated "things" of the Internet will be apps, AI bots, facial recognition software, virtual fences, digital leashes, and, perhaps, cyber death camps.

* * *

That was the second attempt at ending this paper, and it still ended on a dour note. So, let's have some "Fun with Google." Following are two Google searches and the top suggestions they yield. You may have heard of this search exercise, but consider it now in the context of the simulacra of the Google Archipelago. There, now I've gone and taken the fun out of it. But here is fun with Google, as far as it goes:

Google

- 🔍 men can
- 🔍 men can **have babies**
- 🔍 men can
- 🔍 men cancer
- 🔍 men can **get pregnant**
- 🔍 men can **have babies now**
- 🔍 men can**vas shoes**
- 🔍 men can**dles**
- 🔍 men can **cook**
- 🔍 men can**'t have babies**
- 🔍 men can**'t multitask**

Google Search   I'm Feeling Lucky

Report inappropriate predictions

Google

Q women can

Q women can
Q women can **fly**
Q women can**cer**
Q women can **vote**
Q women can **do it**
Q women can**vas shoes**
Q women can**dle company**
Q women can **do anything**
Q women can**didates**
Q women can**didates for president**

Google Search   I'm Feeling Lucky

Report inappropriate predictions

CHAPTER TWENTY-TWO

The "Real Left" Versus "The Left of Capital"

SOME LEFTISTS DEMAND that one recognizes the vast difference between the "real left" and "the left of capital"—or "woke capitalism," bourgeois leftism, or what have you. The left of capital is the visible leftism that permeates most of the social order today—including academia, the media, digital media, and even corporate America. The "real left" is particularly anxious to dissociate itself from the left of capital, given the daily embarrassment that capitalist leftism causes the real left, especially the embarrassments of identity politics, the *avant-garde* of which is the transgender movement.

But I have news for these "real leftists." Never in history has the "real left" undertaken anything of significance independent of the left of capital, or the bourgeois left—not even socialist revolution. The Russian Revolution was not primarily a working-class movement. I am not referring merely to the petty bourgeois intellectual leadership of the vanguard, including Trotsky and Lenin. I am referring to the funding, and organizational and tactical assistance provided by the left of capital. Without the left of capital, a socialist Russian Revolution would not have been possible.

Similarly, the "real left" regularly aids and abets the left of capital. For example, I'm told that the globalism of corporate capitalism and the internationalism of international socialism are utterly incommensurate; they have nothing to do with each other—except that the latter opposes the former. I am not going to entertain this supposed distinction, because it's a distinction that makes no actual difference, or the difference is merely ideological. The real left's internationalism, unwittingly no doubt, helps corporate capitalist globalism, whether the real leftists mean it to or not.

There's no "real left" as such, no Platonic ideal leftism, but only "actually-existing" leftism. "Actually-existing" leftism includes many groups and individuals that the "real left" would scoff at, but without whom they would have no platform or visibility whatsoever.

APPENDIX:

Best Facebook Statuses not included in *Google Archipelago* or *Springtime for Snowflakes*

Michael Rectenwald

March 3, 2019 ·

I'm more convinced by the day that it is leftism and not rightwing ideology that is the choice ideology of the ruling class—the one to perpetrate on the vast majority, that is.

Let's look at what leftism promotes and how it serves ruling interests. First, it is an ideology that suggests only "systemic" change and systemic forces have any efficacy. Individual humans are mere effects of structural conditions and thus their agency is limited if not non-existent.

Under leftism, human agency is efficacious only at the level of the collective, leaving the individual the helpless, hapless victim of circumstance. Environmental determinism is the rule. Environmental determinism is preferable for this defeatist ideology because genetic determinism might afford at least some populations hope, and they can't have that.

Leftism represents the extirpation of all hitherto stable social ontologies: gender, the family, social hierarchies of any kind, localities, churches, anything that might stand between control of the collective and the oligarchy. These must be eradi-

219

cated because they represent barriers to complete social, collectivist control, whether statist or corporate capitalist it does not matter. Today's leftism is corporate leftism, which I explain in my forthcoming book, *Google Archipelago*.

Leftism works for the monopoly capitalist because it discourages and precludes competition, convincing otherwise potential entrepreneurs that they are at a distinct class disadvantage, that no matter what they do, they cannot win, that they will be exploited and that their social position is static at best and sinking at worst. This is a self-fulfilling prophecy. One of the main means of ruling over others is convincing them that winning, rising, improving, or competing is impossible at the outset.

Leftism is for the erosion the nation state, and this serves global capitalists one-wordlists because nation states represent potential impediments to global monopoly capitalism and global governmentality. It is also the only source of individual rights at this point. Eradicate the nation state and privatize all forums of expression and you have a world of non-citizens and people with no rights. This is the objective.

The goal, folks, is "socialism with Chinese characteristics"— for all, not just for China. What that means is veritable monopolies at the top and "actually-existing socialism" for the vast majority. ("Actually-existing" socialism is a term of derogation used mostly by dissidents in socialist countries to refer to what life is really like under socialism, rather than in the perfidious books of Marx and his epigones.) This was the reason that major capitalists invested in the Russian revolution, because they wanted a captive and powerless consumer base, a captive market of workers without any chance that any of them might rise to compete with the monopolists in any of their industries.

This, folks, makes leftism the rational choice of ideologies for the ruling class. Classical liberalism must be banished and branded as an abomination. Anything other than collectivism must be deemed a vestige of unearned "privilege" and eradicated. Leftism is the ruling ideology.

Michael Rectenwald
March 7, 2019 ·
PC and "social justice" have destroyed American culture. The demands that put identity above quality have made it nothing but a "minority" ass-kissing festival day in and day out. These people who think they are disadvantaged are ironically actually advantaged and are getting far more than they deserve based on their "talent" or "accomplishments." But making them feel better is more important than reality and competence. US culture is just a system for giving trophies to people based on their supposed "subordination" status and without any real reference to talent or accomplishment. Get ready for the time when your brain surgeon is selected on the basis of his, her or zir subordination. Or maybe your robot surgeon will have to have the right simulated ethnicity, transgender identity and/or meet other criteria like "having been built in a disadvantaged country." Get ready to die at the hands of political correctness.

Michael Rectenwald
August 4, 2019 ·
Authoritarian leftists need the "dangerous" to justify their control and to disguise it as benevolence.

Michael Rectenwald
August 19, 2019 ·
I think the proper pronunciation for Antifa is Anti-fa, not An-tee-fa. They supposedly oppose fascism and aren't your Aunt Tee-fa.

Michael Rectenwald
August 25, 2019 ·
Socialism-Communism is a production of monopoly capitalists.

Michael Rectenwald
August 26, 2019 ·
Monopolists produce socialism-communism—to eliminate

competition.

Michael Rectenwald
September 17, 2019 ·
Think you might be a woman in a man's body, or a girl in a boy's body? Don't even think about it. Off to the sausage factory.

Michael Rectenwald
October 7, 2019 ·
I'm sick and tired of socialists virtue-signaling with promises of disbursing stolen money.

Michael Rectenwald
October 7, 2019 ·
Totalitarian leftism has been the most pernicious political ideology in history.

Michael Rectenwald
October 10, 2019 ·
#Antifa brownshirts running amok in Minneapolis. When Antifa activists look in the mirror, they are looking at what they pretend to oppose: totalitarians. These Red Guards are the enemies of freedom.

Michael Rectenwald
October 16, 2019 ·
Sanders merely wants to redistribute wealth that only capitalism can produce.

Michael Rectenwald
October 16, 2019 ·
Capital accumulation—in private hands—is necessary for the production of wealth.

Michael Rectenwald
October 16, 2019 ·
Wealth isn't a pie to be shared. Wealth is an oven for baking

pies!

Michael Rectenwald
October 16, 2019 ·
Corporate socialists want reduced expectations for all but their own monopolies.

Michael Rectenwald
October 16, 2019 ·
Woke capitalism is the ideological expression of corporate socialism.

Michael Rectenwald
October 19, 2019 ·
Only individual rights exist regardless of how they are acquired. The rights of collectives always abrogate the rights of at least some individuals. Whenever the "common good" or the good of "the people" is exerted, individuals are killed. The Chinese Communist Party is abrogating individual rights for the sake of the collective. That is always the case where collective rights are asserted. It was the case in the Soviet Union as well. Anytime the interests of a collective are considered the premium, individual rights are shredded. Collective rights always abrogate individual rights. Therefore, the only rights are individual rights. Only leftists believe in group rights. And leftists are always totalitarian.

Michael Rectenwald
October 21, 2019 ·
"Fake news" does not get to the bottom of the media problem. "Fake reality" does.

Michael Rectenwald
October 21, 2019 ·
The new patriarchy: ppl w/penises dominating women's sports, spaces, & feminism.

Michael Rectenwald
October 21, 2019 ·
First of all, stop using the word "gender." The word applied to LANGUAGE not people!

Michael Rectenwald
October 21, 2019 ·
The left is trans-maniacal, anti-scientific, anti-chromosomal, anti-genetics, anti-empirical-reality, mass psychotic, catastrophist, projectionist, Russophobic, conspiracist, & utterly delusional. And they enforce compliance with insanity with totalitarianism.

Michael Rectenwald
October 23, 2019 ·
The political criminality of the left has been extirpated from the historical records.

Michael Rectenwald
October 24, 2019 ·
The "radical" academic left is really a mob of conformist groupthink zombies.

Michael Rectenwald
October 24, 2019 ·
I know the social and linguistic constructivist "arguments" regarding gender and reality and demolish them in *Springtime for Snowflakes*. Most of my friends and followers here have also heard these PC authoritarian claims; we just don't believe them. They are ludicrous on their face. They deny genetics, chromosomes, anatomy, evolutionary history, and empirical reality. The transgender movement would have us buy into their mass delusion, but we refuse. What can't you understand?

Michael Rectenwald
October 24, 2019 ·
I now identify as the King of England. Where is my king-

dom?

Michael Rectenwald
October 25, 2019 ·
The word "gender" should never have been introduced to describe anything associated with human sex difference. Blame John Money for this lunacy.

Michael Rectenwald
October 26, 2019 ·
What is more likely, a bevy of transgender people were suppressed for millennia, or a cultural wave of transmania has ensued in recent years?

Michael Rectenwald
October 26, 2019 ·
Problem: We live in a patriarchy. Solution: Make men into women. New problem: Men running feminism etc. (How feminists cooked their own soup.). H/t Steve Bashir.

Michael Rectenwald
October 28, 2019 ·
Leftist catastrophism: Horse shit is going to bury us alive. Overpopulation is going to cause world starvation. The ozone layer is full of holes; we're gonna roast. Global warming will kill us in twelve years. The catastrophist left wants apocalypse more than any millennialist Christians.

Michael Rectenwald
October 28, 2019 ·
Burning people alive in cages, keeping women as sex slaves, and throwing homosexuals from rooftops makes one an austere religious scholar. Who'd have guessed?

Michael Rectenwald
November 2, 2019 ·
No one can change their sex. Halloween costumes are

cheaper and just as effective.

Michael Rectenwald
November 7, 2019 ·
Academia Today: The Politics & "Studies" of Weaponized Identity & Victimhood in an Intellectual Sewer.

Michael Rectenwald
November 7, 2019 ·
Reconstructing an Intellectual Edifice from the Rubble of Blue Church Disintegration.

Michael Rectenwald
November 7, 2019 ·
The main suffering derived from climate change is the psychological distress suffered by believers in it.

Michael Rectenwald
November 8, 2019 ·
With their constant outrage and suggestions that all their complaints can be redressed, they miss the fact that life is fundamentally tragic.

Michael Rectenwald
November 11, 2019 ·
Adherence to and repeating nonsense demonstrates loyalty like nothing else. It's more meaningful for a political organization than acknowledgements of the truth. Anyone can affirm the truth. Only true believers faithfully affirm nonsense.

Michael Rectenwald
November 12, 2019 ·
"Nothing is more important than that our fellow students feel safe." Not even an education.

Michael Rectenwald
November 12, 2019 ·
Dear ed. board of Frontiers: Twitter isn't an academic forum, hence NO ONE need abide by "academic standards of discourse" on Twitter! & I'm sure your "standards" are DOUBLE STANDARDS & don't apply to leftists calling for Trump's beheading.

Michael Rectenwald
November 14, 2019 ·
The establishment is leftist. That makes me anti-establishment.

Michael Rectenwald
November 16, 2019 ·
The Rockefeller Foundation funded the Frankfurt School Marxist Herbert Marcuse, whose research influenced the CIA, and who worked for the state department.

Acknowledgments

THE FIRST PART of this work is the result of my studies as a Senior Fellow at the Russian Institute, Columbia University, during the years 1952–53. The second part was prepared at the Russian Research Center, Harvard University, in 1954–55, under a special grant from the Rockefeller Foundation. I am much indebted to the Russian Research Center, and especially to its Director, William L. Langer, and Associate Director, Marshall D. Shulman, for their kindness in relinquishing to Columbia University Press their publication rights to the second part.

I also wish to express my thanks to George L. Kline, Columbia University, who prepared some of the material used in the second part of this essay; to Alfred E. Senn, for his assistance with Russian references; and to Arkadii R. L. Gurland, who offered valuable help and comments.

My friend, Barrington Moore, Jr., read the manuscript and helped me as usual with his incisive criticism.

The index was prepared by Maud Hazeltine.

HERBERT MARCUSE

Brandeis University
June, 1957

Herbert Marcuse, *One Dimensional Man*, Acknowledgements

Michael Rectenwald
November 17, 2019 ·
Socialist: George Orwell was a socialist.
Me: Nobody's perfect.
Socialist: Socialism has nothing to do with oligarchy.
Me: You're thinking of the ideological version, not the actual one. Socialism is nothing if not a monopoly controlled by oligarchs who stole their wealth.
Socialist: That's not the *real left* [referring to the left of woke capitalism.]
Me: There is no *real left*, only the left that exists in reality. You're thinking of the *historical left,* which is hardly preferred given that it represents the most murderous political contingent in world history.
Socialist: That wasn't *real socialism.*
Me:

Michael Rectenwald
November 18, 2019 ·
It's a wonder of the world that socialists are so complacent and silent about the vast contradiction that has existed between the working-class rule promised by socialist propaganda and the brutal dictatorship of the party leadership that socialism becomes, Every. Single. Time.

Michael Rectenwald
November 20, 2019 ·
For those on the "actually-existing" left, *belief* trumps empirical reality.

Michael Rectenwald
November 20, 2019 ·
I'm thinking the "resistance" is fundamentally a resistance of REALITY.

Michael Rectenwald
November 20, 2019 ·
I support the side that was actually ELECTED over the side
attempting a COUP.

Michael Rectenwald
November 22, 2019 ·
I read the *NYTimes* & *WaPost* — to keep informed of the
Ministry of Truth's propaganda.

Michael Rectenwald
November 22, 2019 ·
In such fact-free times as ours, one best resists the establish-
ment's "truth."

Michael Rectenwald
November 27, 2019 ·
Ready for the "Thanksgiving is a celebration of colonialist
slaughter of indigenous peoples" posts? Do these would-be virtue-signaling guilt-trippers think they're educating anyone? As
if their cartoon version of history, with its cookie-cutter "White
man bad" shorthand narrative amounts to anything but historical myopia and political illiteracy, excluding thousands of years
of conquest that makes everyone alive a descendent of conquer-
ors.

Michael Rectenwald
November 27, 2019 ·
Fascism is a form of collectivism. It has more in common
with socialism than it does classical liberalism, individualism,
or *laissez faire*.

Michael Rectenwald
November 28, 2019 ·
Marxism's latest pretext for the "necessity" of revolution—
to save "the Planet."

Michael Rectenwald
November 29, 2019 ·
The greatest problem of (post)modern humanity is its intolerance of ambiguity. Thus, the felt need for more masculine women to jump across (trans) sex/gender lines (if only imaginarily), and vice versa. Thus, the need for a distinct "gender" as other than "sex" (difference).

Michael Rectenwald
November 29, 2019 ·
Thank Rousseau's "noble savage" nonsense, including its misinterpretations, for the ridiculous romanticizing of indigenes and the bad conscience liberals and leftists try to foist on the contemporary inhabitants of America, I mean Turtle Island.

Michael Rectenwald
November 30, 2019 ·
When people who adopt a politics whose legacy is political mass murder and imprisonment are telling you what you can and cannot say, it's time not merely to rebut them but to exercise the very freedom they would rescind and take away from you. Such people are totalitarians. They make claims like "speech is wrong when it advocates injustice to others." Imagine that slippery slope. These tyrants believe that their notions of "justice" are sacrosanct. Meanwhile they avow a political ideology whose symbol shouldn't be a hammer and sickle but a slaughterhouse and a gulag. Yet they believe they are somehow endowed with the probity to tell you how to think and what to say. Their claim to be the arbiters of anything is beyond outrageous!

Michael Rectenwald
December 1, 2019 ·
No matter how much one tells the truth about socialism, "the patriarchy," "social justice," or argues that "discursive violence" is an absurd notion based on postmodern theoretical nonsense, one can't win. They're generating idiots faster than we can count them, let alone debrief and reverse the ideological

programming.

Michael Rectenwald
December 4, 2019 ·

"Social justice" activism is cultural and political authoritarianism that *uses* the "oppressed" as props for the power gambits of authoritarians. The end game is to have means for controlling individuals and punishing "deviants" or dissidents. Free thought must be stopped and the means for stopping it is to associate free thought with one sort of horrid ideology or another, and then to punish persons who supposedly espouse said ideology. Meanwhile, the ideology of contemporary "social justice" itself has totalitarian roots in Stalinism and Maoism, in particular the practices of "auto-critique" and "struggle sessions"—which can be seen in the self-criticism and apologies of those attempting to placate Others (autocritique), and in the various forms of callout culture. Listen to this survivor of Mao's Cultural Revolution and notice the echoes and the same terms in the contemporary "social justice" movement. These features of the Cultural Revolution are discussed from around the 37:00 and into a discussion of contemporary Hong Kong: https://www.youtube.com/watch?v=HKiJsU8Is5A

Michael Rectenwald
December 14, 2019 ·

I received a review copy of Stanley Fish's book *The First: How to Think About Hate Speech, Campus Speech, Religious Speech, Fake News, Post-Truth, and Donald Trump*—just in time to ruin my Saturday night. But I won't let it.

The first paragraph of the insert for reviewers should tell you what I mean:

"How does the First Amendment really work? Is it a principle or a value? [???] What is hate speech and ***should it always be banned?*** Are we free to declare our religious beliefs in the public square? [WHAT?] What role, if any, should companies like Facebook play in policing the exchange of thoughts, ideas, and opinions?"

"Should hate speech ALWAYS be banned," he asks—not should it EVER be banned?! "Are we free to declare our religious beliefs in the public square?" he asks. Is this satire? I return a question for an answer-begging-yet-defying question. That's right; Fish actually argues that religious expression should never have been protected by the First Amendment in the first place, and that its protection should be presently excised from the Bill of Rights.

What authoritarian ogre and ideological dictator is this, you ask? The one and the same Stanley Fish, who condemned the Sokal Hoax as "unethical" in the *New York Times*, after Sokal had dutifully and responsibly exposed the truly unethical and fraudulent drivel of postmodern "Science Studies." See *Springtime for Snowflakes* for a full account.

"The First"--a title that incidentally echoes the name of the most important early Soviet censorship agency, "The First Department"—calls for banning public religious expression, for *more* censorship by the digital giants (Facebook, Google, Twitter, et al.), and for banning the "wrong" opinions, among other curtailments. It tries to effect an edginess, with arguments so provocative as to be downright sinister. Yet such an attack on the rights of U.S. citizens must be music to the ears of the authoritarian, wannabe totalitarian left.

The authoritarians on the left are anxious to suppress oppositional perspectives entirely. But given the atrophy of their rational faculties (in both senses), they've been rendered incapable of refutation. Instead, they claim that oppositional views are beyond the pale and don't deserve serious engagement. Thus, snowflake totalitarians that they are, leftists display the obstreperous petulance of adult-sized toddlers, screeching to weaponize their fragility in attempts to suppress oppositional ideas.

But now the boobs can also take refuge in the fuzzy effusions of an esteemed "legal and literary scholar," whose readings of American law appear to be almost entirely without precedent in legal scholarship. But the left is far from demanding that the arguments of their "allies" present the slightest coherence or remotely resemble language use that might make sense. The specious arguments of Stanley Fish, the obscurations of their pet postmodern sophist and slippery Stalinist speech suppressor, will do just fine, at least as far as they are concerned.

Having been written by one whom *The New Republic* calls "a scholar thrillingly authoritative" and "wholly convinced" (by his own sophistry, I suppose), the good news is that *The First* is being outperformed by my own *Google Archipelago*. The latter, written from a libertarian perspective by me, a lesser known scholar than the Fish, is outselling *The First's* repackaged totalitarianism. Thank goodness not everyone can be fooled by the shoddy tropes dished out by Stanley Fish.

My review will appear in a forthcoming number of the periodical *Academic Questions*.

Michael Rectenwald
December 17, 2019 ·
This is the Age of Hyperbole.

Michael Rectenwald
December 19, 2019 ·
The phrase "lived experience" makes me want to reach for my...

Michael Rectenwald
January 4 ·
Leftists say that race isn't a scientific reality; it's a social construct and thus a sociological phenomenon. Then they say their sociology (Marxism) is *the* scientific view of the social order. Then they say that homosexuality is genetic, not socially constructed. The left is a can of tangled worms.

Michael Rectenwald
January 14 ·
Tom Steyer is a billionaire and can't afford a tie that's not cut from the cloth of a kilt?

Michael Rectenwald
January 14 ·
Healthcare cannot be a human right unless it is a human right to force other humans to work for you.

Michael Rectenwald
January 15 ·
The role of Sanders, AOC, et al. is to plow the soil to produce conditions conducive to corporate socialism—that is, monopolies on top, and "actually-existing" socialism, a static condition of reduced expectations and lack of liberty, for everyone else.

Michael Rectenwald
January 16 at 3:51 AM ·
Anyone who says 'it's easy to see where the right "goes too far" but not so for the left,' just doesn't know history.

Michael Rectenwald
January 17 at 4:24 PM ·
As the gulag made clear, many Marxists are fine with slavery.

Michael Rectenwald
February 1 at 5:15 AM ·
True believers tend to take political ideology at face value and think that political opposites are just that, opposing forces that are forever antagonistic toward each other. Thus, corporate socialism can't possibly exist because never the twain—socialism and corporate interests—shall meet—in their minds, that is. Thus, liberal neocons cannot exist because, as they point out in their brilliance, "liberal means the opposite of conservative." When one points to Rachel Maddow as a liberal neocon, they either go into convulsions, deny that she's a neocon, or when very desperate, deny that she's a liberal. But she's both a liberal in the contemporary sense of the term and a neocon. Her support of the war in Afghanistan makes the latter clear. Her support of liberal economic and social policies makes the for-

mer clear. The same goes, to a lesser extent where "liberal" is concerned, for Hillary Clinton. She's definitely a neocon. As for being a liberal, she's good at pretending to be one. This is to say nothing of the fact that the leading neocons were all Trotskyists before becoming neocons.

I would feel badly for such true believers were it not for the ferocity with which they cling to what they've been trained to think about opposing "sides," clueless as to how the ruling elite can use any political mask it wishes at any given time.

Take for example the likely response to the following question by Marxist true believers: "Why did socialism lead to revolution in Russia and not the U.S., when the U.S. had more socialists per capita than the former in 1917?" The answers will follow from some leftist truism about greater organization or the weakest link theory, despite the fact that Marx held the opposite view, which became known as the orthodox Marxist view—that even Marx recanted when it became clear that it wasn't going to hold up. (That is, Marx held that socialism could only take place in advanced capitalist countries and not in backward near-feudal states but recanted when it became clear that Russia might become revolutionary.) The answer to the question, by the way, is ***corporate funding.*** Socialists in Russia had corporate funding. Not so the U.S. socialists—for obvious reasons. Russia posed the threat of throwing up numerous competitors for U.S. monopoly capitalists, whereas the U.S. was an established theater for profit.

Many other examples of these supposed political hybrids exist--but the main point is that they're not really hybrids. Politics is like a game of chess played by the ruling elite. True believers are the pawns.

Michael Rectenwald
February 1 at 2:39 PM ·
On the left coast for some media appearances. I've gone to Starbucks every day since I've been here and ordered "bacon egg bites"—in addition to my iced latte with almond milk.

The cashier has gotten the order wrong every time. I say

"bacon" and they say "veggie." I say "bacon" and they say, "egg whites." Finally, today I asked why no one can hear the word "bacon" and instead substitutes "veggie" or some other PC bullshit in its place. I want to eat my pig, god dammit! Meanwhile, nobody burns more fossil fuels than the people in this hypocrite state, racing around in their luxury cars and SUVs. I don't care, as long they don't try to virtue signal and shame me at the same time.

Michael Rectenwald
February 3 at 6:31 PM ·
My feedback was solicited by a scholar on *academia.edu*. The paper claimed that the U.S. is fascist, that fascism is spreading the world over, that the sky is falling, etc. etc. Here's my feedback:

I think your definition of fascism lacks sufficient specificity and historical grounding. Fascism was born in Italy and thus the use of the term should follow from its inception and development there. That history shows clearly that fascism developed out of the fusion of Marxist syndicalism and nationalism, as brilliantly discussed in the best book on the subject, namely *Mussolini's Intellectuals: Fascist Social and Political Thought*, by A. James Gregor.

"Conjoint political control of government and big business" is nebulous and imprecise. Control by whom? The relationship between business and the state under fascism is best understood as a corporatist one wherein corporate business interests are put at the service of the state. This is not primarily the case in the U.S., where the relationship between big business and state is one of collusion that is more in the service of the corporate capitalist monopolies or would-be monopolies than it is in the service of the state. In the U.S, each side serves and ingratiates itself to the other.

You seem to be under the impression that all imperialist militarism is fascist but that is simply belied historically. Not all imperialism is fascist and not all fascism is necessarily imperialist. The latter point is evinced by the fact that Italian fascism was not imperialist at the outset and wasn't developed for imperialist but rather self-defensive, competitive, and developmental purposes. The prior point is evidenced by the millennia-long history of imperialism that precedes fascism by many hundreds of years.

Some of your claims appear to be no more than hysterical political rhetoric derived not so much from or for scholarship as from and for political advocacy and presentist hyperbole of the "resistance" under Trump. You're just throwing around charged rhetoric for effect and not at all to describe history or contemporary conditions with the slightest modicum of accuracy. It's a shame that academia has become an echo chamber but more a shame that what's echoed is often ludicrous, activist, and propagandist. More after I finish this. The meal is unsavory so several sittings will be required.

Michael Rectenwald
February 5 at 9:53 PM ·
All the pharisees are out in force tonight, telling us how virtuous they are by declaring that they hate Trump more than the next guy and reminding us that they're "profoundly religious." Virtue signal all you want, pharisees. You're nobody's moral superior. You just have an overweening sense of your own moral superiority, and that sense is false. You point to your hatred as proof of your soaring moral virtue. How utterly self-deceived and mistaken you are!

Michael Rectenwald
February 8 at 2:28 PM ·
Diversity = Ideological Conformity
Equity = Inequity for those who don't conform
Inclusion = Exclusion of non-conformists

Michael Rectenwald
February 17 at 4:48 PM ·
Socialism is a ruling class idea and ideology. It's a means of duping the masses into accepting an "equality" of reduced

expectations. Why else would major capitalists be funding it?

CPSIA information can be obtained
at www.ICGtesting.com
Printed in the USA
LVHW081101250721
693623LV00008B/493/J